Making Friends in School:
Promoting Peer Relationships
in Early Childhood
PATRICIA G. RAMSEY

Play and the Social Context
of Development in Early Care
and Education
BARBARA SCALES, MILLIE ALMY,
AGELIKI NICOLOPOULOU, &
SUSAN ERVIN-TRIPP, Eds.

The Whole Language Kindergarten
SHIRLEY RAINES
ROBERT CANADY

Good Day/Bad Day:
The Child's Experience of Child Care
LYDA BEARDSLEY

Children's Play and Learning:
Perspectives and Policy Implications
EDGAR KLUGMAN
SARA SMILANSKY

Serious Players in the Primary Classroom:
Empowering Children Through
Active Learning Experiences
SELMA WASSERMANN

Child Advocacy for
Early Childhood Educators
BEATRICE S. FENNIMORE

Managing Quality Child Care Centers:
A Comprehensive Manual for
Administrators
PAMELA BYRNE SCHILLER
PATRICIA M. DYKE

Multiple Worlds of Child Writers:
Friends Learning to Write
ANNE HAAS DYSON

Young Children Continue to Reinvent
Arithmetic—2nd Grade: Implications
of Piaget's Theory
CONSTANCE KAMII

Literacy Learning in the Early Years:
Through Children's Eyes
LINDA GIBSON

The Good Preschool Teacher:
Six Teachers Reflect on Their Lives
WILLIAM AYERS

A Child's Play Life:
An Ethnographic Study
DIANA KELLY-BYRNE

Professionalism and the Early Childhood
Practitioner
BERNARD SPODEK, OLIVIA N. SARACHO,
& DONALD L. PETERS, Eds.

Looking at Children's Play: The Bridge
from Theory to Practice
PATRICIA A. MONIGHAN-NOUROT,
BARBARA SCALES, JUDITH L. VAN HOORN,
& MILLIE ALMY

The War Play Dilemma: Balancing
Needs and Values in the
Early Childhood Classroom
NANCY CARLSSON-PAIGE
DIANE E. LEVIN

The Piaget Handbook
for Teachers and Parents
ROSEMARY PETERSON
VICTORIA FELTON-COLLINS

Teaching and Learning in a Diverse
World: Multicultural Education
PATRICIA G. RAMSEY

The Early Childhood Curriculum:
A Review of Current Research
CAROL SEEFELDT, Ed.

The Full-Day Kindergarten
DORIS PRONIN FROMBERG

Promoting Social and Moral
Development in Young Children
CAROLYN POPE EDWARDS

(Continued)

Making Friends in School:
Promoting Peer Relationships in Early Childhood

Patricia G. Ramsey

Teachers College, Columbia University
New York and London

Published by Teachers College Press, 1234 Amsterdam Avenue, New York, N.Y. 10027

Library of Congress Cataloging-in-Publication Data

Ramsey, Patricia G.
   Making friends in school : promoting peer relationships in early
childhood / Patricia G. Ramsey.
      p.   cm — (Early childhood education series)
   Includes bibliographical references (p.) and index.
   ISBN 0-8077-3128-5. — ISBN 0-8077-3127-7 (pbk.)
   1. Socialization. 2. Interpersonal relations in children—United
States. 3. Early childhood education—United States. I. Title.
II. Series.
LC192.4.R36 1991
370.19'0973—dc20   91-30224

Printed on acid-free paper
Manufactured in the United States of America
98 97 96 95 94 93 92 91   8 7 6 5 4 3 2 1

To Daniel

Contents

Chapter 5
**Fostering Peer Relationships: Teaching Practices
and Classroom Structures**   **99**

Chapter 6
Social Intervention: When? To Whom? How? And How Much?   **132**

Chapter 7
Activities and Resources for Teaching About Social Relationships **168**

Preface

I owe my interest in children's friendships to a child named Lenny, who was one of those children that new teachers "never forget." Lenny was a puzzle; he was bright and athletic, and could be charming. At the same time, he was often sullen, and frequently hit and kicked other children. As I struggled to neutralize Lenny's more difficult behaviors and foster his positive ones, I found myself frequently confounded by the cycle of Lenny's behaviors and his peers' reactions to them. If Lenny was trying hard to be sociable, his peers often chose that moment to provoke him. If Lenny was being belligerent, his classmates either gave way or tried to placate him and thus reinforced the very behavior they disliked. As I floundered around trying strategy after strategy, I was constantly outflanked by Lenny and his peers. Meanwhile Lenny's behavior became the focal point of the whole class and absorbed much of my energy and that of the other children. In retrospect, I realize that I never took the time to really understand the dynamics between Lenny and his peers, what Lenny was trying to achieve, and how his needs related to his family situation. Instead, I simply reacted to the surface behaviors. This experience taught me to appreciate the complexity of children's peer relationships and to respect their power to influence all aspects of the classroom.

Almost all teachers have had similar experiences and concur that the peer relationships are critical to the overall tone of the classroom and to individual children's school success. We know all too well that children who are feeling alienated or threatened have no emotional or cognitive energy for learning. We all have experienced how the chemistry among the children in the class affects our teaching. Squabbling and tension among groups can undermine the most carefully planned and skillfully implemented activities. In contrast, harmonious groups often "take off" with some wonderful results. Given this common experience, it is surprising that concern about social relationships in schools has not been very prominent in the national educational agenda.

A recent issue of a national magazine was devoted to an examination of the status of education in the United States. The issue included articles about most areas of the curriculum: reading, math, science, history, foreign languages, and the arts. The roles of politics and parents were also addressed. No articles, however, raised any questions about the quality of children's social experiences in schools. Even a commentary about Head Start evaluated the worth of this program solely on its effectiveness for raising children's academic performances and reducing their drop-out rate. The lack of any commentary on these aspects of children's school lives is disturbing, as it suggests that most people in this country continue to think of education only in terms of academic material and test scores. This priority is not surprising: academic achievements usually yield tangible results, whereas social well-being is evident in more subtle ways. When educators are worried about students in the United States being able to compete with their Japanese and European counterparts, they are thinking about their test scores, not their social lives. The astute teacher knows that these two measures are often linked, but may find this connection hard to prove because it is not demonstrable with numbers.

This lack of concern about children's social experiences in schools is even more surprising given the fact that children's peer relationships has been the topic of an enormous amount of recent research in the fields of developmental and clinical psychology. We know so much more than we did, but the information has not yet begun to influence our national educational priorities. In classrooms, however, many practitioners are making peer relationships a higher priority. Preschool teachers have traditionally emphasized this aspect of development. Now, many elementary school teachers are strengthening their focus on the social dimensions of their classrooms by incorporating cooperative learning methods and using children's social relationships and interests to support academic work rather than dismissing them as distractions. With this book I hope to to support these efforts by making concrete connections between research on peer relationships and classroom practices, and to provide teachers with examples and guidelines to stimulate new insights and ideas.

This book is written with the conviction that teachers are first and foremost active learners and creative problem solvers. As a teacher and a teacher educator, I have been frustrated by many of the books written for preservice and experienced teachers. Activity books in which lesson plans are presented in detail are useful, but do not provide the background information needed to help teachers analyze their own situations and make informed choices. At the other extreme, child development text books and compilations of research studies offer valuable insights into children's development but do not help teachers make the connection between research findings and classroom applications. In this volume, I have reviewed and consolidated much of the current research about peer relationships in ways that I hope will be useful for teachers as they analyze their classrooms and design strategies to create positive social environments and resolve individual and group problems.

The first part of this book is written to help readers become more aware of the developmental trends, the group dynamics, and the individual differences that affect peer relationships. To provide a framework for developmentally appropriate expectations and activities for young children, Chapter 2 is a review of aspects of children's cognitive, emotional, and behavioral growth that are related to early social adjustment. Chapter 3 is a closer look at group dynamics and peer culture and how they affect the roles of individuals as well as the overall classroom social climate. Chapter 4 is a description of individual differences in social success and an analysis of why some children are more popular than others. Collectively, these chapters provide background material and multiple frameworks for analyzing individual children's friendships and social skills and the overall social climate of classrooms.

The second part of this book focuses on practical and specific applications of the material discussed in the first part. The primary goal is to help teachers make decisions that lead to effective practices and positive resolutions of social problems. Chapter 5 includes several methods for observing and analyzing classroom dynamics and guidelines for classroom organization and teaching roles. Chapter 6 is an exploration of some of the dilemmas teachers face when confronted with individual and group problems. The numerous examples in this chapter illustrate how teachers can intervene effectively with individuals and groups that are having social difficulties. Chapter 7 is a compilation of specific activities and resources that can be used to expand children's social understanding in a number of areas.

I expect that this book will be used in many different ways. Beginning teachers may find that it triggers some memories about their own school experiences. They may also use it to analyze the social dynamics and teaching practices in classrooms where they are doing their field work and student teaching. More experienced teachers may find that the book affirms ideas and strategies that already they intuitively know and use. Hopefully, this book will also stimulate some reflections about their current practices and ideas for changes they want to make. For students in child development, this book shows how child development research is related to larger questions and can be applied in educational settings.

Above all, I hope that this book challenges some misperceptions, stimulates some discussions, and encourages readers to develop creative strategies to foster children's friendships and to promote positive peer relationships.

Acknowledgments

This book has been a collaborative effort in all respects. Many teachers, children and colleagues have been instrumental in its inception and final production. Although I did the actual writing, this book is largely based on the work and ideas of the staff of the Gorse Child Study Center at Mount Holyoke College. As a group, we spent many hours discussing the issues that this book addresses, and the wealth of insights and ideas that the staff produced inspired me to begin this project. The teachers also generously let me, my students, and my research assistants observe, tape, and interview their children as we conducted the research and compiled many of the examples for this book. Barbara Sweeney, Assistant Director and teacher, provided many wonderful insights about children and was always willing to try new ideas as we experimented with different interventions with individuals and groups. She also provided invaluable administrative and organizational support for the many research projects that contributed to this book. Marguerite Davol generously shared her wisdom of many years of teaching about what works and does not work in classrooms and helped me to maintain an appropriate balance of idealism and pragmatism. As an author of children's books and stories, she also contributed a great deal to the reviews of children's books. Suzannah Heard's strong interest in this area of research and teaching and her active participation in many phases of the research inspired all of us to keep going on this project. I am especially grateful for her detailed observations and analyses that helped me refine my understanding of the unique social world of three-year-olds and the social issues that children face as they enter school. Susan Jensen's curriculum innovations and her work with computers helped all of us to see more possibilities for social engagement in a variety of curriculum areas. Her infectious enthusiasm and her openness in expressing her dilemmas in dealing with various social issues gave this project much of its momentum. Helen Johnson's insights about children's emotional and social needs and her masterful ways of dealing with them have inspired both my interest in this topic and many of the interventions described in this book. Her ability to address children's needs at the individual, interpersonal, and intergroup levels, and her unfailing commitment to create a more just and caring world for children, have helped me keep these multiple perspectives in mind while doing this work. Most recently, Valerie Sawka has provided many wonderful resources and ideas for fostering children's social understanding in a variety of ways. Mary Ellen Marion kept all of us calm and organized so that we could engage in the research and teaching that has led to this book. In many ways, the children of Gorse Child Study Center are the true authors of this book, and I am deeply indebted to them and their parents for their participation and support at all stages of this work.

I am very grateful to Martha Faison, Sigrid Howell, Janet Kennedy, and Polly Strain, all teachers in the Amherst, Massachusetts School System, who reviewed this manuscript in its earlier stages and gave me many wonderful comments and suggestions. They had a formative influence on the tone and substance of this book.

Many colleagues from different institutions contributed to this work. Sherri Oden, who got me interested in this area of research several years ago, has provided wonderful guidance and support for several related research projects and for the writing of this book. Her thoughtfulness and thorough knowledge of the field were invaluable as I was working on the research reviews. Carolyn Edwards also inspired my initial interest in children's friendships and has helped me understand the influences of the larger social contexts on children's social development. I have also used many of her creative classroom ideas in the applications sections of this book. Bob Shilkret was instrumental in my pursuing this area of research several years ago, and I have appreciated his continuing enthusiastic support of this work. Barry Wadsworth read and commented on various parts of this book and helped me integrate issues related to children's cognitive development in a meaningful way. The members of the Writers' Group at Mount Holyoke also offered many helpful suggestions. All of my colleagues in the Department of Psychology and Education at Mount Holyoke College were wonderfully encouraging and patient with me throughout this project, and I am most grateful to them for creating such a supportive environment. The research for this book was supported by a faculty fellowship from Mount Holyoke College and a grant from the National Institute of Mental Health.

Many Mount Holyoke College graduate and undergraduate students contributed to this work with their observations, interventions, and assistance with data collection and analysis. In particular, I wish to thank Carol Lasquade, who helped get this project started several years ago; and Mary Brownley, Leslie Myers, Heather Coons, Deeana Gillespie, and Christina Theokas for their wonderful help in the research underlying much of this book. Most recently, Jennifer West has spent hours proofreading, checking resources, and finding children's books from libraries all over western Massachusetts.

The editors at Teachers College Press have been very supportive during all phases of this work. I thank Sarah Biondello for her constant encouragement and her willingness to be flexible with deadlines. Leslie Williams provided excellent feedback on the original draft and helped me overcome some conceptual and organizational problems in the book. Most recently, Nancy Berliner has patiently supported me through the final phases and has encouraged me to take risks and follow my intuitions. I have especially appreciated her calm organization as we dealt with logistical complexities and tight deadlines.

My family has been wonderful. I cannot begin to express my appreciation to my husband Fred Moseley who has unfailingly provided encouragement, support, and practical assistance at all stages of this project. Finally, Daniel, my newest teacher, has shared with me the joys of infancy and toddlerhood and has provided many delightful distractions and humorous interludes throughout this project.

1 | The Importance of Early Friendships

My happiest memories are playing with my friends in the school playground. We had all sorts of elaborate adventure games that we kept making up and adding to. We created secret names for different areas and . made up code words and strategies to elude our enemies. I can't remember how we thought up all this stuff...people would just play off of each other and the ideas would take off.

I had a very close friend in the second grade. She and I did everything together. People used to call us the Siamese twins. Then I was away for the summer, and when I came back, she had met a new girl and was spending a lot of time with her. I remember being insanely jealous and trying to win her back with all these crazy pleas and threats and bribes. Of course it did not work; I was miserable and sure that I would never be happy or feel good about myself again.

A group of us played a lot of sports...in the summer, it was day after day of baseball. I don't remember it being that competitive; we would switch around so that we did not have set teams. We all shared fantasies of becoming famous players like our current heroes. Sometimes we would enact plays in the games that we watched on TV. We were joined by our common obsession with baseball.

I didn't like school much as a child. I felt stifled and bored by the work in the classroom. What I loved was being with my friends and that is what I looked forward to everyday. We would meet a few blocks away from school and fantasize about playing hooky until we arrived at the door. Time in the classroom was seen as mostly the filler between the beginning of school, recess, lunch, and the end of school. Every minute we were not doing some assignment or under the teacher's direct supervision, we got together and played and talked.

I was pretty shy as a child and not very good at sports. My most excruciating memories are times when we had to choose partners or teams for either sports, class contests, or group work. I remember sitting there with my eyes down trying not to notice that I was always one of the last ones chosen. It didn't matter what the project or activity was, I dreaded having to be with classmates who did not want me.

Three of us formed a club. We had a clubhouse, secret password, and all of that. It was very exclusive: "Members only." I don't remember that we actually did anything as a club; we mostly discussed the rules and how we were going to make the other kids feel bad because they were not allowed to join. It was a great sense of belonging, but I guess looking back, we must have felt pretty insecure to have to be that exclusive.

I fought a lot as a child. For all kinds of reasons, I was a pretty angry kid. I remember that kids used to call me names and provoke me into fighting. I acted really tough so that no one would know how miserable I was. I dreaded going to school, knowing that it was going to be a succession of overt insults and taunts and more subtle signs of dislike. The teacher often tried to pair me up other children for field trips and projects. I can still remember the horrified looks on their faces and their frantic efforts to change partners, when they realized that they were going to have to be with me.

As I heard these comments from my early childhood education students reflecting on their happiest and saddest childhood memories, I thought about a scene that I had witnessed earlier that day in our laboratory preschool.

Clara is hanging onto her mother's hand as she reluctantly walks into the preschool. Her head hangs down as her mother helps her off with her coat. She mutters, "I want to go home with you! I don't want to go to school!" Her mother pats her back and asks her if she would like to play with Marianne, her special friend. Clara looks a little more interested but slowly shakes her head. Then her mother pulls her gently to the door of the classroom. The teacher squats down and quietly welcomes Clara. Clara still looks downcast and hangs back. Then Marianne runs over and exuberantly shouts "Clara, come see the guinea pig!" Clara looks up and smiles hesitantly, and her mother pushes her gently towards the classroom. Clara's smile broadens, she straightens up, and walks to the guinea pig cage with Marianne.

Both observations and self-reports attest to the importance of friendships, not only to children's immediate enjoyment of school and recreational activities, but also to many aspects of their physical, cognitive, emotional, and social development. For both children and adults, friends enhance our pleasure, mitigate our anxieties, and broaden our realm of experience.

Children's peer relationships are also related to their psychological development as adolescents and adults. In a recent review of longitudinal studies of rejected children, Parker and Asher (1987) concluded that children with poor peer relations were at risk for later social and emotional problems. They identified several patterns. Children who were considered aggressive at school were more likely to engage in juvenile and adult delinquency. Nonaggressive rejected children dropped out of school more often than did their popular peers. Shy and withdrawn children appeared to be at greater risk for mental illness when they reached adolescence and adulthood, although the trends were mixed. In addition to these demonstrated outcomes, researchers have speculated that poor peer relations may also be associated with later job and marital problems (Kupersmidt, Coie, & Dodge, 1990). We do not know whether poor peer relationships actually cause the later disturbances or if they are simply symptoms of previously existing disturbances. We do know, however, that negative peer relations cause stress and lowered self-esteem which are likely to aggravate any existing difficulties. Moreover, social isolation reduces children's potential resources for overcoming problems (Coie, 1990). One teacher poignantly described the following situation.

Mara is shy and withdrawn and comes from a very troubled family. I have been trying to find ways of supporting her, but she thwarts my every attempt. She seems so lonely and sad; I thought that I would try to pair her with some of the more sympathetic girls to see if we could substitute some friends for the lack of support she feels from her family. I have tried pairing her with peers on field trips, for special projects, even a high interest game in which she could choose her partner. Every time, it has ended in disaster. Almost as soon as the activity gets started, Mara seems to get offended and then sits there with a sullen expression on her face, staring off into space and ignoring the attempts of her partner to resolve the situation. Even the most good-hearted children have gotten frustrated and have given up. After each one of these attempts, Mara looks even more downhearted, and I know she feels that once again she has failed. It's a terrible cycle: she's lonely and desperate for companionship, yet sabotages every potential relationship. Meanwhile, she just seems to get more and more depressed. Friends, instead of being a source of support, are yet another failure.

In this case, poor peer relations were not necessarily the root of Mara's problems, but they were aggravating her problems because they were a source of pain instead of support.

On the positive side, friendships contribute to children's successful adjustment to school, and this impact, in turn, may have a long-term effect on drop-out and delinquency rates. Ladd and Price (1987) found that children who began kindergarten in a class with several of their friends had more positive feelings about school. During their kindergarten year, these children's satisfaction with school and their academic success were clearly tied to both the maintenance of old friendships and the formation of new ones (Ladd, 1990). Not only do friends ease children's transition into school, but they also help maintain interest and enjoyment in school, as is aptly illustrated by Marianne's role in helping Clara enter the classroom.

Although friendships have always been important to children, recent economic and lifestyle changes have resulted in children spending less time with their families and more time in peer group settings (day care families and centers, afterschool programs, and organized activities). This change means that peer relations now provide a greater proportion of children's socialization experiences. Thus, the quality of these peer experiences may have a growing impact on children's development (Asher, 1990).

Beyond personal well-being and success in school, friendships and positive social development better prepare children to live in the larger social world. Every day we are confronted with examples of inhumanity: random killings, intransigent racism, callous indifference to the plight of poor people, and the casual sacrifice of human lives for minor material gain. These problems stem from causes far beyond the confines of early childhood classrooms, but, by helping children develop a greater awareness and concern for others, and skills in relating to a broader range of people, we can contribute in a small way to improving the state of human relations.

PERSPECTIVES ON EARLY SOCIAL DEVELOPMENT

Daryl was from a single-parent family and had four siblings. Although his mother worked very hard, she was not able to afford many toys for her children. When Daryl first entered preschool, he refused to share anything. A typical scene was Daryl lying on top of the Playdough to prevent any other children from getting it. His teachers responded by providing him with many different materials so that he could become used to getting the resources he needed without fighting for them. They also set up situations where he could play with one other child, but did not have to share materials (e.g., Daryl and a peer would work side by side, each with his/her own puzzle). Gradually, the teachers introduced activities in which the children had to take turns. Over time, Daryl began to trust that his turn would come around and became more willing to let others have theirs. Initially, he shared begrudgingly, often giving peers the minimum access (e.g., a pea-sized piece of Playdough). Gradually, with more experience and more explicit feedback from peers, he began to share more willingly and to see peers as potential companions rather than as intruders.

In early childhood classrooms, young children are gaining social knowledge and learning how to relate effectively to other people. One underlying assumption in this book is that children are active participants in their learning. As they experiment with social interactions, they develop new theories about how the social world works. After a number of teacher interventions and peer conflicts, Daryl began to question the advantages of devoting all of his time to controlling the available materials, and soon realized that letting others use them was more fun and that he could still have access to toys. Social understanding develops as children mature and interact in their social environment. As they become more socially skilled, their peer relations become more sustained and complex. These emerging friendships, in turn, provide a context and a motivation for the development of many social skills.

To support children's social development, we need to understand their developmentally related capacities and potential. A second assumption I maintain is that assessments and strategies related to social competence must take into account children's level of cognitive, emotional, physical, and social development. In their responses to Daryl, the teachers responded to his existing needs. They did not expect him to begin to share immediately; they let him experience satisfying his own needs before they expected him to attend to those of his peers.

A third underlying assumption throughout this book is that children's development must be viewed within their immediate and larger social contexts. Often we think of social development in terms of personal relationships and ignore factors such as discrimination, poverty, and privilege that affect how children learn about other people and themselves. One of my goals in writing this book is to integrate the current research on children's interpersonal competence with the research on intergroup relations and the effects of social and economic conditions on children's development. Because they were aware of the financial circumstances of Daryl's family, the teachers interpreted his reluctance to share as, in part, a reaction to the lack of toys at home, not as evidence of a selfish disposition. This information helped them develop a more effective strategy in their work with Daryl.

DEVELOPMENTAL TRENDS AND GOALS

Children's acquisition of social skills and their engagement in increasingly complex relationships depend on many dimensions of development. To support children's social growth, we need to consider aspects of cognitive and emotional development and how they contribute to changes in social behavior and the acquisition of social skills.

In terms of cognitive development, young children are becoming aware of others' perspectives. They are learning that their needs and viewpoints may differ from those of other people and that they may have to accommodate to these different views in order to engage in meaningful conversations and games. As children become more responsive to others' needs, they gain skills in reasoning about social justice and begin to see themselves as members of a community. They also begin to understand how their relationships with various people (e.g., peers versus siblings) differ in terms of mutual expectations and gratifications. As part of this development, they develop increasingly complex concepts about friendships.

Emotionally, young children are becoming more aware of their own and others' feelings. At the same time, they are learning how to control and modulate their feelings and to conform to specific cultural rules about emotional expression. Children are also dealing with many psychosocial conflicts that are often expressed and resolved through their social play. As children become more self-sufficient, they often feel torn between being independent and dependent and worry about whether or not they are competent; successful resolution of these conflicts is critical to future social and emotional development.

Behaviorally, children are learning specific skills related to initiating and maintaining social interactions. To fully participate in their social environment, children need to learn how to gain entrance into peer groups and how to initiate interactions with individuals. If children consistently fail to make contact, they become increasingly isolated from the mainstream of peer social life. To maintain their interactions, children need to learn how to resolve conflicts and manage aggression. Sustaining peer interest also involves the ability to elaborate the theme of play; the willingness to give as well as to take; and the flexibility to exchange, adjust, and embellish roles in games and fantasy play. As children gain more awareness of others' perspectives these accommodations become easier. Children also become more responsive to others' needs and more motivated and effective in their efforts to help others. At the same time, children also need to learn how to resist peer pressure when appropriate and how to pursue their unique interests without jeopardizing their peer relationships.

All of these developmental trends and goals must be considered in the larger social context. As children are becoming more cognitively aware of other individuals, they need to learn about other groups of people and to see themselves as members of a broad and diverse social environment. Their skills in reasoning about social justice should extend beyond interpersonal conflicts to incorporate an awareness of larger social injustices such as discrimination and poverty. Learning to recognize and express their own feelings should occur in a context that helps children understand that all people have similar emotions even though they may express them differently. With this broader range of emotional awareness, children hopefully develop a concern and a sense of social responsibility for all people, not simply their immediate friends and family. Behaviorally, they need to learn skills in relating to a wide range of people, so that they are not limited to interacting only with members of their own group. As they expand their awareness and range of concern, children also need to gain the confidence and optimism that they can play an active role in creating a more just society.

CONTEXTS OF EARLY PEER RELATIONS

Although the focus of this book is on peer relations in the schools, a number of settings and a wide range of people contribute to children's peer relationships. Social experiences in school are potentially supported, undermined, alleviated, or aggravated by relationships outside of school. For example, active peer involvement in a neighborhood or religious organization might mitigate the pain and isolation of a child who is rejected in school. On the other hand, if children feel torn between the behavioral norms at school and those of their home community, their social experiences in both places may be impaired. Sometimes, school is the place in which children act out problems that they are experiencing in other social realms. Family discord may be reflected in children's hostile or withdrawn behavior with peers. Alternatively, school may provide an escape from family or neighborhood tensions. This section will provide an overview of the nonschool contexts in which children are learning to be social beings.

First, the family has a profound influence on how children approach others. From the time of their birth, children have observed their parents and other family members interacting. Depending on the social encounters that they experience and observe, they develop a generally positive or negative orientation to their social world. They also see how people initiate and maintain contact, resolve conflicts, and express feelings. Major family events such as relocation, divorce, remarriage, and birth of siblings also affect how children respond to their social world. Specific ways in which parents may influence children's social behaviors and competency will be discussed in Chapters 2 and 4.

Second, the neighborhood, which might include other adult caretakers and nonschool peers, provides a wide variety of social experiences. Children who have had the chance to interact with a number of adults often have a wider repertoire of social skills (Pettit, Harris, & Childers, 1989). Neighborhood friends often are more diverse than school friends. They are likely to include more children of different ages; and children who ignore members of the opposite sex at school may play in mixed-sex groups in their neighborhoods. These groups are also usually less closely supervised by adults and so provide children with more experience in developing their own rules and organizations.

Third, many children participate in organized programs in which they may interact with another set of age mates in drama, art, or sports. These activities offer children opportunities to interact around specific skills and interests. Children may also participate in language, religious, and cultural programs designed to maintain ties and identities with particular ethnic or religious groups.

The larger social environment affects all of these contexts. If children are members of groups that have experienced systematic discrimination and a disproportionate amount of poverty, their relations with peers, adults, and institutions may be affected by the stresses and antagonisms that commonly occur under these conditions. On the other hand, children of families who are highly successful in a material way may feel that they have to live up to or exceed their families' success. This assumption may lead them to compete with peers which may undermine their relationships. Because social values and expectations differ across ethnic groups, children from specific groups may learn particular activities and acquire specific social skills.

History also plays a role. During wartime, for example, children may develop friendships around themes that are different than those that might bring children together during a time of exciting space travel. The absence of a parent due to a national crisis will have an immediate impact on the composition of the family network. Parental unemployment or economically forced migration may disrupt a child's early relations with friends and extended family. Parenting and teaching philosophies that are prevalent at a given time also influence the amount and kinds of social pressures and opportunities that children experience.

TEACHERS' DILEMMAS AND CONCERNS

Despite the importance of social development and the vast amount of current research in this area, many educators resist the notion that children's social concerns should be a central consideration in designing classrooms and planning curricula. Teachers often worry that attending to social issues will interfere with their academic goals. This position is reinforced by the media and school systems which evaluate teachers and schools largely on their children's test scores. However, children with social problems often cannot engage in academic tasks and end up disrupting classrooms, keeping other children from their work as well. Thus, even in highly academic classrooms, social issues often intrude.

From quite another perspective, some early childhood educators feel that intervening in children's social development would be "pushing" children too hard. The philosophy of giving children time to grow out of various phases underlies many early childhood curricula and teaching practices. This hands-off approach is positive in many ways because it reflects a respect for children and their individual developmental pace. At the same time, children who are having social problems are often unhappy and may be in a self-perpetuating cycle of antagonistic behavior and rejection. This unhappiness, in turn, often interferes with children's learning, making the process of growing out of a particular phase longer and more arduous.

Some parents and teachers express concerns that the goal of a more active involvement in children's social development is to make every child popular. As one teacher put it, "Everyone is supposed to become a cheerleader." This comment reflects the common misperception that the only end point for social intervention is popularity. Contrary to this linear view, the main goal of social development is to help children find their own ways to interact comfortably with peers and to feel good about themselves while they are doing it. In fact, fulfilling a child's social potential might mean that the child learns to feel alright about playing by herself much of the time. However, children who desperately want to be in the group but are too shy or awkward need to learn enough social skills so that they can become as much a part of the social mainstream as they wish. The aggressive child who is longing for attention, but will settle for being a scapegoat, is probably miserable and is certainly not getting what she wants. Thus, the goal is not to make everyone "popular," but rather to help all children develop ways of interacting with each other that do not involve sacrificing their own interests and priorities for the sake of peer approbation.

Related to this concern about making everyone popular is the worry that socially related interventions and instructions may change children's behaviors in ways that conflict with their families' and communities' values and culture. For example, if a family feels strongly that little boys should be learning only male roles, a teacher's efforts to get the boys and girls playing together in the doll area may meet with some parental resistance. Encouraging children to talk through conflicts may seem naive in neighborhoods in which children see people settling arguments with fights and guns. We must be aware of children's larger social context and how external pressures and future expectations affect children's current functioning. To understand children in the context of their culture, teachers need to be aware of their own biases and how their ideas about appropriate social behavior reflect their own social backgrounds. Supporting children's social development does not mean teaching them specific behaviors, but rather helping them integrate successfully into their social environment.

When we are concerned about the social dynamics in our classrooms or the social development of a particular child, we often are confused about what actually is happening. As adults we can observe the contacts and behaviors of children, but in a sense we are outsiders. We cannot know with certainty how children feel about each other or predict the effects of specific behaviors. For example, a child who appears to be acting in a socially appropriate manner, such as inviting another child to join him, may be rejected despite the positive overture. Often the reason for this apparent discrepancy is not clear; the many dynamics of the local peer culture are subtle and child-defined and perhaps not visible to adults. Because children often create rituals and routines that are designed to circumvent adult restrictions (Corsaro, 1985), they may be intentionally covert. Thus, when we are attempting to analyze or intervene in children's peer relations, we frequently do not have all the information.

Even if teachers and children see the same behaviors, they may not interpret them in the same way because their perspectives are different. For example, the class clown may be seen as rude and disruptive by the teachers, but as daringly witty by peers. Because of this difference, teachers may find it difficult to analyze accurately why some children have more difficulty than others in their social interactions.

During the past 15 years, researchers have identified many aspects and nuances of children's social competence and classroom dynamics. This information can be be used to develop observation techniques and classroom practices that foster children's social development. The following chapters of this book provide an overview of some of this research and its implications for classroom practice.

2

Developmental Considerations

Daniel (2.5 years) is on his way to day care. He is eagerly talking about his friend Andrew who will be there today (Andrew only comes one day a week). "I play with Andrew today!" he crows. As Daniel enters the family day care home, Andrew rushes over and greets him. Daniel begins to hug Andrew and then reaches for the toy that Andrew has in his hand and the two boys are soon scuffling and pushing each other.

Luz (4.5 years) is playing with Gabriela in the block corner. They are collaborating on building a tall tower that will house airplanes and princesses. Suddenly an argument breaks out about the placement of a block decorated with gold braiding. Each child is grabbing this desirable object and scowling at the other one. "I need this block for the crown room!" wails Luz. Gabriela mutters "No, it's my block." Luz releases her grip on the block with a flourish and stomps out of the area informing Gabriela that "I am not your friend any more! And you can't come to my birthday party!"

Asoka, Maria, and Shandra (all in the second grade) have formed a club. It is named after a currently popular rock group. The three girls have made up membership cards and elaborate rules to insure that no nonmembers can enter or even know about the club. The members, however, make frequent, not-so-veiled references to the club and delight in refusing to satisfy their classmates' curiosity. The official purpose and activities of the club are not apparent, as the girls spend most of their time guarding against intruders and insuring each others' loyalty. There is some talk of making bookmarks and selling them, but this project is not yet underway.

These vignettes illustrate some of the similarities and differences in peer interactions at different ages. Many underlying dynamics, such as the desire for resources and the protection of friendships, emerge at all ages. However, children's understanding of their peers and their conceptualization of their relationships change dramatically during the early childhood years. These developments unfold quickly and are complex, since they reflect growth in a number of developmental domains.

11

For organizational purposes, I have divided this review into three domains of development: cognitive, emotional, and behavioral. However, as we will see in the following discussion, these areas of development often are interdependent. This chapter is also organized to view children's development in a series of expanding contexts. The first two sections focus on the development of individuals and the impact of cognitive and emotional changes on children's capabilities to function in social groups. In the section on behavioral development, children's social skills and actions are considered in the larger context of interpersonal interactions and relations. Throughout this review, we need to keep in mind that all development occurs in a social, cultural, and economic context. In the final section I will discuss some of the ways in which these factors influence the social values that underlie relationships and the specific strategies that children acquire. We need to view the findings and descriptions contained in this chapter as examples of how social development occurs with particular children, not as absolute norms of age-expected behaviors.

COGNITIVE ASPECTS OF SOCIAL DEVELOPMENT

Children's cognitive development influences how children process social information: what events or information they notice, how they interpret them, and what reasoning skills they bring to bear on solving problems. Many studies in this area are based on Piaget's theory of cognitive development. However, several commentators and researchers (e.g., Gelman, 1978, 1979; Gelman & Gallistel, 1978) have challenged Piaget's conclusions about the limited cognitive capacities of young children and the abrupt and qualitative changes between each cognitive stage. They have also raised questions about whether or not Piaget's theory, which is based on children's understanding of physical phenomena, can be applied to their understanding of their social environment (Lee, 1989). Despite these shortcomings, Piaget's descriptions of how children construct knowledge and how their thinking changes with age still provide a useful backdrop for understanding how children at different ages understand various types of social information.

Early Cognitive Stages

According to Piaget, preschool children are usually preoperational in their thinking and live in a concrete and, from their perspective, somewhat static world. They cannot yet make logical assumptions or use abstractions, nor do they anticipate events far into the future or make causal connections between past and present events. Because they rely primarily on concrete and observable information, young children often draw conclusions about their peers on the basis of physical characteristics such as appearance, dress, race, and sex. Furthermore, they are likely to think of other people in terms of single rather than multiple attributes. For example, in one preschool, a young boy was labeled as "bad" by many of his classmates. This reputation, as far as the teacher could tell, reflected the fact that he had hit several children in the beginning of the year. Although he had since calmed down, his peers' perceptions were focused on this single behavior. In a similar way, when children talk about their friends, they often describe a concrete activity or event that defines or explains that friendship. As one 4-year-old girl said, "Samir is my friend because he lets me wear his sunglasses."

Preoperational children rely on concrete perceptions and have difficulty making mental transformations, so they are often confused by physical changes. The classic example of this pattern is their inability to comprehend that an amount of liquid in a container is conserved when it is poured into a different-sized container. As with physical phenomena, preschoolers often define friendships in very concrete ways. When Luz stomps off from Gabriela, she declares that the friendship ended. This announcement reflects the typical preschooler's view that "friends are the people I play with." Because Luz is angry at Gabriela and no longer wants to play with her, the friendship is over. At this point she does not understand that the underlying attraction and affection continues and that she and Gabriela will once again be friends as soon as they have gotten over their anger.

Young children are often described as egocentric because they cannot coordinate multiple pieces of information and have a difficult time seeing their own and others' social perspectives simultaneously, as is illustrated by Daniel's grab for Andrew's toy. Preschoolers are interested in other people, enjoy their companionship, and often "feel along" with others, but have a hard time consciously anticipating what others know, see, or feel. For this reason, their contacts with peers sometimes seem to be disjointed. Piaget describes the "collective monologue" in which participants converse, but each on his or her own topic and without any real effort to communicate. Young children also tend to be immersed in their own needs, as is amply illustrated by children's conflicts over possessions, turns, and rules. (Specific developmental levels in children's abilities to take others' perspectives and to reason about social justice issues will be discussed in more detail later in this chapter.) Children, however, are not absolutely bound by their egocentrism. In many instances, they carry on relatively coherent conversations and show some capability to adjust their needs to those of others, which suggest that children's social knowledge may develop more quickly than their physical knowledge (Lee, 1989). As teachers we need to be aware of individual differences in children's level of awareness, yet realize that overall young children operate most often from their own needs and interests and rely primarily on concrete information for making social decisions.

Between the ages of 5 and 7, children begin to use logic, make mental transformations, recognize causal relations, and differentiate multiple points of view about the concrete world around them. As they enter the concrete operational stage of cognitive development and rely less on their immediate perceptions, they are no longer easily fooled by changes in appearance. They can control their thinking and become able to consider several alternatives when trying to solve problems. Because they can manipulate information better, they can engage in transitive thinking (e.g., if Rory is taller than Bonnie and Bonnie is taller than Ellen, then Rory is taller than Ellen) and class inclusion (e.g., a person can be a member of both the boy group and the whole classroom). As children gain the ability to consider multiple pieces of interconnected information, they can grasp some of the complicated dynamics of their classrooms. A 7-year-old child was deliberating about the guest list for her birthday party. "I *want* to invite Sara and Emily and Lucinda, *but* Lucinda and Sara just had a fight, so I can't have both of them. Also if I invite Emily, Beth will be hurt if I don't invite her, but if I invite her, then I really need to invite...." This example also illustrates how these older children are much more aware of peers' feelings and the fact that their own actions can affect others' sense of well-being.

Children from 5 to 7 are still bound to fairly concrete information and rarely think in the abstract. Although they see friendships as extending beyond their immediate contact, they rely on concrete manifestations such as the rules and rituals of the second-graders' club described earlier. As illustrated by the emphasis on exclusionary loyalty to the club, friendships at this age cannot sustain too many disruptions or betrayals.

During the early elementary years, children are increasingly aware of actual and potential social problems, but their ideas for solving them usually rest on single, concrete solutions (e.g., dividing resources into absolutely equal shares; poverty would be solved if rich people would give their money to poor people). As with their preschool peers, however, young elementary school students often display social sophistication that exceeds the limits that characterize their stage of cognitive development. For example, one group of first graders developed an elaborate behavioral code for deciding when it was alright and not alright to yell at another peer. As a group, they were able to consider many perspectives and nuances of behavior that might not have been obvious to individuals working independently.

Processes of Cognitive Development

Piaget described the process of cognitive development as being a continuous cycle in which children develop ideas and categories which help them see life more predictably. When they encounter events and objects that violate their expectations, they experience disequilibrium. For example, after a child has decided that "all four-legged creatures are dogs," she may begin to notice differentiations such as differences in names, sizes, and sounds that challenge that assumption. At this point, the child may experience uncertainty as she tries alternately to integrate new information into a category that no longer works and to develop a new set of categories (e.g., horses, cats, and dogs). These periods are times when children are in a state of disequilibrium and offer many possibilities for cognitive growth. In one classroom (Edwards, 1986) the teachers noticed that their 3-year-old children assumed that age and size were inextricably correlated. The teachers presented the children with a skit in which two birthday cakes, one with many candles on it and one with only a few, were to be presented to two people named Carolyn, one short older woman and one tall college-aged woman. The children had to decide which cake belonged to which person named Carolyn. At first they agreed that the taller person was older and should get the cake with the most candles. However, as the teachers asked them to explain why, the children began to notice other features such as grey hair and "broken skin" (as one child described wrinkles). As they talked, the children experienced disequilibrium in trying to reconcile their conflicting assumptions. This confusion pushed them to observe more carefully and to develop new hypotheses about what attributes actually define age. In another classroom, two first-grade boys had had a fight and were adamant that they would never be friends again. The teacher read and discussed stories in which friends are reconciled after a conflict (e.g., *Happy Birthday, Ronald Morgan; Rollo and Juliet Forever; Hating Book; I'm Not Oscar's Friend Anymore*). As the two boys heard these stories, they began to question their assumptions and to see the potential resilience of friendships. When we are working to foster children's social development, we often challenge their beliefs and support them as they construct new levels of social understanding. In short, we can take advantage of the motivation that results from the state of disequilibrium; children are confused, curious, and want to find out more.

Vygotsky (1978), like Piaget, viewed children as actively constructing their knowledge and also focused on ways in which this process occurs. In contrast to Piaget, he saw cognitive development as occurring in a social context and studied the role that social interactions play in facilitating it. He introduced the concept of the zone of proximal development to describe the difference between a child's current level of independent problem solving and her potential level of problem solving that is evident when she is being assisted or guided by an adult or a more mature peer. For example, children on their own may resolve conflicts by hitting each other and grabbing objects. With a teacher's guidance, however, they may be able to express their feelings verbally and work out a mutually acceptable resolution. During this process, the children are using their potential skills, i.e., their zone of proximal development. As teachers organize groups and help children initiate and maintain peer interactions and relations, they often think about children's potential development and the type of support and guidance that would be most effective for each individual. Although these teachers may not consciously use the term "zone of proximal development," they are applying Vygotsky's principles to engage children at their highest potential skill level. For example, a teacher may pair a child with low social skills with a more sociable peer in the hope that each will learn from the experience. The child who has difficulty in social situations may be challenged and encouraged to interact more adeptly in his encounters with his sociable model. The latter, on the other hand, may find that trying to interact with his less skilled partner challenges him to be more conscious of another's perspective and to develop new approaches to engage this child. Both children are extending their skills and are functioning in the zone of proximal development. (The practical applications of the concepts of disequilibrium and the zone of proximal development will be discussed in more detail in later chapters.)

The following sections include more specific descriptions of several aspects of children's cognitive development that relate to their social understanding: awareness of others' perspectives, reasoning about social justice, and concepts of friendships.

Awareness of Others' Perspectives

A critical component in children's increasing ability to interact with others is their ability to coordinate their own perspectives with those of other people. For example, the young child who can see only her own desire to use the tricycle may be limited to complaining and perhaps hitting the child who currently has it. However, if she can think about the other's point of view, she might be able to come up with a suitable toy as an exchange item or suggest a game in which she and her antagonist can both use the tricycle. These strategies require that the first child have some idea about the desires and preferences of the other child and be able to anticipate his response.

Children's awareness of others' perspectives develops rapidly during the early childhood period. These changes can be seen in the increasing complexity and length of their social interactions, which will be discussed later in this chapter. The cognitive aspects of these developments have been studied in depth by presenting children with different hypothetical social scenes and having them respond from different points of view. Children's responses on the interviews may not be the same as their reactions to live social situations, but the interviews do provide some insight into children's capacities to see multiple perspectives.

Selman (1980, 1981) has written extensively about how children develop the ability to see and coordinate relationships between different people's views, and to understand the psychological characteristics and capacities of others. By presenting children with several hypothetical stories of interpersonal dilemmas, he identified five levels of coordination of social perspectives.

Level 0, which characterizes children from the ages of 3 to 7, is called the egocentric or undifferentiated perspective. In this phase, children recognize thoughts and feelings within themselves and others, but cannot distinguish their own feelings from those of others. For example, they often bring new possessions to school and gleefully draw attention to them and assume that their classmates will be equally interested and excited. They do not anticipate the possible envy or disinterest that their peers might feel. Because they do not see other points of view, they also have trouble distinguishing between the overt actions and covert feelings of others. For example, if a classmate accidentally knocks down their block tower, preschoolers often assume it was a purposeful act, despite protestations to the contrary. Sometimes young children learn to talk about others' perspectives without really understanding the concept. One teacher reported that a 3-year-old child who had been hitting his peers came into the classroom one morning saying that he was going to "be nice" to his peers and "not do things that hurt them." Within a few minutes, however, he was attacking another child.

At *Level 1*, characteristic of children from the ages of 4 to 9, children are able to differentiate perspectives. They can see that others' views and feelings might be different from their own and that two people might react differently to the same situation. A child at this level who is considering whether or not to bring a new possession to school may anticipate that other children might feel envious because they do not have a similar treasure and that she might be required to share the object. Moreover, because they are more aware of different perspectives, children at this age are able to distinguish between accidental and intentional acts. The accidentally spilled paint is likely to elicit a sympathetic and helpful response, which is not the case in the preschool.

Level 2, which embraces the ages from 6 to 12, marks the onset of the ability to take a self-reflective or reciprocal perspective. At this level, children learn that they themselves can be the object of another's thoughts and feelings. During this period, they often become quite judgmental about their peers, but at the same time are very concerned about whether or not they themselves are liked. A child at this level might worry about bringing an object to school because it might not be an "in" thing to do. He is also likely to be aware of the social consequences of "showing off" and may develop elaborate schemes for deflecting this criticism (e.g., making very off-handed references to the possession and hoping that he is encouraged to show it).

The final two levels do not begin to develop until after the early childhood years. *Level 3*, which emerges between the ages of 9 and 15, denotes the ability to take a third-person or mutual perspective. It marks the beginning of children's ability to stand outside of an interaction and see the protagonists' and the outsider's perspectives. At *Level 4*, adolescents and adults are able to see that the coordination of perspectives involves a multidimensional process that may be occurring at several different levels. Individuals at this level become attuned to hidden meanings and contradictory motives. As they approach adulthood, adolescents also become aware that some perspectives (e.g., nationalism) are shared by a whole group and therefore are societal perspectives.

According to Selman's findings, most preschool and early elementary school children are at Level 0. However, the onset of Levels 1 and 2 also occurs during this period, so there may be a considerable range among children's abilities to coordinate social perspectives. This ability may also vary across situations. When children are angry because they cannot get another child to do what they want, they have a harder time seeing their antagonist's view than they would under more emotionally neutral circumstances. If the other person is a friend or someone who is very clear about his/her feelings, then children may be more accurate in their perceptions.

In actual practice, children may exceed the developmental levels identified by Selman. Analyses of young children's naturally occurring conversations have shown that children are more able to "tune into" others' perspectives than might be assumed from their responses to hypothetical situations (Lee, 1989; Rizzo, 1989). Children's responses to hypothetical situations may underestimate their actual capabilities. When children are confronted by actual social problems, they might be more motivated to think about another's perspective than they are in an interview. Because even very young children resonate to others' emotions (Hoffman, 1981), children can empathize and communicate on an emotional plane before they are consciously aware of others' perspectives. Furthermore, interactions with peers and teachers may also cause children to function at a higher level, in their zone of proximal development. For example, if one member of a pair in conflict points out that his opponent has hurt his feelings, the latter may become more aware of his protagonist's feelings than he would be otherwise. Likewise, a teacher's suggestions about possible solutions may induce the antagonists to consider solutions more sophisticated than ones they could have invented independently.

Reasoning About Social Justice

Parallel to children's increasing ability to coordinate social perspectives is their ability to decide what is fair. Many studies on moral reasoning have used Kohlberg's dilemmas and criteria to ascertain different levels of moral reasoning. Although his model is intended to be a life-span theory, most of the changes that it describes occur in adolescence, so it provides a less adequate account of the changes occurring in the early years (Damon, 1983). Damon's model of the early development of positive-justice reasoning (1980) fills in this earlier gap because it focuses on children from the ages of 4 to 11.

Knowing how children reason about justice enables teachers to understand how children view and resolve conflicts. Often resolutions and explanations that make sense to adults fail to work with young children because they cannot understand the more adult-oriented concepts of fairness that underlie them. By keeping the following levels of reasoning in mind, teachers can be more effective in helping children to develop their own solutions.

Damon's levels of positive-justice reasoning are parallel to Selman's levels of coordination of social perspectives. At *Level 0-A*, which is typical of early preschool children, children's ideas about positive justice reflect their own wishes. As one would expect of children in Selman's Level 0, young preschoolers do not easily differentiate their own perspectives from those of others and simply assert rather than justify their wishes. The child who more and more loudly demands an extra cracker at snack without attempting to justify or negotiate illustrates this level of reasoning. *Level 0-B* is characteristic of the older preschool child (ages 4–5). By this time, children are still egocentric in their perspectives and guided by their own wishes, but have learned that they need to make some justification in order to get their way. Their reasons, however, are often irrelevant to the issue and ultimately self-serving. "I need another cracker because I'm the biggest person at this table!" is a typical justification at this age.

Damon's *Level 1* is parallel to Selman's Level 1 in which children can differentiate their perspectives from others, but only in a concrete way. At *Level 1-A* of children's positive-justice reasoning (ages 5–7), children recognize the need for fairness, but can think only in terms of strict equality. A group of children may painstakingly count the number of crackers (often down to the extra crumbs) and divide them equally among the claimants. They are also concerned about their peers' rule infractions and often become classroom enforcers or tattlers. At *Level 1-B* (ages 6–9), children have developed some ideas about reciprocity and merit. They might either trade snack food or argue that one member deserves more because she did something particularly helpful or challenging that day. The exchanges are done in a very precise fashion and justified by concrete reasons.

Damon's *Level 2* occurs after the early childhood years. After 8 years of age, children are more aware of moral relativity and understand that people can have equally valid yet different points of view. They also begin to recognize that different principles such as merit and equality may sometimes be in conflict and have to be weighed against each other. With this awareness, they realize that problems may have a number of valid, yet competing, solutions. Children can only reason at these levels after they have developed the ability to take the third-person or mutual perspectives that characterize Selman's Level 3.

As children experience the many conflicts that arise in classrooms and among family members, they develop and discard hypotheses about what is fair. Often they experience bewilderment, but these moments are excellent ones for helping children begin to reason at a higher level. By engaging in conflicts and negotiations, they are also exposed to others' ideas about fairness that further stimulate the development of more sophisticated ideas.

Concepts About Friendships

As children engage in different peer relations, they define and refine the concept of friendship and develop hypotheses about how friendships work. They demonstrate their increasing sophistication both in their actions with friends and in their ideas about the concept of friendship. Most of the research on this question has been done by interviewing children about their friends (e.g., Berndt, 1986; Selman, 1981). Not surprisingly, children's responses reflect the same kind of cognitive shifts described in the previous sections on coordinating social perspectives and reasoning about social justice. In fact, Selman (1981) makes very explicit connections between levels of perspective-taking and concepts of friendship. Although the exact terms have varied, the following sequence has been identified in several studies.

Infants and toddlers, who are still in the sensory–motor stage of cognitive development, cannot, of course, describe their conceptions of peer experiences. Toddlers, however, do seem to differentiate familiar and unfamiliar play partners. When they are with familiar peers, they engage in more reciprocal play, such as alternating the roles of chaser and chasee (Howes, 1987b), and more social pretend play (Howes, Unger, & Seidner, 1989) than they do when they are with unfamiliar peers. Interestingly, toddlers have fewer and more stable relationships than do preschoolers (Howes, 1983). For these very young children, one or two familiar peers may be a source of security in the absence of parents, whereas preschoolers are more independent and interested in exploring their social options.

During preschool, children form "playmateships" in which children think of their most frequent companions as their friends (Selman, 1981).

Friendships are defined by the current situation. Children sometimes say "I can't be your friend today" when they really mean "I'm playing with somebody else right now." Because frequency of association is often determined by availability and proximity (e.g., the child in the apartment upstairs), some friendship choices may reflect convenience more than personal preference for that particular child. Despite the transitory nature of early peer relations, many young children do develop strong preferences for particular peers. Their choices usually reflect similarity of play styles and activities that directly affect the quality of their interactions. Thus, children who like to build with blocks, enjoy rough-and-tumble play, or prefer quiet table activities gravitate toward each other and become frequent companions. If these activity preferences change, then the relationship is likely to dissolve. As one would expect of young children in Selman's egocentric level of coordination of social perspectives, these children see friendships in terms of their own immediate pleasure, not as a long-term commitment to a particular person. Although some friendships at this age are quite stable, they often end when one partner is absent for a period of time during which the other partner may become involved with other peers.

Children in late preschool and early elementary school see friendships as relationships of one-way assistance (Selman, 1981). Children are beginning to see the difference between their current playmates and long-term friends. One child, who was just beginning to make this differentiation, made the distinction between "buddies" and "friends." The latter were the children he was playing with at that moment, but if he was not playing with a particular child, he would reassure himself and the child by saying, "But we're still buddies, right?" Although these children are now able to differentiate their own perspectives from those of others, they still see peers in terms of their own needs. Best friends are peers who are successful in anticipating and meeting each other's needs. These relationships are more stable than those of early preschoolers because they depend on shared knowledge developed over time rather than on a momentary attraction. At the same time, children's own needs still predominate, and they often pressure their friends to comply with their wishes by threatening to end the friendship (e.g., "If you don't let me have my turn now, I won't be your friend."). Thus, these relationships are quite fragile, and rather small external events can end them. For example, if two companions begin to get interested in different types of activities, or new friends, they may not sustain efforts to maintain the relationship for very long.

In the early elementary years, children begin to form friendships that are described by Selman as Fairweather Cooperation. In these relationships, children recognize the two-way nature of the relationship and the need to adjust to each others' preferences and interests. These relationships are more stable and flexible than those of the earlier years and often involve long-term cooperative projects such as building a clubhouse or forming a sports team. However, they continue only as long as they serve the needs of both children. When reporting on why friendships end at this age, children often describe "huge fights" that resulted when one partner defected to a new friend or violated the trust of the other. Although sometimes children do reconcile, these events can end forever the trust and mutual interest that the two friends once shared.

In adolescence, relationships become more psychologically intimate and less dependent on shared activities. Now the partners feel a loyalty to and trust in the relationship itself and work to insure that minor arguments and events do not disrupt it. The relationship also shifts from an activity focus to a haven for personal support and disclosure. Because they are so intimate, partners in these relationships become very possessive and feel betrayed if the person who knows so much about them leaves them for another peer.

Finally, adults engage in autonomous yet interdependent friendships. They no longer need to possess each other absolutely in order to feel psychologically safe and intimate. They also understand that friendships can continue despite distance and long periods without contact.

Based on his observations in a first-grade classroom, Rizzo (1989) has questioned whether or not Selman's levels truly reflect children's practical understanding of friendships. The first graders he studied appeared to have a commitment to relationships and an understanding of what it takes to maintain them that was more advanced than Selman's levels suggest. In their day-to-day interactions, children have the benefit of feedback from their peers and may mutually adjust their behaviors almost intuitively. Furthermore, their desire to maintain friendships may motivate them to be more responsive and flexible and to push themselves to develop interactive skills that are beyond those that they can describe in an interview. By using both interview data and observations, we can gain a fuller picture of how children act with their friends and how well they understand these processes.

EMOTIONAL ASPECTS OF SOCIAL DEVELOPMENT

Recognizing and Expressing Emotions

Emotions provide the energy that drives or disrupts many social interactions. When people are enjoying each other, conversations and play flow smoothly; when there is mistrust or anger, the tension either makes the interaction explosive or, if it is covert, causes the interaction to limp along in a stilted manner. Thus, learning how to recognize emotions in oneself and others and how to express them effectively are crucial components in the development of social skills and peer relationships.

Basic emotional responses of joy, anger, fear, disgust, and interest are evident in facial expressions during the first year of life, and the ability to experience these reactions may be inborn (Izard, 1977). These feelings also appear to be universal, as cross-cultural studies have shown that people all over the world make similar facial expressions and report similar physiological reactions in response to the same emotions (Singer, 1984).

As children develop, they go through several different levels of skill development in the integration and differentiation of emotions (Fischer, Shaver, & Carnochan, 1989). Their emotional responses change from simple reflexes (e.g., a newborn's undifferentiated crying), to goal-directed behaviors (e.g., a toddler's struggles to retrieve a desired object), to representational enactments (e.g., a preschooler's role play about an angry mother), to symbolic expressions (e.g., a second grader's elaborate insults designed to hurt a peer).

With age, children become more skilled in recognizing the emotions of others. During the first year of life, infants learn to recognize emotions of their caretakers and use that information (e.g., a parent's encouraging smile versus a look of fear) to regulate their own behaviors (Lamb & Campos, 1982). Preschoolers' abilities to recognize others' emotions appear to develop more quickly than one might expect from the egocentrism described by Selman (Zahn-Waxler, Cummings, & Cooperman, 1984). Children as young as 3 years of age are able to identify happy and sad faces and predict what situations might produce each reaction (Borke, 1971). During their early elementary years, children learn to recognize more complicated emotions (e.g., frustration, shame) (Zahn-Waxler, Iannotti, & Chapman, 1982). Children's abilities to monitor their own emotions are related to their skills in identifying facial expressions of other people (Eder & Jones, 1989). Thus, familiarity with one's own feelings may be related to more accurate perceptions of their peers' emotional states.

With their increasing skills both in expressing emotions and in recognizing others' responses to themselves, children begin to conform to cultural rules about emotional expression. As early as preschool, children begin to mask or feign emotional reactions. For example, they learn that "big boys don't cry" and that girls scream when being chased by a group of boys. In elementary school they may conceal feelings of discouragement or inadequacy by bragging about a failed test. As they learn that expression of emotions may not always be a good idea, they begin to discuss others' emotional experiences as a way of pretending that they themselves do not have certain feelings (Barden, Zelko, Duncan, & Masters, 1980). Rules about emotional expression often fit rigid gender stereotypes, as can be seen from some of the foregoing examples. Cultural rules about when and how emotions can be expressed can sometimes create problems for children who come from backgrounds that are different from that of the teachers and the other children in their schools. They may find that teachers and peers do not know how to "read" their feelings and that they are ridiculed for the ways in which they express or suppress their emotions. In one classroom, a child who was from a culture that stressed reticence in the expression of personal feelings was intimidated by his more expressive and boisterous peers, who responded to his reticence by trying to provoke him to get mad. His more expressive peers seemed to be uneasy about not knowing how the child felt. He, in turn, became increasingly withdrawn in the face of these provocations.

In the early development of their emotional control and expression, young children are emotionally labile (Maccoby, 1980). They are often flooded by emotions which disorganize their behavior. As teachers well know, children's excitement over a new toy or activity can easily get out of control. During their early childhood years, children learn how to modulate their emotional reactions so that they can organize their behavior to respond to situations more effectively. For example, they learn not simply to hit at a child who takes their toy, but to argue or negotiate, or to find an adult who can assist in resolving the conflict.

Affective expressiveness is an important element in interactions. Emotions inject life into peer interactions and help sustain and invigorate preschool children's play (Sroufe, Schork, Motti, Lawroski, & LaFreniere, 1984). The introduction of dramatic events, such as robbers in the housekeeping corner or a "flood" in the sandbox, enliven the ongoing play and make it much more engaging for all children. Children's glee as well as feigned fear is often the glue that holds an interaction together. In a recent observation, a 5-year-old and 6-year-old had just met each other and were tentatively finding common ground, when they discovered a muddy area in the yard. As they began to squish the mud and smear it on some sand box toys (and themselves), they became more and more exhilarated. They played gleefully for over an hour, wallowing in the mud and then cleaning it up by throwing water all over everything. Children who convey a generally positive affect and express their negative and positive emotions appropriately are more socially competent and better liked than those who are either emotionally "flat" or inappropriate in their expressions (Sroufe et al., 1984). These patterns are not exclusively related to negative emotions. Sroufe et al. described how one child who was always smiling inappropriately was avoided and disliked by his peers.

Emotions are an inextricable part of social interactions and relationships. Learning to be aware of one's own emotions, to recognize others' feelings, and to express emotions genuinely and appropriately are critical components of early social adjustment.

Psychosocial Themes

Children are often ambivalent about growing up. One day they may be ready to conquer the world, the next day they may want to retreat from all these challenges. During childhood and adolescence, they experience this conflict along many different dimensions. How these tensions are resolved influences children's long-term emotional and social well-being. The conflicts that children are currently experiencing often emerge as themes in their social play. These themes illustrate ways in which social and emotional development interact to the mutual benefit of both domains. Children's play provides an outlet for emotional tension and an opportunity to resolve emotional conflicts. For example, a child who is torn between being independent and dependent may enact the role of a bad baby. At the same time, common emotional concerns facilitate peer interactions. As one child begins to enact the misbehaving baby, the other child seems to know instinctively how to play the irate mother. Often this apparent familiarity is a reflection of shared age-related concerns and common play roles and scripts.

The most comprehensive model of psychosocial conflicts was developed by Erik Erikson (1963). In his life-span model he articulates how, at each stage of childhood and adulthood, we face a particular developmental crisis. This model, which was developed in the United States in the 1950s, may not be as applicable to females as it is to males and may not accurately describe experiences of people growing up in very different societies. However, despite its potential bias, this theory shows how at least some children experience the ambivalent processes of development and how these themes affect children's social development.

According to Erikson (1963), young children have recently emerged from the crisis of Trust versus Mistrust that characterizes their psychosocial development during infancy. In their early peer relations, young children are still looking for evidence that they can trust the larger social world. To develop that trust, children need peers that respond to their needs in a predictable and appropriate manner (Buzzelli & Fine, 1989). Children are more likely to avoid peers who behave erratically. They also ensure predictability in their peer interactions by developing a number of routines in which they follow prescribed scripts. In a classroom of 3-year-olds, two shy girls established a ritual of starting the day in the housekeeping corner, donning the same clothes, and enacting the identical shopping trip day after day. After they completed this routine, which seemed to provide them with some security and confidence, they then went on to other activities and peers.

As toddlers, children experience the crisis of Autonomy versus Shame/Doubt, according to Erikson. At this age they strongly assert their will, yet worry about pleasing adults and possibly losing them. Preschoolers often enact this conflict with scenes of "bad" children being scolded by an irate mother or games involving "bad guys" versus "good guys." In many fantasy sequences, children deliberately violate the "rules" of the house game or jail game, and wait to be caught and punished.

Preschool children are typically in the Initiative versus Guilt stage and are often exuberantly exercising their new physical and cognitive powers on the world. This sense of freedom, however, often carries with it an awareness of their relative powerlessness and a concern that they may lose the security of their caretakers. These concerns get played out in many dramatic themes such as lost–found, danger–rescue, and death–rebirth (Corsaro, 1985), in which they conquer or gain control of the feared event.

Kindergarten and early elementary school children are likely to be moving into Erikson's fourth stage of Industry versus Inferiority in which children focus on mastery and competence. Children are more likely to engage in joint projects and to want to have some tangible outcomes of their work, rather than enjoy the free-flowing play of their younger peers. At this age, children begin to worry about their relative level of competence and compare themselves with their peers. This focus introduces a comparative and sometimes competitive element into peer interactions. They begin to enjoy games that have specified rules and clear outcomes and are increasingly interested in who is winning and who is losing.

SOCIAL SKILLS AND BEHAVIORS

During the early childhood years, children go from making their first tentative peer contacts to being able to sustain long interactions in the context of ongoing relationships. This rapid development means that groups of children are constantly changing over the year and that, in any classroom, children may be functioning at a number of different levels. Successful social behavior requires a number of different skills, which are discussed in this section. They include initiating social contacts and entering groups, maintaining social encounters, resolving conflicts, controlling aggression, and responding prosocially to the needs of peers. Almost all of the studies cited in the following review were done in the United States and many were conducted with middle-class children. Thus, the particular behaviors described may not be applicable to all children. However, the underlying developmental trends are likely to show up in a wide variety of cultures and communities.

Initiating Contacts and Entering Groups

In order for children to engage in a peer interaction, they have to enter an ongoing group of peers, initiate a contact with a friend or acquaintance, or be approached by other children. As will be discussed in Chapter 3, interactions in preschool classrooms are short, so children are constantly having to gain entry into new groups. This process is made more difficult because children who are already engaged with each other tend to protect their interactive space and reject newcomers (Corsaro, 1981, 1985). In elementary classrooms, interactions are more sustained, but groups are also more rigid, making it harder for children to engage peers who are not their usual friends.

Children's entry strategies and their rate of success have been studied by a number of researchers. The following observations illustrate some of the different types of strategies and responses that occur in early childhood classrooms.

Marisa (3.7 years) walks over to a table where Irina is working with Playdough. She watches for a moment, then pulls out a chair and carefully sits down. She takes a small piece of Playdough from the mound in the center of the table and begins to roll it while humming quietly to herself. Irina looks up as Marisa approaches, smiles briefly, and then returns to her work. They continue working with no interaction.

Elena (4.5 years) arrives at the door of her classroom, bursting with excitement. She rushes over to a table where four children are working on art projects. She cries out, "Look at my new sneakers! They are pink and have hearts on them!" Two of the children glance in her direction, but do not make any response to her. Elena then grabs Steven's arm (he is sitting closest to her) and commands, "Look at my new sneakers!" He pushes her hand away and growls, "Cut it out!" Elena looks bewildered and slowly walks over to a teacher and quietly tells her about the new sneakers.

Jeremy (5.4 years) is scanning the room where several groups of children are playing in a variety of activities. His eyes fix on two boys, Alberto and Ron, who are building with blocks. He goes over to them and watches with interest as they construct a garage. They continue working and do not appear to notice him. Jeremy then squats down and places a block on the periphery of the building and says quietly, "This could be the air pump." Ron looks over, smiles, and says, "Yeh! And here's the place to fix the tires!" Jeremy sits down close to the two boys and they begin to discuss the various aspects of the garage as they continue to place blocks on the structure.

Lon (6.4 years) walks over to two boys who are standing at the pencil sharpener in the back of the room. As he vigorously sharpens his pencil, he asks quietly, "We gonna play...today?" One of the two boys nods his head and the other surreptitiously gives the thumbs up sign. The three boys, all glancing at the teacher in the front of the room, return to their seats.

As the teacher dismisses the class for recess, Adrian (7.2 years) approaches Lianna. "I have a new jump rope, do you want to jump rope with me?" Lianna looks disconcerted and watches other girls form into groups. A member of one of these groups looks over at Lianna. "Hey, Lianna, are you coming?" Aletha demands impatiently. Lianna looks back at Adrian and stammers, "I'm sorry, I can't...I already promised...." Her voice trails off and she rushes over to the other girls. Adrian looks downcast and wanders off by herself.

In their attempts to initiate contacts, children use a number of different strategies that range from fairly passive ones, as illustrated by Marisa's entry and Jeremy's initial approach; to more active ones, such as those used by Lon and Adrian; to demanding ones, as illustrated by Elena's attempts to gain attention. A number of specific entry strategies, responses, and outcomes have been identified in a variety of research projects (e.g., Dodge, Pettit, McClaskey, & Brown, 1986; Putallaz, 1983; Putallaz & Gottman, 1981; Ramsey, 1989b; Ramsey, 1989c). Children's responses to entry attempts vary from welcoming to rejecting and include acceptance (e.g., "Here, you can have this truck."), acknowledgement (e.g., target child smiles briefly and then returns to what s/he was doing before), no response (e.g., target child appears not to notice the approach of the newcomer), and rejection (e.g., "Get out of here! You can't come in!"). Outcomes are usually measured by the affective tone and level of involvement and include the following: positive social interactions (e.g., the children sit down and do a puzzle together), negative interactions (e.g., fights, continued squabbling), no interactions (e.g., one participant leaves the area), and parallel play (e.g., both children stay at the puzzle table, but work on their own puzzles and do not have any interaction).

The types of strategies that children use are highly associated with particular responses and outcomes (Ramsey, 1989b; Ramsey, 1989c). The most passive strategy is called "wait and hover." Entering children simply approach and watch what is going on with no verbal or nonverbal attempt to initiate contact. Often children seem to use this approach as a way of learning what is going on so that they can make a more successful entry bid later. Still unobtrusive, but somewhat more active, is synchronous behavior typified by Marisa's entry. In this case, children make no overt request to join, but simply begin doing the same thing as the other person(s) and quietly blend into the ongoing activity. Both of these entries are most likely to elicit passive responses from the target children. They may not respond at all or briefly acknowledge the presence of the newcomer, in either case making no effort to accept or reject the newcomer. As children more actively seek contact, they often make sociable overtures such as greetings, invitations, comments about similarities between the enterer and the target(s), and references to friendship. These bids most often receive accepting and welcoming responses from their targets. This type of entry is illustrated by Adrian's approach to Lianna. Despite her sociable tone and intention, Adrian was rejected. In this case, ongoing friendships and classroom status had a mediating effect on the effectiveness of her entry bid. (These factors will be discussed later in this section.) Another active approach is informational statements or questions. Lon's contact is an example of this approach. These entry approaches usually elicit a favorable response, but do not necessarily evolve into social interactions because often the informational exchange is all that is required, and the children then return to their previous activity. Children sometimes make overt requests to join a group (e.g., "Can I play with you?"), which is another active bid. These requests are often turned down, possibly because they are stated in a way that almost invites rejection. Also, often embedded in requests is the desire to obtain a particular resource (e.g., a share of the Playdough, a turn on the bouncy ball), so that targets' responses may also reflect a desire to protect their resources. Some entries are attempts to control the behaviors of the target children and include bids for attention, illustrated by Elena, demands for materials or access, or disruptions of the ongoing activity (e.g., knocking down the block structure, telling the players that they are playing with the wrong rules). Not surprisingly, all of these attempts to control are met most often with resistance and rejection.

Success in entry attempts appears to be related to two factors besides the specific strategy used (Putallaz & Wasserman, 1990). First, if the entering child adapts and contributes to the targets' ongoing play, she is more likely to be accepted. Second, how children sequence their strategies has an impact. Many successful entries consist of an initial hovering approach, during which the child learns what is going on and gets an initial reading of the targets' response, and then makes a more assertive bid. This approach also allows children to save face by withdrawing before making an overt bid if they think that rejection is a likely response. At the same time, children can be too hesitant. Children who approach others in a confident and positive way are more likely to meet an accepting response than those who are very tentative (Mize, Ladd, & Price, 1985). Jeremy's successful entry illustrates both of these patterns; he begins by observing and then fits smoothly into the ongoing play. Elena's entry illustrates the opposite effect. Her initial approach was highly directive, and she was oblivious to the ongoing activity of the group. Needless to say, her peers experienced her arrival as an undesired disruption and reacted accordingly.

As children become more cognitively aware of others' perspectives, they become more effective in initiating peer contact. In one study of preschool children in age-segregated classrooms (Ramsey, 1989b), the youngest children (3-year-olds and 4-year-olds) most frequently waited and hovered or engaged in synchronous behavior. Low-risk entries such as these enabled the younger children to initiate interactions and enter groups without explicitly requesting permission or drawing attention to themselves. The kindergarteners, however, used more assertive strategies such as sociable comments and actions and informational questions and comments. This change suggests that children gain both confidence and skills in initiating contacts during their preschool years. The older children also became more subtle and diplomatic in their rejections. Instead of overtly rejecting a newcomer, they often permitted his entrance and then simply left the area and went on to another activity.

Children become increasingly skilled at engaging peers during the early elementary years (Dodge et al., 1986). However, their opportunities to initiate contacts decline as the overall social structure becomes more rigid, and children stay in their established groups for longer periods of time (Putallaz & Wasserman, 1989). As groups coalesce, outsiders find them harder to enter and soon no longer try. Children's friendship choices and status begin to have more impact on whether or not an entry is accepted. Adrian's approach was rejected primarily because she was low status (based on sociometric data) and did not belong to the same group as her target (Lianna). Her expectation that a new jump rope might be enough to convince Lianna to forego playing with her usual cohorts suggests that she is naive about how classroom relationships function. This strategy might work in a preschool classroom where groups are more fluid and children more entranced by novel toys, but not in a classroom where groups are clearly formed and generally recognized by all the children. (The effects of social status and friendship patterns will be discussed in more detail in Chapter 4.) Despite the increasingly rigid social structure, older children are more aware of the initiator's feelings and more subtle in their rejections. Whereas preschoolers frequently use overt rejections, elementary school children more often simply ignore the newcomer (Shantz, 1987). As illustrated by Lianna's response to Adrian, they are more uncomfortable at having to reject a peer, even one they do not like.

During their early school years, children are gaining many skills in initiating contacts, but at the same time, they confront an increasingly rigid social environment. Thus, efforts to help children develop entry skills may have a greater chance of success if done during the preschool years when changes in behavior are more likely to result in greater group acceptance.

Maintaining Social Interactions

Once children have made contact, they then confront a number of challenges in maintaining interactions with each other. The level of social participation often shifts during the course of an interaction, but there are some overall developmental trends that affect the length and quality of children's interactions. In general, as children's peer relationships become more stable and their communication skills increase, their social play becomes more sustained and complex.

Prior to the preschool years, infants and toddlers go through four stages of social engagement (Howes, 1987b). First, infants younger than a year begin to recognize a peer as a social partner by sharing the manipulation of objects and imitating and touching each other. Second, young toddlers (13–24 months) engage in complementary and reciprocal play in which partners exchange both turns and roles in action (e.g., chaser and chasee). Often children develop fairly stable partnerships in which they share these action routines. Third, in the late toddler period (25–36 months), children begin to communicate meaning and can arrive at shared understanding of the content of the interaction. Social pretend play begins to emerge at this point, and children assume complementary pretend roles such as father and baby. Finally, they become aware of group membership and the behavioral characteristics of individuals in their group. They can now use language to communicate their wishes, and the simple behavioral routines of toddlers become the more complex games and fantasies of preschoolers.

In her observations of preschool children in 1933, Parten identified six levels of social participation that are still used today by many teachers and researchers. The levels of play are (1) *unoccupied behavior*, in which a child is aimlessly wandering or momentarily watching others; (2) *solitary play*, during which a child makes no effort to engage others and plays with toys that are different from those of children around her or him; (3) *onlooking behavior*, in which the child intently watches a particular group of children and may talk with them, but makes no overt effort to join the group; (4) *parallel play*, during which children play with the same toys or activity and are close to each other, but play independently and make no effort to engage each other; (5) *associative play*, during which children are engaged in similar materials and activities, converse about what they are doing, and exchange materials, but do not attempt to organize the activity into a joint project or shared fantasy; and (6) *cooperative organized play*, which is group play in which the members are clearly identified and are organized around a shared goal or fantasy (children have differentiated roles and tasks so that the efforts of one member are complemented by another).

In a more recent study, Parker and Gottman (1989) identified three levels of interactive play. Their first level is *coordinated cooperative play* or peaceful companionship, which is analogous to Parten's associative play. The next level is *joint activity*, in which children do something together and so must manage conflict and excitement. The highest level is *fantasy play* that involves children creating their own world and continuously negotiating roles, actions, props, and settings. These last two levels are subcategories of Parten's level 6 cooperative play.

During the preschool years, children increase their time in the higher levels of social participation. Although Parten found that parallel play is most common for all preschool children, she noted a dramatic shift in the other levels of social participation from 2 years to 4.5 years. The time spent in associative and cooperative play increases, and conversely the time spent in unoccupied, solitary, and onlooker behavior decreases. The duration of children's social interactions also increases during this period (Ramsey, 1990). Cognitively, these shifts parallel children's increasing ability to coordinate social perspectives, which enables them to sustain more complex social interactions.

Play has a cognitive dimension as well as a social one, which is often divided into four categories: *functional play*, which consists of simple repetition (e.g., swinging); *constructive play*, in which children manipulate objects to construct or create something new; *dramatic play*, in which an imaginary situation is introduced; and, finally, *games with rules*, in which children agree to play according to a set of predetermined rules (Smilansky, 1968). Children shift from functional play to games with rules as they go through their preschool years, but this change is not linear: a child might be engaged in functional play in one activity and dramatic play in another during the same day. These levels of play interact with the level of social participation (Rubin, 1977). For example, a child is more likely to engage in functional play when she is alone, or in a parallel play situation, whereas dramatic play and games with rules occur more often in cooperative situations.

During an interaction, children's level of participation often shifts in levels of involvement. Among preschool children, episodes of parallel play often precede associative or cooperative play, suggesting that young children may need a transition between solitary and interactive play (Bakeman & Brownlee, 1980). Children often have to work quite hard to gain and maintain higher levels of involvement. Parker and Gottman (1989) described this process as a series of small tentative steps which are slow escalations of play and which do not always evolve into coordinated play. To facilitate this process, young children often try to maintain a climate of agreement by identifying commonalities, even ones that are trivial. One group of 4-year-old girls always found one color that their clothes had in common and called themselves the "blue team" or "green team" or whatever the common color was that day. Children also solidify their current partnerships by rejecting other classmates (e.g., "Me and Jesse are friends so you can't be our friend today.").

In middle childhood, groups are more defined and children consciously identify themselves as members of a particular clique. In their study of children's conversations, Parker and Gottman (1989) found that among elementary school children gossip about other classmates was the most common topic. It both reaffirms the boundary between insiders and outsiders and establishes the norms of that particular group. For example, if two children are belittling a third's style of dress, they are reassuring themselves that they are correctly attired and are part of the inside group that knows the difference. The social interactions at this age are longer (Putallaz & Wasserman, 1989) and relationships more stable, and children now participate in many ongoing cooperative ventures such as sports teams, clubs, small businesses, and plays. Reflective of their need for mastery as well as their increased social skills, children at this age engage in games and activities that have clearer structures, rules, and tangible outcomes, quite unlike the free-flowing play of their early childhood years.

We know less about the social participation patterns of these older children because they are more difficult to study. First, the structure of most elementary school classrooms does not allow for the spontaneous contacts of most preschools, so children's peer preferences are less obvious. Most studies of social patterns at this age have focused on playground behaviors (e.g., Ladd, 1983; Putallaz & Wasserman, 1989) and are thus confined to short recess periods. These older children are also more conscious of observers and therefore less easy to watch when they engage in spontaneous behavior. Furthermore, they are more independent and spend more social time away from direct adult supervision. Consequently, teachers often have to rely on more indirect information, such as the groups that form on the way out to recess, children's facial expressions when they return, and their manipulation of the seating and grouping system to be with friends, in order to learn about the nature of children's peer contacts.

Peer Conflicts

Although we tend to view peer conflicts negatively, they play an important role in children's social development. They challenge children's assumptions and force them to see others' perspectives. In a recent review of the literature on conflict, Carolyn Shantz (1987) stated that "conflict is an essential impetus to change, adaptation, and development" (p. 284).

Social conflicts occur when the goals and/or behaviors of two or more individuals or groups are incompatible. They span the range between mild disagreements over the possession of a toy to international wars over land. Although aggression often occurs during these disputes, it should not be equated with conflict, because it can occur outside of conflicts, and many conflicts do not involve aggressive acts. Developmental trends in aggression will be discussed in more detail in the next section.

Conflicts have been most commonly studied in preschools, so we know less about the frequency and type of disputes that occur in elementary class-rooms. In her review of studies of social conflict in preschools, Hay (1984) found that the number of conflicts in a classroom varies from 2.4 to 23.0 per hour. Some of the variability reflects the different sizes of classrooms (obviously, more children means more potential antagonists) and methods of observation. In over half of the studies, disputes occurred from 4 to 10 times an hour. The episodes are usually quite short, ranging from 12 to 31 seconds, although here again there is considerable variability depending on how researchers define the onset and offset of a conflict episode. In one study, Dawe (1934) observed that quarrels lasted for an average of 23.6 sec-onds. Overall, conflicts are rare, and are brief in duration in most preschool classrooms (Shantz, 1987).

The causes of conflicts change during the early childhood years. The most common (71%) area of conflict among preschoolers is the control and use of objects (Hay, 1984). Their next most frequent arguments involve efforts to control the behavior of their peers (e.g., "Stop chasing me!") (Shantz, 1987). Entry attempts fall into this category of disputes because children often end up quarreling when a newcomer persists despite being rejected. During the preschool years, object disputes decrease and social control conflicts increase (Dawe, 1934). Kindergarten and elementary chil-dren often argue about rule violations. If their peers do not follow classroom procedures or game rules, they often engage in lengthy legalistic arguments. Their conflicts also focus on academic and skill competition as they vie to outdo their peers. At any age, the surface cause of the conflict may not be the real issue. For example, a child who is feeling rejected by his former best friend may start a fight over imagined rule infractions.

In order for a conflict to occur, one child or group must first make a ver-bal or nonverbal move that is then opposed by another. Children employ numerous strategies and tactics in their efforts to pursue their goals (Shantz, 1987). Often the tactics vary according to the type of conflict. For example, if a child wants to get an object away from a peer, then her strategies are likely to be directed toward gaining physical control over the object. How-ever, an argument over a rule may involve legalistic verbal exchanges.

The types of strategies also change during this period as children learn to use less physical force and more indirect efforts to gain compliance from peers (Selman and Demorest, 1984). Initially, children rely on more primitive strategies that involve simply overcoming another's wishes by physical force or by flight. Later, children use forceful verbal strategies such as threats or appealing to authority. As children become more aware of their protagonist's state of mind, they begin to employ tactics of friendly persuasion. Parkhurst and Gottman (1986) found that children older than 5 years of age use tact, deference, and common interests in their efforts to gain compliance, whereas younger children's polite efforts are limited to the use of commonality. Older children are more rewarded for their use of tact, since their peers respond favorably to tactful overtures. Younger children, however, respond more frequently to power assertions (e.g., "We need that right now!") than to polite requests.

Following the opening move on the part of the first protagonist(s), the second member(s) resist(s). Several kinds of oppositions were identified by Eisenberg and Garvey (1981): (a) a simple "no"; (b) a reason for opposing (e.g., "I'm using it now"); (c) a counterproposal (e.g., offering a substitute object); (d) a temporizing move (e.g., "You can have it in five minutes"); and (e) an evasion or a hedge (e.g., directing their opponent to another activity). The second type was most frequently used by children in both preschool and early elementary school, suggesting that these children have learned that refusals must be bolstered by reasons in order to be effective. The subsequent moves of one or both parties can either escalate or mitigate the conflict. Repeated and vociferous demands are likely to aggravate the conflict. On the other hand, efforts to explain one's position, propose alternatives, or suggest a compromise give the opponent "something to work with" (Eisenberg & Garvey, 1981) and may lead to a successful resolution.

Most conflicts are settled by the children, with no adult intervention (Shantz, 1987), and the resolutions usually involve a win/lose outcome. In object and territorial conflicts, defenders are more successful than invaders (Ramsey, 1987; Shantz & Shantz, 1985) because they can lay claim to the rule of "I had it first." They may also be more persistent because they are already invested in the object, whereas the invader has not yet played with it. After a conflict in which one child submits to another (e.g., withdraws or gives up the contested object), the pair is more likely to separate. However, when the protagonists make conciliatory gestures (e.g., offering an object or affectionately touching) the social interaction is likely to continue without any disruption (Sackin & Thelen, 1984). The relationship between antagonists also influences the outcome of a conflict. Conflicts between mutual friends, as opposed to those between nonfriends, are less intense and more likely to result in equal outcomes and continued social contacts (Hartup, Laursen, Eastensen, & Stewart, 1988). Although children settle many disputes on their own, teachers can help children learn more effective conflict resolution techniques, as will be discussed in Chapter 6.

Children's ideas about conflict resolution change as they become more aware of others' perspectives (Selman, 1981). In response to hypothetical conflicts, younger children suggest strategies that rely on either physical force or threats to leave the interaction. As they grow older, children see that the psychological effects of the conflict are important, but only from one perspective. Their solutions reflect two new themes: one is to undo the harm (e.g., "Take back what you said!") and the second is to compensate the injured party (e.g., "Do something nice so he'll feel better."). By around 8 years of age, children begin to realize that all participants are psychologically affected by a conflict and that a successful resolution must satisfy both parties, not just one. Adolescents realize that conflicts may at times be caused by personality differences and that resolving them may strengthen a relationship and allow the expression of personal feelings.

Although conflicts frequently disrupt classrooms, they also provide an impetus for children to increase their social understanding. When children encounter opposition, they often experience some disequilibrium and are motivated to reconsider their previous positions. As teachers guide children through conflict resolutions, they are often working with children in their zone of proximal development as they help them develop new levels of awareness and to practice new skills.

Expression and Control of Aggression

Aggression is distinct from conflict but often occurs during disputes, and so is included in this section rather than in the one on emotional development. Since children's level and frequency of aggressive actions peak during the early childhood period, it is a topic of concern among early childhood educators. Aggression has been the subject of hundreds of studies, but this discussion will be limited to a review of the general developmental trends in children's expression and control of aggression.

As children become more aware of others' perspectives and more able to control their emotions, their expressions of aggression change. As toddlers, children often have unfocused temper tantrums which decrease during the preschool period (Goodenough, 1931; Hartup, 1974). Children at ages 2 and 3 are most often aggressive after their parents have thwarted their efforts, but during preschool their aggression becomes more focused on peers and siblings. Most aggressive actions at this age are physical (hitting, kicking, etc.) and are focused on gaining control of objects and space. This goal-oriented aggression is called *instrumental aggression*. During the preschool years, children begin to retaliate when they are frustrated or angry with another peer. In this case, they are not simply pushing a peer out of the way when they want access to an object, but are using aggressive actions as a means to hurt that person. This type of aggression is called *hostile* and is often done verbally (threats, taunts, insults) as well as physically. In order to use these tactics successfully, children need to be aware of others' perspectives so that they can reliably predict what actions or comments will hurt them. Children also become more accurate in determining appropriate targets for aggression. Preschoolers often direct their anger at peers who have injured them by mistake because they cannot distinguish accidents from intentional injuries. However, from kindergarten to fourth grade, children learn to recognize the difference between accidental and intentional actions and aim their aggressive actions accordingly (Dodge, Murphy, & Buschbaum, 1984).

Young children often engage in playful aggression that includes pretending to scare each other (e.g., monster roles), feigned fighting (e.g., playful wrestling), and teasing (e.g., exchanging insults). This play is distinct from serious aggression as it is usually accompanied by laughter and role exchanges (e.g., the chasers become the chasees) that maintain a positive mood and equilibrium. These episodes rarely evolve into serious fights (Smith & Lewis, 1985). In fact, rough-and-tumble partners often describe each other as friends (Humphreys & Smith, 1987). As will be discussed in Chapter 4, some children have a harder time than others maintaining the playful quality of these interactions and are more likely to precipitate a shift to more serious aggression. In general, however, playful aggression is not the same as serious aggression, and as teachers we must be able to distinguish the two and devise appropriate responses. Sometimes children need help seeing the differences and recognizing the point at which they begin to cross the line between playful and serious aggression.

During their early childhood years, children's aggression becomes more focused and more controlled. The unfocused temper tantrums of toddlers give way to more directed actions that are used either to gain control of an object or to hurt another person. As children become more aware of others' perspectives, they become more accurate in selecting their victims and in devising ways to hurt them. At the same time, they also learn how to diffuse aggression with humor and playful actions, which enables them to reduce the intensity and frequency of aggression as they get older.

Prosocial Behavior and Altruism

As well as learning how to manage conflicts and aggression, young children are also gaining prosocial skills such as helping, sharing, and comforting. These skills, in turn, facilitate the development of children's relationships.

At a very early age, children show some ability to empathize with others and help them. When they hear a distressed cry, newborns often begin to cry (Sagi & Hoffman, 1976) as though they too feel the other's pain. After doing extensive research about the early onset of empathy, Hoffman (1981) concluded that the ability to empathize is an inborn trait. Toddlers often show signs of concern when another child is hurt or crying and make attempts to comfort that child. Typically their efforts are egocentric. For example, they may bring their own teddy bear to a crying child, assuming that the child will respond to it the same way that they do. Thus, although very young children cannot cognitively see another's perspective, emotionally they resonate to another's distress. Children at this age also share objects (Rheingold, Hay, & West, 1976) and help parents with housekeeping chores (Rheingold, 1982).

The development of prosocial behavior during childhood is difficult to assess because age trends differ according to the type of behavior (Eisenberg & Mussen, 1989). Preschool children express concern over each others' welfare and show great interest when a child is hurt or upset (Corsaro, 1985). However, children at this age rarely share unless they are responding to a direct request and are more likely to share if the solicitation comes from a child who has previously shared with them (Birch & Billman, 1986). When they do share, it is often in a begrudging manner as illustrated in the following example:

> Kuan and Arndt are playing with peg boards; the box of pegs is on Arndt's side of the table. Kuan asks Arndt for some pegs. With an exasperated sigh, Arndt carefully counts out three pegs and gives them one at a time to Kuan. "That's all you get!" he announces as he bends over his board.

Preschoolers also often resist helping; we all know the many ploys children use to avoid clean-up. However, their willingness to help increases during the preschool years. Initially, their helping acts are limited to those they do in the context of sociodramatic play, but, in the late preschool years, they begin to perform real helping acts (Bar-Tal, Raviv, & Goldberg, 1982). This study also showed that comforting actions increased during the preschool years, but that sharing ones decreased. The mixed findings about the development of prosocial behavior during the preschool years may reflect two somewhat conflicting developmental trends (Bar-Tal et al., 1982; Yarrow & Waxler, 1976). As they grow older, children develop more awareness of others' perspectives, increased capacity to empathize, and greater competence to provide assistance, all of which might lead to increased prosocial behavior. At the same time, they are also becoming increasingly competitive, achievement-oriented, and protective of their privacy, trends that may reduce their willingness to assist others.

During the elementary years, children's altruism shows an overall increase, although the trends are somewhat mixed. Helping in emergencies increases during elementary school years, but then declines as children become aware of the potential embarrassment of the victim (Midlarsky & Hannah, 1985). Sharing, however, generally increases from the ages of 6 to 12 (Eisenberg & Mussen, 1989). These shifts parallel children's increasing ability to coordinate social perspectives, which enables them to respond to more subtle cues and to balance their own needs with those of others. They also become more aware of the negative social consequences of being seen as "selfish." As they grow older, children feel more competent and responsible which also contributes to their willingness and ability to help others. During this period, their motives shift from being self-related to altruistic as they become more aware of others (Eisenberg & Mussen, 1989).

Prosociability is a fairly consistent and stable characteristic as it does not change dramatically over time or across situation. In one longitudinal study, most children's modes of responding to distressed companions were similar at the ages of 2 and 7 (Radke-Yarrow & Zahn-Waxler, 1983). Children who respond prosocially in one context are likely to do so in another. However, some situational factors appear to influence whether or not children respond prosocially. In particular, children are more likely to help if the beneficiary is a friend, when they are in a positive mood, and when the need of the other is obvious (see Eisenberg & Mussen, 1989, for a full review).

ENVIRONMENTAL INFLUENCES ON SOCIAL DEVELOPMENT

In the previous sections of this chapter we focused on social development in individual and interpersonal contexts. At this point the perspective broadens as we consider children as members of particular social groups.

Children learn about other people and develop their social skills in complex environments. Bronfenbrenner (1979, 1986) describes children's developmental environment as four concentric circles which include (a) the *microsystems* of the family, school, and neighborhood; (b) the *mesosystems*, which include the relationships between elements in the microsystem such as family and school, neighborhood and school, and home and neighborhood; (c) the *exosystems*, which are institutions that have the power to affect the child's life, but the child does not participate in them; they include parent workplaces, school and planning boards, and systems of social support; and (d) the *macrosystems*, which include cultural values, the ideology of the social group, and social attitudes such as discrimination. All of these environmental factors affect children's social development in various ways. For example, if children are members of a group that is the target of discrimination (macrosystem), they are affected by the resulting limitations on their parents' job opportunities (exosystem). These limits, in turn, have an impact on the resources available to the family and the community in which they live (microsystems), and on the ways in which families and communities interact (mesosystem). Within the microsystem, the lack of available resources, the frustrations that parents experience at work, the tensions in the community that reflect the lack of economic opportunities, and the inadequate social and medical services all have a direct impact on children's daily lives and their interactions with the people around them.

The economic system in which children are raised has a direct bearing on all of these environments and the specific social skills that children learn. For example, children in nonindustrialized societies usually live in extended families and have many more responsibilities such as assisting in farming or taking care of young children. Because of their upbringing and relationships with others, they have a much higher rate of prosocial behaviors than do children raised in industrialized societies (Whiting & Whiting, 1975). For children in nonindustrialized societies, the developmental trends toward increasing prosocial behavior may not be diverted by the contradictory emphasis on competition and individual achievement that children encounter in the United States.

In short, children are developing in a context that includes their place in the larger economic system and the culture and history of their families and social groups. Child-rearing practices are developed by each group to teach the skills that are most adaptive for functioning in their specific social context (Ogbu, 1983). Thus, middle-class parents insure that their children acquire skills to succeed in middle-class environments such as schools and businesses. However, parents who live in environments with marginal resources teach their children how to exploit those meager resources as best as they can (Ogbu, 1983). Although some of these tactics, such as "hustling," may violate certain norms of the middle class, they should be viewed as survival strategies, *not as evidence of individual pathology or poor parenting*. Because of these differences, definitions of social competence often vary across groups and sometimes between home and school. These discrepancies, in turn, can create confusion and alienation for young children who are trying to bridge the gap between the two worlds. When interpreting children's behaviors, we constantly need to ask ourselves if we are applying norms and expectations that are congruent with children's real life experiences.

Social Networks

One aspect of children's microsystem is the social networks that are available to children. These networks influence not only the processes by which children develop social competence but the types of skills that they learn

(Tietjen, 1989). For example, children who spend their weekends helping their grandparents are gaining different skills than those who are taking art and music lessons during the same time. The composition and size of children's networks are influenced by many contextual factors such as socioeconomic status, race, type of community, and occupation of parents. For example, children in black, one-parent families tend to have networks comprised of relatives, whereas their white counterparts have networks comprised primarily of nonkin.

Role of Parents

Parents and other family members comprise the child's first social environment and therefore have a formative influence on children's social behavior. Children, however, also affect parents, and parenting behavior is, in part, a reaction to the temperament or behaviors of their particular children. A number of studies have identified particular factors that appear to be most relevant to children's social development. First, children develop their interactive styles from observing their parents in social encounters with each other and with other family members and friends. For example, if parents are very shy and avoid contacts with many people, their offspring are likely to have less social exposure and learn fewer social skills. Second, the quality of the relationship between the parents and child also affects their social adaptation to the peer group. Children who are securely attached are able to develop more positive peer interactions, whereas children who are either avoidant or anxious in their relationships with their caregiver(s) are less successful in forming peer friendships (Sroufe & Fleeson, 1986). Third, children's social behavior is related to their parents' childrearing styles, particularly their levels of control and warmth.

Parents also play a managing role in children's social lives that influences the kinds of contacts that children have in their early social development. In this role they influence several facets of children's lives (Parke & Bhavnagri, 1989). First, parents select (within their means) the neighborhood and community in which their children live. The number of children in the neighborhood, the proximity of the houses, and the safety of the environment all influence the frequency of their children's peer contacts. As children get older, they are able to spend more time outside of the immediate environs of the house, and their use of the neighborhood changes. Second, parents participate in children's organized activities and facilitate children's entry into organized social programs. Third, parents also initiate and arrange social engagements for their children. This role is particularly important during the early preschool years when children have limited mobility and ability to make these arrangements. After 4–5 years of age, children begin to make their own arrangements. Fourth, parents also monitor and supervise children's social activities. This role changes as children develop. Parents more often directly observe their preschoolers' social interactions and can significantly increase the social-interactive competence of their preschool children by helping them when they encounter difficulties. They may help children resolve conflicts or provide ideas and props for maintaining interest in the ongoing play. As children get older, parents supervise from a greater distance. They are aware of children's social activities and often assist in making arrangements, but are less often physically present. However, parents at this stage still offer advice to help children become more adept at managing their peer relationships.

The managing role of parents is affected by demographic factors such as socioeconomic status, race, culture, and job opportunities. Level of affluence and discrimination have considerable influence on parents' choices of where they live. These constraints limit their control over important environmental factors, such as the safety of the neighborhood and the proximity of other families, which influence the types of social opportunities that are available to their children. Work demands on parents also affect their involvement in children's activities, the roles they are able to play in facilitating a child's entry into school and neighborhood groups, and their ability to supervise their children's social activities.

Overall, parents play a decisive role in children's social adjustment. More specific ways in which childrearing styles and values affect children's social competence and levels of peer acceptance will be discussed in Chapter 4. However, the larger social context must always be kept in mind, as parents and children are interacting in a complex social environment that not only offers support but also imposes constraints.

3

Social Dynamics of Early Childhood Classrooms

Two teachers were comparing notes: "My group this year is so industrious," commented one teacher, "they are all eager to get down to work; there does not seem to be a lot of concern about who is friends with whom. They all get along. What a contrast to last year!" Her companion countered, "Lucky you! My group seems very tense. There are a lot of splinter groups, and everyone seems obsessed by the rivalries between the groups. Everything we do—circle time, field trips, projects—all become an arena for playing out these rivalries and in-group–out-group stuff."

The social dynamics of each classroom influence the quality of teachers' and children's social experiences. They are a crucial backdrop for attempts to foster peer relationships and to make judgments regarding individuals' social adjustment. In our efforts to create more positive classroom climates, working with the existing and evolving dynamics is easier than constantly fighting them. In cases where the dynamics are shifting in a negative direction, early recognition of the trend and its possible causes enables teachers to intervene in a more effective and timely way. However, pinpointing specific classroom dynamics is difficult because they are, by definition, an interplay of a number of constantly changing factors. Furthermore, each group of children creates a unique set of dynamics as individual children and teachers interact within the context of the particular constraints and opportunities of each setting.

A number of recent observational studies have identified common classroom dynamics, factors that contribute to them, and the changes that occur during the year. The subtle nature of these dynamics requires qualitative data as well as quantitative measures of larger patterns. Fortunately, two recent ethnographic studies (Corsaro, 1985; Rizzo, 1989) provide many new insights into the dynamics of classroom environments. The authors have also contributed to observation strategies by using an innovative combination of methods that include video and audio taping, ethnographic field notes, and interviews with informants. Their methods can be adapted to help teachers monitor the evolving dynamics in their classrooms. Because of the amorphous, transitory, and idiosyncratic nature of classroom dynamics, research findings cannot provide absolute predictions, but rather can serve as a guide in terms of what to look for. For example, teachers can develop observation plans to monitor the dynamics in their own classrooms using the guidelines presented in Chapter 5. These methods are based on techniques used in ethnographic and sociometric research, but are adapted for classroom use.

Many factors influence the dynamics of each classroom. Among these are the social and personal concerns of children that change during the early childhood years. The first section of this chapter will focus on how these concerns affect the ways in which children interact. Time of year is another relevant variable, since levels of familiarity and group coalescence and hierarchies develop over time. Because children often select friends on the basis of proximity and similarity, the presence of different sex, racial, cultural, and socioeconomic groups in the classroom also may affect grouping patterns. The individuals themselves, their range of skill levels and personality traits, and the chemistry among them influence the interactions and climate of the classroom. Furthermore, the children, as they become familiar with each other, create a unique peer culture that reflects their particular developmental issues, interpretations of adult roles, and reactions to the expectations and constraints of the teachers. Finally, the physical setting, the availability and roles of the adults in the classroom, and the structure of the day have an impact on the types and frequencies of peer interactions that occur.

CHILDREN'S SOCIAL CONCERNS

As children develop their social skills, awareness of others, and concepts about friendship, their abilities to sustain interactions and maintain relationships change. As a result, their concerns shift from focusing on their immediate playmates to solidifying more long-term relationships. Their psychosocial issues also change, which affects the themes that dominate their peer contacts. Furthermore, as academic expectations increase, children create ways of adjusting to more curtailed social opportunities in their classrooms.

Preschool Children

Preschool children are primarily concerned with finding playmates who have similar activity preferences and play styles. Because the attractions are concrete (e.g., a child is playing with an intriguing toy; a child is enacting a particular role), contacts are often quite transitory. Corsaro (1985) compares preschool social interactions to an adult cocktail party in which participants in one conversation are often scanning the room for other potential and perhaps more attractive encounters. As a result, people spend a great deal of time and thought initiating and ending contacts. Unlike their adult counterparts, who consciously employ a number of tactful stratagems to move from person to person, preschoolers often move from group to group quite spontaneously. Furthermore, their approaches and responses to newcomers are likely to be fairly abrupt and frank. The following example illustrates the rapidity with which interactions begin and end:

> Laila and Mandy are making birthday cakes with the Playdough. All of a sudden four children come around the corner, on their hands and knees and barking in squeaky voices. Laila grins and cries out "Hi, puppies!" and jumps up, throws herself on her knees and joins in the barking and crawling. Mandy protests, "Laila, we haven't finished the birthday cakes yet!" Laila responds in her puppy voice, "Puppies can't make birthday cakes!" and moves off with the puppies.

Because of the the fluid structure in most preschools, in which children can come and go at their own will for at least a part of the day (usually referred to as "free play"), children have the opportunity to engage with a number of different peers. At the same time, they frequently are abandoned by their companions who may decide to play with someone else or simply tire of a particular activity. Thus, children are often in the position of needing to initiate new play contacts. As described in the previous chapter, children employ a number of entry strategies which have different degrees of success. The children are, however, often dealing with two conflicting goals. Not only do they have to initiate contacts, but, at the same time, their awareness that peer engagements are fragile and transitory compels them to resist the advances of peers who are trying to achieve the first goal (Corsaro, 1981, 1985). Thus, over half of children's entry attempts meet with initial resistance (Corsaro, 1985). Not surprisingly, children have more success when initiating contact with a single individual than when they are trying to enter an ongoing group (Ramsey, 1989c). Children are more successful in entering groups if they adapt to the ongoing play, as mentioned in Chapter 2. This approach may work because it poses less of a threat to the ongoing interaction.

In their attempts to either gain access or to resist newcomers, preschool children often refer to friendship (Corsaro, 1985). "We're friends, right?" is often used as a ploy to gain admission to a group. "You're not our friend today" is a common justification for refusing entry. The spurned child may then threaten not to invite any of the group members to an imminent (within the next year) birthday party. To adults, these seemingly casual references to friends or denial of friendship often sound fickle or cruel. However, when preschool children are referring to friendship, they are seeing friendship as a current state of playing together, not as an ongoing relationship. Thus, the affirmation or denial of friendship does not have the same impact that it would on older children or adults.

Although preschoolers do not conceptualize friendship as a long-term relationship, many do develop fairly stable networks of frequent play partners that enrich their social experiences and enhance their social development in several ways. When initiating contact with their frequent companions, children are more likely to meet with success (Corsaro, 1985; Ramsey, 1989a). These relationships also provide a context for more domestic and adventure fantasy play (Roopnarine & Field, 1984) which is the highest level of peer interaction at this age (Parker & Gottman, 1989). Contacts between friends are more likely to include reinforcing actions such as helping, inviting, complimenting, and showing affection (Masters & Furman, 1981). These interactions also last longer and are more vocal (Howes, 1987a). Furthermore, children respond more positively to the emotional needs of friends than to those of acquaintances (Costin & Jones, 1989). For children who are at risk for poor social adjustment, a stable friendship lessens the impact of peer rejection (Howes, 1987a).

The dynamics of preschool classrooms change during the year. When unfamiliar children come together, they quickly begin to sort out preferred peers. In an observational study of the first several weeks of a preschool, Roopnarine (1984) found that the number of new playmate combinations decreased steadily after the second day. As their range of contacts narrowed, children's level of social participation increased. During the first 17 days, the amount of joint positive play increased, whereas the amount of time spent in parallel play decreased. Using an experimental situation, Doyle (1982) found that when preschoolers were with familiar partners, their play was more active, competent, and cognitively mature than when they were with unfamiliar ones. Thus, the nature of children's contacts changes with familiarity, which means that the dynamics of a classroom change during the year.

As children shift from being strangers to being friends, they go through four stages (Gottman and Parkhurst, 1980). First, children try to interest each other in an activity. Then the two participants engage in social comparisons to find common ground. Third, their talk shifts to the activities they are doing or planning to do. The final two phases are the initiation of fantasy and extension of fantasy play. The relationship can falter at any point if children discover that they do not have enough in common to continue interacting. During the first few weeks of school, children are going through a similar process with a number of different peers as they begin to settle on their primary group of playmates.

The degree and types of changes in social patterns vary across age groups. In a study of age-stratified preschool classrooms (Ramsey, 1989a), the 3-year-old children became more socially active during the school year. The number of teacher contacts and solitary play episodes decreased, and the frequency of their peer initiations increased. In the spring they began to reject each others' entry attempts more often, suggesting that they were learning to protect their interactive space. The 4-year-old children seemed to be in a period of consolidation; they progressively had longer interactions with a more limited group of peers. Related to this increased selectivity, they showed a marked increase in same-sex preferences. The trend towards gender segregation continued during kindergarten. These children also appeared to be refining their social skills; they increased their use of friendly entry strategies and were more accepting of each others' entry bids. During the preschool years, children initially increase their level of social activity as they become more comfortable in peer settings. They then begin to differentiate play partners and narrow their range of contacts, particularly along gender lines.

Early Elementary Classrooms

Many of the same dynamics that occur in preschool classrooms are present in elementary schools. However, as children enter the more academically oriented structure that typifies most elementary programs, new social concerns emerge. Their motivation for having friends shifts from the single goal of having someone to play with, to more varied goals such has having friends to help them with schoolwork, to provide needed materials, and to provide reassurance that their work is adequate (Rizzo, 1989).

In addition to the new needs that friendships satisfy, the ways in which they are played out also change from the preschool years. Opportunities for social contact are more limited in most elementary school classrooms, so children often plan their social time quite carefully. Because recess is the primary occasion for children to be with their friends, they frequently reduce uncertainty and delays by prearranging activities and groups. Thus, peer contacts are not as fluid and spontaneous as they are in preschool settings, but are deliberate and planned. Another constraint is that children are usually assigned to desks or work areas so that neighbors and work partners are predetermined. In the classroom that Rizzo studied, children changed seats once each month and thus were frequently recreating their play and work groups. Not surprisingly, close friends often tried to manipulate the system so that they could continue to sit close to each other. Rizzo also noted that interactions were often disrupted by frequent and abrupt transitions imposed from the outside. In preschools, interactions usually end with one partner voluntarily leaving the situation, but in the elementary school, interactions often end when one participant is called for reading group, or when gym period begins, or when recess ends. As a result, children are often engaged in unfinished interactions which may be continued in surreptitious ways (e.g., passing notes or multiple trips to the pencil sharpener or water fountain).

Another constraint is the introduction of tracking. In the first grade that Rizzo studied, children quickly became aware of which were the higher and lower reading groups. Not only did they spend more time with children at their own level, but they also began to tease or reject peers who were not as "smart" as they were. In this way, ability grouping influences children's contact patterns and peer perceptions at an early point in their elementary years. The effects of tracking were illustrated dramatically in a study that compared social patterns in classrooms structured around academic competition and ability groupings with those in which children worked together in interest groups (Bossert, 1979). The classrooms in which children publicly demonstrated their academic competence, with a heavy emphasis on oral recitation and testing, were conducive to the development of more performance-homogeneous friendships than the classrooms with interest groups and a multitask organization. In the latter classrooms, friendships developed from shared interests and group experience. Most striking was the alteration in friendship patterns when the children changed settings. When children who were in a multitask classroom went into a competitive one the following year, they soon abandoned previous friends and exclusively interacted with peers at their academic level. The reverse pattern occurred for children going from competitive to multitask classrooms.

Children in early elementary school have a more sophisticated understanding of friendships and are clearer than preschoolers about what they expect from friends. Disputes between friends often reflect one partner's desire to get the other one to conform more closely to his idea of what a friend should be (Rizzo, 1989). Children have shifted from a focus on momentary playmateships to expectations of one-way assistance (Selman's, 1981, Level I), in which they want the relationship to continue, but on their own terms.

In his analysis of how friendships are formed, Rizzo concluded that most friendships evolved from more spontaneous mutual enjoyment, rather than from deliberate efforts to make a friend. He described one friendship which began when two girls who happened to be sitting next to each other started pretending their feet were stuck in their chairs. This spontaneous event evolved into a long interaction in which the girls fantasized what life would be like if they could never get their feet unstuck. They subsequently sought each other out and became frequent companions.

Children's peer preferences are not limited to social friends. They also develop activity partnerships in which they collaborate on projects (Oden, 1988). These relationships may overlap with friendships, but are not necessarily the same. For example, two children who enjoy drawing cartoons may end up working together on a class comic book and in the process share materials, advice, and feedback, but not necessarily engage in personal discussions or make plans to play at recess or after school.

As friendships become more defined, children clearly distinguish between friends and nonfriends in their actions. When disputes occur between friends, the protagonists rarely ask the teacher to intervene, whereas teachers often get drawn into conflicts between nonfriends (Rizzo, 1989). Friends are also more responsive to each other. When 7- and 8-year-old children watch cartoons with a friend they are more likely to look at each other and share laughter than when they are paired with a stranger (Foot, Chapman, & Smith, 1977). Apparently, if children are friends, these contacts increase the arousal and enjoyment of both parties; if they are not friends, then such overtures may seem intrusive and may not be reciprocated.

Elementary school children begin to show evidence of reputational bias in their responses to peers (Hymel, Wagner, & Butler, 1990). Unlike preschoolers, who respond primarily to the specific actions of their classmates, elementary school children are now able to think about their peers' overall behavior patterns. Their perceptions and interpretations tend to be quite rigid and biased because they cannot integrate a lot of conflicting information about their peers. Unpopular children are blamed for more than their share of negative events, and popular children are given greater credit for positive behavior than is warranted by their actual actions; the same behaviors that are accepted by peers when enacted by popular children are rejected when done by unpopular children.

The social dynamics in the elementary classrooms change during the year. Rizzo noted that early in the fall, the first graders most eagerly sought out siblings, neighborhood friends, or classmates from their kindergarten class during recess. Initially, children's play partners and in-class work contacts were quite separate. As the weeks passed, however, they became more involved with their current classmates and were increasingly likely to play with them. To some extent, the constraints of the environment contributed to this shift because children from different classes were less predictably available during recess, due to schedule variations and changes. Also, as children worked and played with their current peers, they developed more grounds for sustained interactions.

DOMINANCE HIERARCHIES

As the dynamics of specific groups develop, teachers often notice that some children are more dominant than others. In a number of studies (e.g., LaFreniere & Charlesworth, 1983; Strayer & Strayer, 1976; Strayer & Strayer, 1980), observers have been able to identify dominance hierarchies in classrooms by noting which children win peer conflicts. These hierarchies are based on the assumption that if A consistently wins over B and B overpowers C, then A would win over C. Although occasionally a lower ranked child vanquishes a more highly placed peer, these hierarchies are quite stable. Once they are established, the frequency of conflict diminishes, leading some researchers to conclude that a clear dominance hierarchy creates a sense of social order and helps reduce conflict (Strayer & Strayer, 1976). However, not all studies have revealed clear dominance hierarchies. Corsaro (1985) reported that he did not observe any evidence of hierarchies in the classrooms that he studied. In some cases, children play in separate groups so that hierarchies develop within those groups, but not across the whole classroom (Lasquade, 1988). Thus, a linear dominance pattern may not always emerge. Moreover, the establishment of a hierarchy may not necessarily lead to a reduction in aggression (Pettit, Bakshi, Dodge, & Coie, 1990). Despite these mixed findings, the concept of dominance can provide a useful framework for teachers to examine the power differentials that do exist among their children.

The ways in which children exert their dominance appears to change between preschool and early elementary school. Hold (1976) found that preschoolers relied more on aggression to assert themselves than did the kindergarten children. Also, children see dominance hierarchies more clearly as they get older. In a series of studies in which children were asked to assess which of their classmates were "tough" (Edelman & Omark, 1973; Omark, Omark, & Edelman, 1975), preschool and kindergarten children did not have a consensus about who were the "toughest" people in their classroom, whereas the children in elementary school did.

One question is whether the most dominant children are also the most popular. On one hand, power might evoke peer admiration, but, on the other hand, imposing authority through aggression might lead to peer rejection. Dominance often involves power assertion and aggression, but children can also influence peers by initiating activities, inviting others to join, persuading peers to accept their opinions, or enacting or suggesting creative ideas. Children's reactions to different dominating behaviors appear to change with age. Younger preschoolers like their aggressively dominant peers, but by kindergarten, children prefer classmates who assert themselves in more positive ways (Lasquade, 1988). As children progress through the early elementary grades, they increasingly discriminate between aggressive dominance and positive leadership (Pettit et al., 1990). Young preschoolers may admire the power of the aggressively dominant children, but with experience they learn to prefer the more socially skilled leaders in the class.

Although clear dominance hierarchies may not always emerge or be that consistent in a classroom, the identification of children who exert more power is helpful in trying to work with the existing social dynamics and making timely and effective interventions when necessary. As teachers, we also need to be alert to power differentials that are getting too wide and to children who are getting locked into dominant or submissive roles. Specific strategies to balance these relationships will be discussed in Chapter 6.

INTERGROUP DYNAMICS

Young children tend to select friends on the basis of proximity and similarity of surface features (Epstein, 1989). Because preschoolers have little control over the people they come into contact with, proximity is often a decisive factor, and they generally accept the idea that their friends are the children next door, the cousin upstairs, or the offspring of their parents' friends. During early childhood, however, the importance of proximity declines as children both broaden their social contacts and gain more control in arranging social events. Emphasis on similarities, however, increases as children get older. During early and middle childhood, surface similarities (e.g., play preferences, age, gender) are more important, whereas deeper similarities (e.g., personality characteristics) are more likely to influence friendship choice in adolescence.

One of the major goals in children's social development, as discussed in Chapter 1, is to help them learn to interact comfortably with a wide range of people. However, because children's early friendships are usually determined by proximity and/or similarity, their contacts with children who are from different backgrounds may be limited. As teachers we are often frustrated by the seemingly inexorable cleavages (gender, race, or social class) that develop despite our efforts to counteract them. Although the underlying causes of proximity and similarity are common to all of them, each difference presents a particular challenge to classroom cohesiveness. Therefore, this section provides an overview of the developmental and environmental issues that are specific to each difference. Because reactions of both adults and children often reflect the attitudes of their community, teachers need to be aware of local perceptions, values, and tensions in order to anticipate and understand children's reactions to members of different groups. For example, in a community where parents are consciously trying to display gender-neutral roles, children may have different perceptions than those in a community in which the roles are rigidly defined. Reactions to racial and ethnic differences may vary according to the number of people from diverse groups and the presence or absence of tension between groups. As shown in the following sections, we have some ideas about how these different dynamics may affect children's relationships, but the specific inter-group affiliations or tensions that will develop in a particular classroom cannot be predicted. Specific strategies for assessing intergroup relations and promoting more positive cross-group contacts will be discussed in more detail in Chapters 5 and 6.

Gender Differences

In one kindergarten, the teachers realized that the "circle" for group time was two parallel lines, one of boys and one of girls, because no one was willing to sit next to a member of the opposite sex. The teachers decided to intervene and assigned places that alternated boy, girl, boy, girl. The next day they received a phone call from a concerned parent saying that her son wanted to drop out of school because he had to sit between two girls at circle time. This anecdote illustrates the strong same-sex preference and cross-sex aversion that typify most groups of children. Same-sex preference dominates children's choices of friends at all grades, although cross-sex contacts follow a curvilinear pattern: they decrease from preschool to middle school and then increase during adolescence (Epstein, 1986).

Teachers who attempt to organize nonsexist classrooms and convey the idea that boys and girls can be friends are often frustrated by children's resistance. In one study, Serbin, Tonick, and Sternglanz (1977) found that if preschool children were specifically reinforced for cross-sex play, they increased their rates of cross-sex contacts. However, as soon as the reinforcement stopped, the play returned to the original same-sex patterns. Similarly, in the elementary school, mixed-sex work groups increase the overall cross-sex interactions outside of the work groups, but children's same-sex preferences do not weaken (Lockheed, cited in Maccoby, 1986). Classrooms in which teachers consciously try to use nonsexist language, role modeling, and materials, and actively encourage children to play a variety of roles, may have fewer sex-typed behaviors than other classrooms, but the same-sex preference remains strong (Swadener & Johnson, 1989). One teacher, after struggling to come to terms with the different ways in which boys and girls played in her kindergarten, decided simply to accept the differences and work at helping boys and girls negotiate their use of the classroom and find common ground, but not to force them to change their play (Paley, 1984).

A related question is what happens when boys and girls do play or work together? Not surprisingly, the boys are often more assertive and dominate the interactions. In cross-sex entry attempts, girls are more tentative with boys than they are with girls; boys, however, are more imperative with girls than with boys (Phinney & Rotheram, 1982). In one study of second- and third-grade math work groups, boys were found to prevail more often than girls even though the two groups were equally capable (Wilkinson, Ludlow, & Chiang, 1985).

Maccoby (1986) suggests several hypotheses that might explain this seemingly universal pattern of gender cleavage. First, with early socialization, children learn to enjoy sex-typed activities and behaviors and are drawn to each other when they observe each others' play styles and activity preferences. As all teachers know, preschool girls tend to congregate in the art and housekeeping areas, and boys engage in more active play with blocks and trucks. In elementary schools, boys are often seen at recess playing vigorous physical contact games, whereas girls tend to play games that require more precise physical skills and social coordination such as jump rope. Maccoby also hypothesized that children recognize members of their own and the opposite sex and are drawn to same-sex peers because they are more confident of what to expect. Conversely, they avoid cross-sex peers because they are unsure about how they will behave and are more uncertain of their own roles. Third, based on a study in which same-sex toddler pairs interacted more readily than cross-sex pairs did, even when all gender cues were minimized, Maccoby proposes that there are basic inherent same-sex compatibilities that do not depend on socialization.

Regardless of its precise origin, gender cleavage quickly becomes self-perpetuating. Children engage in sex-typed play which brings them into more contact with same-sex peers. They also quickly learn that peer acceptance depends on conforming to sex-typed roles. Damon (1977) describes 6-year-old children's outrage at boys who played girl-type games. Children who cross over the gender divide are often accused of "liking" someone of the opposite sex or being a member of that group (Thorne, 1986). As children spend more time in sex-segregated play, each group begins to form its own culture with clearly defined characteristics (Maccoby, 1986). Boys play in larger groups that tend to be outdoors and involved in rough and aggressive play that focuses on dominance. Girls, on the other hand, prefer to congregate in smaller groups and form more intimate friendships. Their interactions are more likely to be conversations instead of physical activities and to be oriented around turn-taking and the maintenance of open communication and closeness. Because children readily divide themselves by gender, teachers often unintentionally support and reinforce this segregation by using gender as a way of organizing their classes into sides for contests or forming lunch lines (Thorne, 1986). As gender segregation becomes more complete, children who like members of the opposite sex find it increasingly difficult to maintain cross-sex contacts. Cross-sex friendships frequently "go underground." Boys and girls who play together in their neighborhoods frequently ignore each other when they are in the public arena of school.

Gender cleavage begins before preschool and becomes increasingly entrenched during the early childhood years (Ramsey, 1989a). Young preschoolers prefer their own sex, but still play in many mixed-sex groups. During their fourth year, children's preferences for same-sex peers increases dramatically, suggesting that this year may mark the beginning of the establishment of separate peer cultures and more rigid sex roles. Sex-segregation continues to increase during the elementary years and is reaffirmed by children's engagement in "borderwork" between the two groups (Thorne, 1986). These interactions include contests (e.g., boys' and girls' spelling-bee teams), cross-sex chasing games that sometimes include a threat of kissing or pollution rituals (e.g., giving "cooties" to each other), and invasions in which one group (usually boys) disrupts the play of the other.

In some settings, however, boys and girls manage to interact in a mutual and productive fashion. Thorne noted that the boys and girls she observed did work together in situations in which mixed-sex groups were formed by the teachers and were engaged in absorbing tasks. In these situations, gender was less salient, and children engaged in cross-sex contacts in a relaxed and productive manner. Often neighborhood groups, extracurricular activities, and some sports teams provide settings in which boys and girls can collaborate. Although children are unlikely to do a lot of cross-sex socializing, they can learn to work together and to respect each other.

Racial Differences

Race underlies many of the divisions and inequities in our society and, therefore, it profoundly influences the relationship between families and the economic and social structures in our society. These disparities, in turn, affect the environments in which children are raised (Bronfenbrenner, 1986) and inevitably have an impact on our children's intrapersonal and interpersonal lives. However, it is difficult to predict the precise effects of racial composition on classroom dynamics because racial identities and cross-racial relations vary widely across and within racial, ethnic, social-class, and regional groups. Moreover, our knowledge base is sparse because most studies of racial differences and attitudes have been done from a Euro-centric perspective, and we know relatively little about the life experiences and perspectives of non-European–American children (Spencer, 1990).

This section will review a few major research findings to provide readers with an overview of some of the issues involved in working in either multiracial or monoracial classrooms. However, much of the research discussed in this section is based on comparisons and relationships between African–American children and European–American children, and may or may not be applicable to children from other groups. Thus, this review is intended not to provide answers, but rather to raise questions to guide readers in learning more about their particular children. As teachers, we need to be familiar with the history and current status of the groups in our communities in order to understand more precisely what conditions, tensions, and disparities are influencing children's perceptions of themselves and their peers.

Although the salience and affective content of their racial concepts may vary, all children probably go through a similar developmental sequence as they become more aware of race and form racially related perceptions and attitudes. Based on extensive research, Katz (1976, 1983) postulated that children go through the following phases in their acquisition of of racial attitudes. First, infants and toddlers seem to notice racial differences as they often react with surprise when they see a racially unfamiliar person. By the ages of 3 and 4, children have a rudimentary concept about race and can easily label and sort people by racial traits. At this age, they may begin to absorb and repeat evaluative comments about their own and other racial groups, but do not really understand their implications. Katz's third phase is called conceptual differentiation, during which children clarify which physical characteristics are associated with particular racial groups. During their early elementary school years, children learn that racial attributes are permanent characteristics and distinct from temporary skin color changes caused by exposure to the sun. At this time they also develop more definite concepts and feelings about their own and other racial groups, which usually reflect the attitudes that they have been exposed to in their families and communities. By around 10 years of age, children's attitudes have crystallized and, from this point on, they may be more resistant to changing their beliefs and perceptions. This model suggests that children's ability and willingness to make cross-racial friends may diminish over time unless they are in situations that promote cross-racial affiliations and respect. Thus, attention to these issues in their early years is crucial.

Promoting cross-racial respect and positive racial identities is difficult because we live in a racially divided society, and, throughout the history of the United States, race has determined a person's status and her or his access to opportunities and privileges (Gibbs & Huang, 1989). According to John Ogbu (1978, 1983), most nonwhite racial groups in this country are viewed and treated as castlike minorities. Although many members of these groups function very successfully in the broader society, people of color are more vulnerable to being stigmatized and excluded from higher status opportunities and roles and relegated to menial jobs and poor neighborhoods and communities (Spencer, 1990). The resulting economic hardships cause stresses on families that may adversely affect children's socioemotional functioning (McLoyd, 1990). Aside from the material deprivations, constant exposure to racism means that many families live in a state of "mundane extreme environmental stress" (Peters, 1985), the day-to-day tension of enduring racially related episodes that may vary from annoying to life-threatening. For example, trips to restaurants and stores, which might be pleasurable family outings, are often ruined by overt or covert discriminatory actions on the part of waiters or salespeople (Peters, 1985).

The economic and societal disparities are reflected in school curriculum and the media. Children of color grow up in a world dominated by positive images of European–American history, lifestyles, and heroes and heroines. Often their own group is invisible in the media or portrayed in negative stereotypes. Not surprisingly, many children become alienated by this combination of constant exposure to and exclusion from more affluent and privileged lifestyles and come to distrust and resist mainstream institutions such as schools because they do not want to be forced to "act white" (Slaughter-DeFoe, Nakagawa, Takanishi, & Johnson, 1990). In contrast, many European–American children grow up in monoracial communities or attend segregated schools and have little awareness of other racial groups. In the absence of cross-race contact, they often develop erroneous and negative perceptions about unfamiliar groups (Ramsey, 1991a).

Current efforts to create more racially and culturally inclusive curricula potentially benefit the education of all children. Children whose groups are underrepresented in the traditional curriculum may feel more hopeful and less alienated when learning about their own people and histories. Conversely, racially isolated white children learn that theirs is not the only way of life and begin to see their own group in a broader and more realistic perspective. Although these efforts cannot neutralize the divisiveness of the larger social and economic inequities, they can help children develop more cross-racial connections and respect. Ways of making classrooms and the curricula more inclusive will be discussed in more detail in Chapters 5 and 6.

The racial divisions and inequities in the larger society are also mirrored in children's peer relationships at school. Not surprisingly, European–American children show an earlier, stronger, and more consistent own-race bias than do their African–American peers (Fox & Jordan, 1973; Katz, 1983; Newman, Liss, & Sherman, 1983; Ramsey & Myers, 1990; Rosenfield & Stephen, 1981; Stabler, Zeig, & Johnson, 1982). Conversely, African–American children are more neutral in their preferences (Harrison, 1985) and tend to be friendlier to their cross-race peers than white children are (Hallihan & Teixeira, 1987). Findings about the extent of racial segregation in early childhood classrooms have been mixed. Because sex is a more reliable predictor of play style and activity preference, young children in racially mixed groups often form friendships based on sex rather than on race (Singleton & Asher, 1977, 1979). However, patterns of same-race preference have been observed in some preschools and kindergartens (Finkelstein and Haskins, 1983; Ramsey & Myers, 1990). Racial segregation often becomes more pronounced during the elementary school years as children develop stronger racial identities and affiliations (Aboud, 1987; Schofield, 1981). These trends are exacerbated by the formation of ability groups that often reflect biased expectations about children from different ethnic groups (Holliday, 1985; Rist, 1973).

From the children's perspective, same-race preferences probably reflect both proximity and similarity. Because of the racial divisions in our society, families usually live in segregated neighborhoods and socialize within their own groups, so that young children are unlikely to have cross-race friends either prior to coming to school or in their neighborhoods. White children, in particular, rarely have any different-race members in their immediate networks (Cochran & Riley, 1988). In terms of similarity, young children can see that they look different from their cross-racial peers, and as they get older, they may also begin to notice differences in dress, interactive styles, and languages that reflect the cultural heritages and contemporary styles of specific racial groups. As a result, members from different groups may find each others' behaviors to be unfamiliar (Rotheram-Borus & Phinney, 1990) and possibly threatening (Schofield, 1981). In the next section, the implications of these cultural differences will be discussed.

Cultural Differences

Young children cannot understand the concepts of national origins because they do not yet grasp the significance of a country or region (Lambert & Klineberg, 1967; Piaget, 1951). However, they do react to the unfamiliar behaviors, languages, or dress of people from different cultural backgrounds. For example, children frequently describe someone with an unfamiliar accent as "talking funny." Because children tend to gravitate toward peers whose responses are predictable and with whom they can share similar fantasies and activities, they may avoid children who seem strange, even if they cannot identify or understand the sources of this unfamiliarity. Cultural traditions may influence children's greeting styles, their willingness to engage in certain types of play, or their knowledge about certain cultural mores (e.g., childhood rhymes, TV characters). In a study of Canadian classrooms containing both French- and English-speaking children, Doyle

(1982) found a striking amount of segregation between the two ethnolinguistic groups. Moreover, same-group play lasted longer and involved more
conversation and fantasy play than did cross-group contacts. Because many
children were competent in both languages, Doyle concluded that the segregation was not simply a matter of linguistic fluency in the less familiar
language. Rather she attributed these patterns to the following cycle: children play less actively with dissimilar partners and do not develop common
repertoires, which, in turn, means that their play is less engaging and
active; children then select their familiar and similar playmates more often,
which precludes opportunities to create the same kind of shared repertoire
with the dissimilar children. Doyle also found that members of the group
that was in the majority in a particular classroom were likely to be preferred
by both groups. Thus, children recreated the status of majority and minority
groups within the each classroom.

Longstreet (1978) identified five aspects of ethnicity which influence
social style and potentially disrupt communications among members from
different groups. The aspects include

1. *Verbal communication*—language and conventions about when and how
   speech is used
2. *Nonverbal communication*—body language and gestures
3. *Orientation modes*—behavior patterns (such as accustomed sitting positions) that are learned socially but which do not have any communicative intent
4. *Social values*—roles and priorities that are common to a particular group
5. *Intellectual modes*—individuals' learning styles and preferred ways of
   learning.

These differences were vividly illustrated in a cross-ethnic and cross-social
class comparison of children's social interactive styles (Rizzo & Corsaro,
1991). Children in the white middle-class preschool tended to be very concerned about the needs and feelings of others, and were easily upset if peers
threatened to deny them friendship. In general, their peer interactions and
their feelings about them were fragile. The African–American and Hispanic children in the Head Start program used a lot more teasing and oppositional and competitive talk with each other, but, unlike their middle-class
counterparts, the Head Start children were not intimidated or upset by it.
In fact, the authors felt that with these exchanges the children created
assertive and competitive friendships and a sense of group solidarity.

These differences can potentially affect many facets of children's social
interactions. Children may express their ideas and feelings in different
ways; they may have learned divergent rules for how to initiate and con-

tinue conversations; they may enact domestic and occupational roles differently; and they may have a variety of preferences for particular kinds of academic tasks and afterschool activities. If the two groups described by Corsaro and Rizzo in the preceding paragraph had been together, they might easily have misunderstood each other. The teasing and oppositional style of the Head Start children might have been perceived as aggressive and intimidating by the middle-class children. Conversely, the Head Start children might have been bewildered at the fragility of the middle-class children's interactions and feelings. A Japanese–American friend of mine, who grew up being told that she should only talk if she had something really important to say, describes her bewilderment when she started school and was surrounded by chattering Anglo-American children. These differences do not affect the overall social development of children, but they may lead children to limit their interactions to peers with whom they have more common ground and an easier time finding connections.

Lifestyle differences, while not necessarily related to ethnic background, may also contribute to classroom divisions. One teacher reported that some children who were devoted to particular television shows and characters formed a group that excluded their peers whose parents did not allow them to watch these shows. Family constellation can be another factor; children may be wary of peers whose lifestyle is unfamiliar, such as having gay parents, living in a communal setting, or being in a foster family.

Proximity may also limit cross-cultural contacts because many neighborhoods are segregated by ethnic group. Children's parents may socialize within their groups and want their children to attend after-school and weekend programs that bring them into more contact with the traditions and people from that culture. These differences are often exacerbated by prejudicial attitudes about particular groups. As discussed in the section on racial differences, certain groups are stigmatized which affects not only the experience of the members of that group, but also other people's perceptions of that group, creating an even wider gap among cultural groups. For all of these reasons, children may have very little early contact with members of different cultural groups and may not have an opportunity to get beyond their initial reactions to unfamiliarity.

Socioeconomic Differences

As with cultural differences, young children are not consciously aware of social class (Naimark, 1983; Ramsey, 1991c). However, because of similarity and proximity, class-related segregation often emerges in classrooms with children from different socioeconomic groups. As mentioned previously, childrearing goals and methods often vary across socioeconomic groups. These differences reflect the social and economic roles of specific groups (Ogbu, 1983) and, in turn, affect the behavioral goals and patterns of the children. For example, low-income elementary school children, who are more likely to end up in manual-labor or menial jobs, tend to use more nonverbal reinforcements with their friends. Their middle-income counterparts, who are being groomed for professional and bureaucratic positions which require highly developed verbal skills, use more verbal reinforcements (Gottman, Gonso, & Rasmussen, 1975). As with cultural differences, these style differences are not indicative of social competencies or deficits, but may cause children from different backgrounds to be less comfortable with each other.

Much of the research on social class differences has focused on the social deficits of low-income children. For example, in a study of social-problem-solving skills, low-income children used a narrower range of strategies and more aggressive actions than did their middle-income counterparts (Shure & Spivak, 1974). Likewise, a number of researchers (e.g., Fein & Stork, 1981; Rubin, Maioni, & Hornung, 1976; Smilansky, 1968) have concluded that low-income children engage in less sociodramatic play and are more often on the periphery of the play that occurs in socioeconomically integrated classrooms. These studies and findings have been criticized because the settings and assessment instruments potentially favor middle-class styles of play (McLoyd, 1982). Usually the interviewers and observers were from the middle class, which adds another source of potential bias. In a study of preschoolers who attended socioeconomically segregated schools, I found that, although both social-class groups had similar distributions of popular, rejected, and average children, the teachers of the low-income children consistently rated their children as less socially skilled than did the teachers of the middle-income group (Ramsey, 1988). If teachers regard low-income children more negatively, then classrooms are likely to be less comfortable places for these children. This pattern may contribute significantly to findings that suggest that low-income children are socially deficient and peripheral.

To avoid biasing our judgments of children from different groups, we must distinguish between style (i.e., the social conventions and mannerisms of specific individuals and groups), and competence (i.e., individual levels of effectiveness in establishing and maintaining positive relationships). Because styles vary across socioeconomic status (and cultural) groups, children who are equally competent may behave differently because they are expressing and responding to different group norms. In one study, Wright, Giammarino, and Parad (1986) found that the popularity of individual children with similar behavior patterns varied across groups. Similarity between an individual's behaviors and the group norms appeared to be a mediating factor in the child's level of peer popularity. In the face of many commonly held assumptions about the deficits of low-income children, we as teachers need to scrutinize our own assumptions and reactions and be alerted to the attitudes expressed by children in our classes.

Proximity is also an issue in cross-class contacts because neighborhoods, social groups, and preschools are usually economically segregated. In one town, the kindergarten and first-grade teachers often spoke about the segregation between the low- and middle-income groups that occurred from the very beginning of school. Not only did the two groups come in with different home experiences, but many already knew members of their own group as a result of attending either a federally funded preschool program for low-income children or local tuition-based nursery schools and day care centers that served middle-income families.

Thus, although young children do not really understand the concept of socioeconomic status, they may react to some of the cross-class differences in social and play styles. Because schools are usually oriented to the values and subject matter of the middle class, low-income children may feel less at home and function at a lower level than do their middle-income peers. Furthermore, teachers' reactions to children from different socioeconomic groups may imply that one group is smarter and more advanced than the other. These influences, combined with the lack of proximity and familiarity, may impede contact between children from different social-class groups

Needless to say, poverty and inadequate resources impose terrible burdens on children and on their families and can jeopardize development in all areas, and we cannot dismiss these deprivations as mere differences in lifestyle. However, we must be sure that we do not exacerbate economic disadvantage by undermining the social skills and styles that children have developed, even though they may be less compatible with the current structure of the classroom.

INDIVIDUAL DIFFERENCES

The children in any class present a perplexing array of individual differences that challenges efforts to create a socially cohesive classroom. To highlight these issues, this section will focus on research related to mainstreaming children who have been identified as having special needs. However, the problems experienced by this population are common to children with average abilities who, for a variety of reasons, do not fit easily into the social fabric of the classroom. Thus, these issues are potentially relevant to all children in classrooms.

Many teachers are frustrated because mainstreaming special-needs children into regular classrooms has not resulted in the social integration of these students. These concerns are valid; many studies have shown that special-needs children are often quite isolated and rejected in their mainstream classroom (Gerber, 1977; Goodman, Gottlieb, & Harrison, 1972; Iano, Ayers, Heller, McGettigan, & Walker, 1974; Taylor, Asher, & Williams, 1987). Based on this research and their own experiences, some practitioners have raised the question of whether mainstreaming does, in fact, fulfill its goal of placing children in the least restrictive environment. The social isolation that many mainstreamed children experience may be more limiting than the supportive environment of a special education classroom (Osman, 1982).

In an effort to understand why this pattern has been so persistent, one of my students systematically compared the social interactions of learning disabled students when they were in the resource room and in their regular classrooms. She found that even though these children were only mildly impaired, they were quite withdrawn in their regular classrooms. In contrast, they were very socially active when they were in the resource room, so their reticence was not simply a reflection of poor social skills. To some extent, the problems seemed to relate to the issue of proximity and familiarity. First, the children were out of the classroom a fair amount of time so they did not know their classmates as well. Second, because of scheduling, they often entered the classroom during the middle of an activity and had to remain on the periphery until it was over. Third, the teacher seemed protective of these students and rarely asked them to perform in front of the class or to answer questions, so they were less visible to the other children.

Besides the issue of proximity, special-needs children are often seen as "different" and usually as deficient in some way. If children cannot do some of the physical or academic activities that dominate children's interactions, then there are fewer opportunities to initiate relationships and less common ground on which to maintain them. Some emotional disabilities cause children to act unpredictably, and they become less trusted by their peers. For example, children with impulse control problems often are seen as "bad" by their peers, who are unable to interpret the actions as anything other than misbehavior.

Milder and less visible impairments that appear unrelated to social skills may still have an impact on children's abilities to interact effectively with others. Learning-disabled children, perhaps because their difficulties are more subtle, are often isolated because they do not meet children's and teacher's expectations to keep up socially (Osman, 1982). In fact, learning disabilities are often accompanied by delayed social awareness, impulsive and distractible behavior, poor physical coordination, and low self-esteem, all of which can make social contacts more difficult. Mildly retarded children often display high levels of shy and avoidant behavior and report that they feel a lot of social anxiety (Taylor et al., 1987). Thus, their peers may easily overlook or ignore them. One study showed how developmentally delayed children can become increasingly isolated over time (Guralnick & Groom, 1987). The classroom consisted of three groups: developmentally delayed and normally developing 4-year-olds, and normal 3-year-olds. Although developmentally they were more similar to the 3-year olds, the delayed 4-year-olds preferred to interact with their age mates rather than the younger children. However, the delayed children had limited entry skills and were not sought out as social resources by their age mates. Over time, they became increasingly isolated from both the younger and older children.

Although they are not dealing with a lack of skills or capabilities, gifted and talented children do not always fit into their classrooms very comfortably. They often have more sophisticated interests and perceptions and do not communicate effectively with their peers. In one kindergarten, a very precocious boy often told clever jokes that the adults appreciated. His peers, however, did not understand his witticisms and dismissed them (and the child) derisively.

When children of different abilities interact, their interactions are more likely to be strained and unequal. Social interactions between retarded and nonretarded peers often have a lower level of social responsiveness and fewer joint activities than encounters between two nonretarded friends (Siperstein, Brownley, & Scott, 1989). Also the roles may be more rigid. In this study, the nonretarded children were more frequently in leadership roles than were their retarded peers. Thus, simply encouraging social interactions between mainstreamed and nonmainstreamed children is not enough. We also have to facilitate equal and positive interactions and relationships.

In spite of these difficulties, isolation and inequality are not inevitable. First, the degree of disability may make a difference. In some classrooms, children who are classified as mildly impaired interact with the nonimpaired children as frequently as the children in the latter group interact with each other (Guralnick, 1980). Second, the type of disability may influence peers' acceptance. In a study of mainstreamed hearing-impaired children, Kennedy and Bruininks (1974) did not observe any signs of rejection. Children who cannot hear can still engage in physical activities, which, for young children, is often the most salient mode of interaction. Furthermore, hearing-impaired children develop alternative means of communication that enable them to participate in play and academic activities. In one classroom, the children reported that they liked their hearing-impaired classmate because he taught them sign language (Swadener & Johnson, 1989). In contrast, children may feel more impatient with classmates who cannot contribute emotionally or cognitively to the flow of ideas and activities that constitute children's play.

The age of the children also seems to be a factor. Younger children are more accepting of mainstreamed classmates than are older children (Goodman et al., 1972). In one preschool classroom, the social profiles of impaired and nonimpaired children became more similar during the course of the year, suggesting that the groups were becoming more integrated as they spent time together (Dunlop, Stoneman, & Cantrell, 1980). I recently observed a young preschooler with fairly severe impulse control problems. He frequently hit children with almost no provocation, usually causing great distress. His peers (ages 3–4 years), however, did not really reject him. They became more wary of him during the year, but continued to invite him to join them and to express concern when he was upset. At these younger ages, social groups are more fluid and children are less bound by reputations, so the peers may be more receptive to children with a range of skill levels and emotional patterns. Moreover, the types of projects that preschoolers do are usually more process-oriented and less likely to highlight children's differences in abilities.

Some classroom variables also appear to make a difference in the integration of mainstreamed children. Swadener and Johnson (1989) found that, if teachers modeled their enjoyment of interacting with mainstreamed children and facilitated the interactions between the two groups, the mainstreamed children entered more fully into the classroom social life. They also reported that timing the children's absences from class to minimize the disruptions made a positive difference, as did the involvement of the mainstreamed children in afterschool activities. Special-needs children are more socially integrated in classrooms where teachers closely monitor the level of social integration, provide activities to develop social skills and positive peer relations, and explicitly instruct children who are lacking in social skills (Odom, Jenkins, Speltz, DeKlyen, 1982). Other types of interventions, such as pairing a mainstreamed child with a well-liked peer, organizing the classroom around cooperative activities, and finding ways of highlighting the skills of each child, also can increase the level of integration (Osman, 1982). More specific strategies will be discussed in Chapter 6.

PEER CULTURE

When children begin school, they are entering a new culture—the school culture (Fernie, Kantor, Klein, Meyer, & Elgas, 1988). They are expected to learn how to participate in routines such as circle and snack, how to use particular areas of the classroom, to follow rules governing behavior, and to participate in rituals such as birthday celebrations and goodbye songs. Although many routines are common to all classrooms, each year children have to adjust to new expectations and subtle differences in teaching styles and classroom environments. The transition from preschool to elementary school often requires a whole new behavioral repertoire as children face more exacting behavioral and academic demands.

Against this backdrop, children create their own peer culture. As they interact day after day, children invent routines that reflect age-related concerns and perceptions of the adult world, and create a sense of group identity, all of which comprise a local peer culture (Corsaro, 1985).

As teachers often notice, similar child-initiated themes emerge every year, yet each group is unique in the way they enact them. In his preschool observations Corsaro identified several recurring themes that reflect Erikson's (1963) stage of Initiative versus Guilt. Children's concerns about physical power and potential harm and mortality emerge in their danger–rescue, lost–found, and death–recovery enactments. Their need to control these potentially scary events leads children to conquer them over and over again. Different groups may gravitate towards specific media figures or objects, but often the underlying theme is the same. In one 4-year-old classroom, children played at being the Headless Horseman all year long, even though the television show that precipitated this interest was shown only around Halloween. During that time in the same school, another group of 4-year-olds were engrossed in Masters of the Universe characters. Particular objects often become significant artifacts in peer cultures. In one classroom, the possession of sticks distinguished group members from nongroup members (Elgas, Klein, Kantor, & Fernie, 1988). Children in another classroom used bristle blocks made into CB radios to signal their membership in the "Emergency" group.

In the elementary schools, when children are more concerned about mastery of skills (as indicated by Erikson's stage of Industry versus Inferiority), peer acceptance, and academic competence, the themes often reflect concerns about groups, friendships, and school work (Rizzo, 1989). Children's conversations frequently focus on skills they have mastered (e.g., "I did the whole story in cursive!") or ones they wish they could learn (e.g., "This picture is dumb, it doesn't look anything like...!") They also engage in a lot of comparison of work and teachers' comments on it. Their concern about friendships and groups often emerges in the formation of exclusive clubs or claiming an area of the playground for a particular group. Children also reassure themselves about their peer acceptability by gossiping about other children in their class (Parker & Gottman, 1989).

Another type of ritual that groups of children develop is humor routines. These can be enacted with group glee which is more typical of younger children, or take the form of joke themes in older groups (McGee, 1979). Young children often play off each other with nonsense words or bathroom-type words and sounds, and enjoy distorting real words ("crackers, plackers, frackers!"). They often repeat each others' words with great hilarity, but with no real point to the joke (e.g., "You're a silly Billy!" "You're a silly Billy Dilly!" "You're a poopy silly Billy Dilly!"). Kindergarten children often get very attached to a particular joke format that is repeated endlessly, but with no meaningful punch line (e.g., "Knock knock." "Who's there?" "Nubie." "Nubie who?" "Nubie Dubie Tubie!" outburst of laughter.) In the elementary years, children begin to understand double meanings and riddles so that "knock-knock" jokes, and others begin to end in real punch lines (e.g., "Knock knock." "Who's there?" "Orange." "Orange who?" "Orange-cha glad it's me?"). At all ages, humor routines tend to be repeated over and over, often with elaborations. The audience knows to laugh heartily when the joke has reached its climax, regardless of whether or not it culminated in a discernible punchline.

Greeting rituals are also common, yet distinct in individual groups. In a recent study (Ramsey, 1989c), I found that one group of 4-year-olds talked a lot about each others' clothes when they were trying to make contact (e.g., "We both have blue sneakers on."). Whereas another 4-year-old group in the same school used bathroom talk as their means of initiating contact. Often attempts to engage another child include references to a highly desirable object in that culture. For example, children in the classroom where sticks were valued frequently approached peers by brandishing sticks and making shooting noises. Older children often mimic the greetings and stances of popular media heroes when they approach peers.

Many routines in the peer culture develop in opposition to the adult and school culture (Corsaro, 1985). Children often collaborate in their efforts to circumvent adult rules. Teachers are all familiar with the Lego and stick guns that can be easily hidden or transformed to avoid detection. One group gathered on top of the climber and played "firefighters." Gleefully they would point their stick "hoses" at objects and people below and shout "Fire! Fire!" Although the disguise was thin, the children could justify their actions as acceptable play. During the times when children are expected to pay attention to the teacher (e.g., circle time), children develop many ways of continuing their communications and disrupting the teacher's plans. In one kindergarten, two boys always deliberately mixed up the words to the songs, causing great hilarity among their peers. In elementary school when teachers start to curtail children's time for social interactions, children develop ways of communicating secretly with sign language, notes, and nonverbal gestures (Hatch, 1986). Children also help each other with school work, in violation of the rules, and egg each other on to avoid work. Children also often "forget" the rules and "play with the limits" to circumvent the rules (Hatch, 1986). They may "forget" to do particular assignments or to follow some procedure. To gain more social time, children often go to the pencil sharpener several times an hour and each time grind away at their pencils while talking with the children in the area. They are not directly violating the rule but are bending it as far as possible.

Many themes are common to all classrooms of children at the same age, but each group is unique because of the individuals involved. Often a particular routine is limited to one particular subgroup in the classroom. However, if it looks exciting or involves high-status children, others may begin to imitate or attempt to join it. For example, one group of kindergarten girls became very involved with "having babies." Initially most of the other children were not involved, but as the play got more exciting, others began to participate as doctors and babysitters. In the classroom with the high-status group who used sticks (Elgas et al., 1988), nonmembers began to carry sticks in hopes of being identified as members of the group. A second-grade teacher reported that suddenly everyone in his class was stumbling around with their sneakers untied as they rushed to conform to the latest fad, initiated by a few of the more sophisticated children.

Together these themes and routines create a local peer culture that provides a shared context in which children initiate and maintain contacts and develop a group identity. Although teachers may find certain behaviors and routines of the peer culture annoying and disruptive, this aspect of classroom life is valuable to children. By developing these routines children are learning to cooperate, to invent, to interact in a greater range of ways (e.g., using humor to diffuse conflicts), and to gain independence from adult authority. By recognizing the peer culture and the possible functions that it is serving, teachers can interact with it more effectively. For example, teachers can help children make props to support their play (e.g., capes to facilitate superhero play) and help children find acceptable and safe ways of enacting their themes. To illustrate this point, Elgas et al. (1988) contrasted two approaches to getting children to stop playing "shoot 'em up" with sticks. One teacher tried to convince the children that the sticks were musical instruments and the children could march in a parade around the room. The second teacher "assumed" the sticks were firehoses and began to enact the role of a firefighter. The first approach was rejected because it did not incorporate the excitement and action of the children's game; the second one worked because it fit the children's mood and interests. The peer culture is also a source of feedback, as children often enact the ways in which the classroom and the adult world are meeting or failing to meet their needs. If children are constantly finding covert ways of expressing aggression, perhaps they need more safe arenas to enact aggressive themes (e.g., learning how to wrestle, hearing stories about strong heroes and heroines). Children who are spending a lot of time and energy trying to communicate surreptitiously with each other may be reacting to a paucity of opportunities to have social interactions. Teachers can also use their knowledge of the peer culture to help children who may not be "in tune" with their peers enter into the mainstream of social play. They might be able to point out to children how their styles differ from that of their peers and help them find more common ground. Sometimes they can correct misunderstandings if a child is not familiar with some of the common themes. One teacher described how a young child who had not seen much television was approached by a peer asking him to play "Batman and Robin." The child replied "You mean Robinhood?" and his peer, looking puzzled and a little scornful, walked away. The teacher, realizing that the differences in these two children's backgrounds was interfering with their ability to communicate, had each child describe and draw some of their favorite characters. As they shared their stories, she helped them to see how their respective heroes had many things in common and encouraged them to create fantasies which incorporated both types of characters.

As adults we can never see all the nuances of the peer culture of their group, because many aspects are deliberate efforts to deceive us. Moreover, some themes and their importance simply are not visible to adult eyes. However, the more aware we are of the "underlife" of the classroom, the more effective we can be in working with it.

CLASSROOM ENVIRONMENTS AND SOCIAL DYNAMICS

Besides the concerns, interests, and social patterns of the children, the physical structures, the types of materials available, and the roles of the teachers also influence the social dynamics of the classroom. Most researchers studying these classroom environment effects have focused on preschool classrooms, so we know less about how elementary school classrooms either support or inhibit social interactions and relationship building. Because traditionally many elementary school classrooms and materials were designed to *limit* social interaction, this question has been less relevant to elementary school teachers. However, many elementary teachers do make adaptations to encourage more social exchange, and, in many cases, the same principles that have been found in preschool studies can be applied to elementary school classrooms. This section will include a brief review of studies on the effects of different aspects of the classroom environment. Potential applications for both preschool and elementary classrooms will be discussed in more detail in Chapter 5.

The kinds of spaces that are available for children influence the sizes of groups that gather. For example, large areas designed for gross motor play usually attract groups of four or more children (Vandenberg, 1981). The structure of the space also has an effect on the types of interactions that occur. When they are in enclosed spaces, children are more likely to engage in cooperative play, probably because children are in closer contact with each other and less distracted by external events (Field, 1980). However, these places may also stimulate more territorial disputes (Ramsey, 1986a). In lofts and other single-entranced spaces children frequently cooperate in their efforts to repel the advances of peers attempting to enter. They may physically block the entrance or stand there "shooting" at potential invaders.

The available materials in each area also stimulate different kinds of play. Complex materials and areas, such as well-equipped block corners and role-playing areas, are often the locations of more interactive and imaginative play (Tschantz, 1985). When children are in art activities they are usually engaged in parallel and constructive play; in blocks they also play constructively but are more likely to interact (Pellegrini, 1984). The kinds of materials also reflect the philosophy of different programs, which may vary in their social goals. For example, children in Montessori schools tend to engage in more constructive play and less dramatic play than do children at more traditional preschools (Rubin, 1977).

The schedule of the day also has an impact on children's social participation. Children's play becomes more complex after 10 minutes or more have elapsed, and programs with play periods of 30 or more minutes are most conducive to cooperative play (Tegano & Parsons, 1989). Children apparently need time to explore the available materials, establish themselves in a group, and find a common theme that can be developed. Thus, schedules that allow for longer play periods and do not force children to change play areas every few minutes provide more opportunities for cooperative play. However, if children are getting into social "ruts" and are limiting themselves to repetitive play with the same partners, then teachers may want to encourage children to switch activities and partners at various times of the day.

The number of adults in the classroom and the roles that they play also influence the level of children's social participation. Children seem to get involved in more cooperative play if fewer adults are present (Field, 1980). Conversely when they are in adult company, children engage in more onlooking and unoccupied behaviors and have fewer cooperative interactions (Pellegrini, 1984). Of course, adults are often in an area because they are providing instructions, directing activities, or reprimanding children for misbehavior, all of which are contradictory to cooperative play. If children are attempting to circumvent adult rules and strictures, then obviously an adult presence has a repressive effect on children's play. On the other hand, adults often facilitate children's interactions. In a study of the year-long evolution of circle time, Kantor, Elgas, & Fernie (1989) showed how the teachers used both modeling and direct instructions to help children learn to take turns in a conversation and to respond meaningfully to each other.

Structuring activities so that children are encouraged to work in cooperative groups (e.g., cooperative learning, projects) without direct teacher guidance enables children to develop more stable and reciprocal relationships and higher rates of cross-sex and cross-race contacts and friendships. These strategies also reduce the numbers of children who are isolated from their peers (see Epstein, 1986, for a review). In Chapters 5 and 6, ways of adapting activities to be more collaborative and cooperative will be discussed.

Many physical, temporal and personnel factors are related to different levels and types of peer interactions. As we arrange our classrooms, decide on daily schedules, hire and train teachers, and incorporate volunteers, we should keep in mind the subtle ways in which these factors affect the social dynamics of classrooms.

4

Individual Differences in Peer Relationships

Ms. L. is scanning the playground as her second graders race around playing a variety of games. She sighs as her eyes alight on Marc who is sitting (as always) by himself on a bench. His shoulders are hunched, his face thrust forward, and his eyes staring at the ground in front of him, looking as though he had lost his last friend...which is the case. Once again he has been left out of the boys' game of kickball.

Jamaal saunters into his kindergarten class, and immediately three children race over to see him. "Jamaal, you should see the new trucks in the blocks! I saved you one!" Ernie shouts. The other two begin to clamor for Jamaal's attention. Jamaal looks around, smiles, and says, including everyone in his invitation, "Let's go then!" All four children run over to blocks.

Irma Lee is absent today. At circle time, Mr. J. asks his 4-year-olds who is missing today. The children all look around, but no one can guess who the missing child is.

These narratives will seem very familiar to most teachers who often are troubled and perplexed about the differences in popularity and social success that they observe among the children in their classrooms. Up to this point we have focused on the commonalities among children: Chapter 2 reviewed the developmental trends in early peer relations and the related cognitive and affective changes, and the preceding chapter on classroom dynamics discussed the development of children's interactional patterns and peer culture. In this chapter, the perspective shifts to individual differences in children's peer relations, and we will look at some of the dimensions and causes of these differences.

Concerns about children's popularity and the negative effects of rejection have been the primary force behind much of the current wave of research in social development. Likewise, teachers often find themselves thinking more about the social dynamics of the classroom if they have a child who is clearly rejected or withdrawn. An immensely popular child also may trigger ruminations about the social patterns of the classroom. Although children who are at the extreme ends of the popularity continuum are likely to draw more adult attention, they should not be seen in isolation from the dynamics of the whole classroom and of the larger social environment. Classroom social patterns and intergroup relationships often influence individuals' levels of acceptance.

This chapter begins with an overview of methods that researchers have used to measure the popularity and social adjustment of individual children and provides suggestions for potential classroom adaptations of some of these assessment techniques. The next section includes behavioral profiles of the four types of children that have been identified from many studies: popular, rejected, withdrawn, and controversial. In the third part of the chapter we will review factors that contribute to the development of differences in social status and social adjustment. Finally, we will consider findings from longitudinal and intervention studies that offer some insight into the stability and changeability of children's status.

MEASURING CHILDREN'S SOCIAL STATUS AND ADJUSTMENT

When we measure children's peer relations we must first make a distinction between popularity and friendship. Being generally liked by one's classmates is not the same as having a close friend. Likewise, children who are generally rejected may have one partnership that in some ways protects them from the ill effects of their unpopularity. Both kinds of information are useful. By knowing which children are friends, we have a clearer view of the group dynamics and can anticipate children's reactions to changes in work partners and seating plans. Awareness of the status of particular children gives us an idea of how well specific children are faring in the social life of the classroom.

Sociometric Measures

The most common way in which children's social status is measured is by having children classify their classmates according to how well they like them. In terms of administering the assessment, preschool children are usually interviewed and shown photographs of their classmates; elementary school children do these tasks as pencil-and-paper activities in the classroom. Researchers usually use one or both of the following two procedures.

First, in a nomination procedure, children name the three classmates whom they like the most and the three whom they like the least. For younger children, these questions are often framed in more concrete terms such as "Which three kids would you invite/not invite to your birthday party?" In a second method, children rate all of their classmates on a 3-point, 4-point, or 5-point scale in terms of how well they like each of them. Both techniques are quite reliable, but the rating scale is considered a more accurate measure with preschool children (Asher & Hymel, 1981; Asher, Singleton, Tinsley, & Hymel, 1979). The rating scale also provides more information because it tells us children's feelings about all their classmates, not just the ones they nominate. The distribution of ratings reveals whether a child and the class in general feel generally positively or negatively about their peer group.

For research purposes, the status of each child is calculated using several different formulas. Teachers, however, can look at the proportional numbers of positive and negative nominations or ratings that each child receives to get a general idea of how well liked a child is in comparison with the other children in the class. If a child receives mostly positive ratings or nominations and few or no negative ones, then s/he is popular. If the reverse pattern is evident, then that child may be a rejected child. Children who receive almost no nominations or only midscale ratings are referred to as neglected. They do not seem to have much impact on the social environment, positively or negatively. If a child gets a lot of high and low nominations or ratings, the child is considered controversial, suggesting that s/he has a considerable impact on the social dynamics of the classroom, but that the peers are not in agreement about whether the impact is positive or negative. Children whose ratings and nominations do not fit into any of these more pronounced patterns are considered average.

In addition to providing information about children's level of peer acceptance, these measures also allow teachers to see which children consider each other as friends and what particular friendships or antagonisms are developing or waning. Often children name peers with whom they would *like* to be best friends rather than children they actually play with. Awareness of these one-way admirations can help teachers identify relationships they might want to encourage.

Peer Descriptions

In addition to assessing whether or not children are liked by their peers, teachers may find it useful to learn how peers perceive each other. One way to gain this information is to have children describe their classmates and record their comments. Preschool children, because they tend to see peers in very immediate and concrete terms, usually describe physical characteristics or a particular event. For this age group, children's comments show what information is salient to peers, but they may be a less accurate measure of overall social adjustment. Elementary children, however, are able to provide more general behavioral descriptions. To see what specific roles children play in the class, teachers can play a game called "Guess Who?" in which they ask children to match classmates with specific characteristics (e.g., "I am thinking of someone who always is willing to help." I am thinking of someone who starts a lot of fights."). An alternative method is to pretend that the children are casting a class play and have them assign roles to specific classmates. To avoid embarrassment, these questions should be asked in a private situation. Some methods have been developed to elicit similar discriminations from younger children by using pictures of different types of actions (e.g., hitting, talking with a lot of people, sitting alone). Teachers and researchers have also used "classroom friend" dolls, made by mounting classmates' photographs on blocks. With these dolls, some children spontaneously enact their perceptions about their classmates' actions and friendship patterns. A more elaborate version of this technique involves providing children with a replica of the classroom to see where they place themselves and their peers and the kinds of activities they have them do. This activity has been used to assess individual children's level of awareness of social dynamics (Wexler-Sherman, Gardner, & Feldman, 1988) as well as their perceptions of individual classmates.

Teachers, parents, and administrators often express concern about encouraging children to express negative feelings and perceptions about classmates. They worry that children will be anxious about what others are saying about them and that these procedures will exacerbate any existing tensions. Preschoolers, because they are not that aware of what others think of them and do not see relationships as long-term entities, are less likely to experience this discomfort. Many preschool teachers informally collect this information with little difficulty. However, for elementary school teachers, these procedures are more difficult. Researchers have an advantage because they come in from the outside and make it clear that the children's responses will not be seen by anyone that they know. Teachers, on the other hand, cannot separate their questions from their day-to-day interactions with children and need to find more subtle ways of gaining this information. They can include these questions in different writing assignments (e.g., "Write a story about going to a secret place with your three best friends..."; "If you were stuck in a blizzard, which classmates would you want to have with you and what would you do?"). They can also have informal conversations with children about peers they prefer as work and play partners, perhaps as part of setting up seating arrangements and work groups. Some teachers are comfortable asking questions about positive feelings and characteristics, but are reluctant to ask about negative ones. This information, although not complete, is still valuable. A lot can be learned about the negative side of the social scale by finding out who and what children avoid mentioning when talking about their preferred peers.

Sociometric procedures rely on the assumption that children have preferences for some peers over others. In some communities, this kind of differentiation may violate norms that stress a more inclusive and cooperative lifestyle. In one preschool classroom, children became upset when asked to choose three children to invite to their birthday parties. One child protested, "But, they're all my brothers and sisters!" In these settings, sociometric questions may be less relevant because children may be more inclusive and less likely to reject each other. If children are uncomfortable answering these questions, we should not push them, but instead use observations to see whether or not some children are more well-liked than others.

Teacher Rating Scales

Research projects on children's status and social adjustment often include teachers' assessments of the children in their classes, and some of these techniques are potentially useful in classrooms. Teachers are constantly monitoring children's development, so having a separate rating system may seem redundant. However, an external system can be a useful framework for stepping back and looking at children comparatively. One of the most commonly used scales for early detection of social and emotional problems is the Teacher–Child Rating Scale published by Primary Mental Health Project. One advantage of this system is that it includes a Child Self-Rating Scale that parallels the teacher ratings. By using both of these, teachers and guidance counselors can get a more complete picture of how children are functioning in the classroom. The items on these scales are listed in Appendix 1, but readers who wish to use these instruments should contact Primary Mental Health Project for the manual and scoring system. Often, individual teachers or school staff develop their own checklists that address their specific questions and philosophies. A more thorough discussion of how these checklists can be constructed is included in Chapter 5.

Behavioral Observations

As teachers know, actually seeing what children do and how their peers react to them is, in many ways, the most authentic and useful type of information. Teachers are observing constantly and often make mental or written notes of children's behavior. Researchers have developed many different scales that can make this process more systematic. Several observation techniques are described in Chapter 5 and can be used to analyze children's level of peer acceptance. To analyze individual differences, researchers often observe specific children for a period of time (e.g., 5 minutes) and systematically go through the whole group. While they are observing they sometimes use a checklist in which they simply indicate whether or not specific behaviors, such as sharing or hitting, occurred within that time. Alternatively, they write or dictate a narrative or make a video recording of all the actions they observe and later analyze the whole observation for particular behaviors. Obviously, this kind of systematic attention to a single child for a prescribed time period is not feasible for teachers. The following adaptation, however, can be integrated with teaching responsibilities. Each day a teacher can select a child to watch more closely, particularly during social interactions. If volunteers or students from local colleges are available, they can assist in recording children's behaviors or relieve the teacher so that he can have some uninterrupted time to watch the children. The observations should focus on children's entries into groups, ways that others approach them, and their skills in maintaining peer interactions. With this method, teachers can identify children who seem to be frustrated and/or self-defeating in their efforts to establish either momentary contacts or long-term partnerships. They can also make a note of children who may be feeling pressured because they are "too popular."

Because many critical behaviors (e.g., entries into groups, rejections) may occur rarely in classrooms, researchers sometimes use contrived situations to get a more systematic view of how children enter groups and begin relationships. Typically, the subject child is ushered into a room where two "host" children are already playing. The subsequent interactions are not supervised, but are videotaped and later analyzed to assess the entering child's skill in initiating contact and entering an ongoing group. Often the "host" children are asked to rate the entering child on his or her social skills after the interaction is over. Another technique that researchers use is to assemble groups of unfamiliar children and have these groups meet weekly for a month or 6 weeks. They closely observe initial contact behaviors and the subsequent establishment of status and peer preferences. Although this kind of methodology is not available to classroom teachers, it does suggest that close observations at the beginning of the school year can reveal how children initiate contacts and establish relationships. The entry of a new child into the class can also provide the opportunity to see how this process occurs. When teachers change work groups or seating arrangements, they can watch to see how particular children negotiate these new social situations.

Social Problem-Solving Skills

Because children's social problem-solving skills potentially contribute to their social adjustment and peer relationships, researchers (e.g., Ladd & Oden, 1979) have designed tasks in which children respond to hypothetical situations. The presented problems usually include some or all of the following: a child's attempt to enter a group, a confrontation with rejecting peers, a peer's request for assistance, and a conflict. With preschool children these tasks usually are administered with small dolls (Getz, Goldman, & Corsini, 1983; Ramsey, 1988); with elementary children cartoon pictures or verbal stories are used (e.g., Ladd & Oden, 1979). In studies of children's interpretation of social events, subjects have watched videotaped vignettes (e.g., Dodge, Pettit, McClaskey, & Brown, 1986). To get more realistic responses, some researchers (e.g., Putallaz, 1983) have set up situations in which children are confronted by various problems enacted by peer confederates. Children's responses to these situations are rated by whether they are prosocial or aggressive and by the number of strategies that children generate. One of the earlier tests of children's problem-solving skills, the Preschool Interpersonal Problem Solving Test (PIPS) developed by Spivak and Shure (1974) focused primarily on the number of different strategies that children had in their repertoires. Spivak and Shure used pictures to present two situations to children, a conflict with a peer and a conflict with an adult, and gave the children several opportunities to generate a range of solutions. Children's responses to hypothetical situations do not necessarily correspond to their behavior (Ramsey, 1991b) and their relation to social status has varied across studies. However, children's hypothetical solutions do give us some information about their interpretations of social information and their repertoire of potential responses.

One drawback of these kinds of assessments is their heavy reliance on verbal interviews. Children from some cultural and social class groups may find this kind of exchange uncomfortable and therefore be less responsive. The recurring finding that low-income children performed less well on these tasks has led some researchers to question the validity of these measures for all children (e.g., McLoyd, 1982; Ramsey, 1988). Classroom teachers, however, can introduce social problem-solving activities in a much more informal way and therefore avoid possible class and cultural bias.

Social problem-solving scenarios fit easily into early childhood curricula. Many children's stories describe social dilemmas that can provide a good background for individual or group enactments or discussions about social strategies. Teachers can also use puppets or flannel board characters to stimulate children's thinking about social problems specific to their particular classroom. These discussions can both give teachers an indication of the types of social problem-solving skills children have and help children think of more strategies. Specific curriculum ideas are discussed in Chapter 7.

CHILDREN FROM DIFFERENT STATUS GROUPS

This section includes an overview of the four identified status groups: popular, rejected, neglected, and controversial. These status categories are useful to organize perceptions of children's behaviors, but they should be applied cautiously. Many children appear to have some of these qualities associated with a particular category, but may not necessarily fit into this group; not all classrooms have children that fit all of these status categories. Moreover, each classroom has a number of average children who are functioning well and do not fit any of these behavioral profiles. These children, although not as visible, are crucial players in the classroom dynamics. They form the core of the classroom and are often instrumental in ameliorating the status of children at the extremes. For example, a child who has been rejected may learn enough social skills to be accepted by peers considered average, but is not likely to become a member of the popular group.

The research on different status groups has tended to focus on individuals' traits and behaviors and to attribute children's successes or difficulties to their social competence or deficiency (Hymel, Wagner, & Butler, 1990). Classroom dynamics, however, also play a large role in how well individual children fare in a specific group. The process by which children attain their status is complicated and reflects each child's unique social history in that group.

The research on social status has included many of the measures and methods described in the previous section. Most studies include a sociometric measure in which peers rate or nominate each other, and at least one behavioral measure which may be in-class observations, lab observations, peer descriptions, assessment of social problem-solving skills, or teacher rating scales. The following profiles are brief summaries of the research in this area and do not provide an exhaustive account of the many subtle nuances that distinguish individuals and relationships. Instead, they describe some salient features that might alert teachers to specific types of dynamics or individual needs in their classrooms.

Popular Children

Chandra is a bright, attractive 5-year-old. Her classmates eagerly seek her out for a number of reasons. When she is playing with her peers, she often comes up with good ideas for elaborating on their play. Recently she inspired her classmates to use the blocks to make beds on which they would sleep and fall off with great hilarity. She is also very aware of others' feelings. Because she is such a popular playmate, her current companion(s) often try to exclude potential competitors. Chandra is clearly uncomfortable about these conflicts and usually tries to find a way to include the newcomer into the play without hurting the other children. In one observation, her playmates were rejecting an attempted entry into houseplay; Chandra resolved the conflict by announcing that there could be "two daddies" in order to create a role for the newcomer.

As can be seen in the description of Chandra, children who are well-liked by their peers are usually very capable and more cognitively, socially, and emotionally mature than their peers. Although the evidence is mixed, popular children are often more physically attractive (Coie, 1990). During elementary school, academic and athletic competence also begins to play a role in children's popularity (Coie, Dodge, & Kupersmidt, 1990). In observations of their entry strategies, popular children use a range of strategies (Dodge, Schlundt, Schocken, & Delugach, 1983) and know how to move effectively into a group situation by varying their strategies from more passively waiting and watching to more actively joining the play. They also focus on the group and the ongoing activity rather than on themselves or some extraneous event. Overall, popular children approach groups with expectations of acceptance and strategies that minimize their risks and increase their chances of being accepted (Putallaz & Gottman, 1981). They also differentiate among the needs of individual peers. One well-liked child who usually used verbal initiations was observed using almost all nonverbal ones when addressing a child who spoke only a little English (Hazen, Black, & Fleming-Johnson, 1984). Throughout their interactions, popular children show more communicative competence (Hazen et al., 1984). They address their peers more clearly and direct their comments to all of the children they are playing with, not just one child. When approached by other children, they are also more responsive than their less popular peers. In general, they seem to be more aware of other individuals and more sensitive to the nuances of social interactions.

Popular children are more positive, lively, and appropriate in their expressions of emotions (Sroufe, Schork, Motti, Lawroski, & LaFreniere, 1984). They are not emotionally bland; they approach peers with smiling expressions, and their feelings are usually appropriate to the situation. In their play, they often become excited (e.g., "Oh no! A shark is attacking us!" or "Let's try to hit the ball 10 times in a row!") and elicit the enthusiastic participation of their peers. At the same time, their emotions do not get out of control; they are able to modulate their expressions, even when they are very upset.

Popular children appear to feel positively about themselves. Boivin and Begin (1989) found that these children rated themselves more positively than average children on academic, athletic, social acceptance, and self-esteem dimensions. Whether this positive self-esteem results from or contributes to their popularity is unclear. These children appear to be in a positive cycle in which they interact positively with others, which, in turn, makes them feel more positively about themselves, so that they approach social interactions with good humor and confidence.

In terms of their social problem-solving skills, popular children are described by their peers as more likely to use calm discussion and less likely to retaliate angrily when confronted with a conflict (Bryant, 1989). Peers also described them as helpful and considerate and more likely to follow rules, especially those governing peer interactions (Coie et al., 1990).

In short, popular children often have some physical and developmental advantages. Possibly because of these physical attributes per se or because of their positive effect on others, popular children become aware of others' perspectives more quickly. In turn, they have a larger repertoire of social strategies that makes them more successful in gaining group acceptance and maintaining interactions.

Rejected Children

Helen is quiet and awkward. In her efforts to make contact with her third-grade classmates, she either hovers around looking uncomfortable or blurts out a comment that seems out of place. As an only child of parents who recently immigrated from an Eastern European country, she is unaware of many of the cultural mores of her peer group. Her clothes are sturdy and plain, and contrast sharply with the more flamboyant clothes of her peers. She is a stickler for classroom rules and frequently criticizes her peers for infractions, evoking jeers and rejection. Several other children in the class speak English as a second language, and Helen's English is more fluent than some others', but she has a harder time picking up on the jokes and nuances. Sometimes she seems paralyzed with self-consciousness, but, at the same time, often makes abrasive comments.

Randy is an active 3-year-old who likes to be involved in everything. In his eagerness, he often blunders into an area, destroying everything in sight (block structures, "tea parties," Playdough birthday cakes, etc.). His classmates frequently object, often telling him they hate him and ordering him to leave. He is also a volatile child and frequently hits and kicks others when he is frustrated. After the first few weeks of school, Ms. W. has noticed that the other children are avoiding Randy and often refer to him as "the bad boy."

Because of the concern about the effects of rejection, unpopular children have been studied a great deal. Readers interested in this research may want to read Asher and Coie's recent book, *Peer Rejection in Childhood* (1990), published by Cambridge University Press. Over the last 7 or 8 years, researchers have identified different types of rejected children and a number of factors that appear to contribute to peer rejection. Still, many questions remain about how to most effectively prevent this pattern from becoming established and how to intervene when it does.

Some physical and developmental attributes appear to be associated with rejection. Lack of physical attraction appears to contribute to rejection, particularly for girls (Coie, 1990). Lower verbal maturity also has been associated with rejection (Rubin, 1983). Rejected boys spend more time off-task and have more academic problems than their average peers (Coie & Dodge, 1988).

Rejected children show many different profiles, but usually fall into two main groups: aggressive-rejected and withdrawn-rejected (Asher & Williams, 1987; Crick & Dodge, 1989; French, 1988). The first group is characterized by pervasive aggressive behavior that includes both verbal and physical attacks on peers. These children appear to be impulsive and frequently interpret others' actions as threatening; they then react aggressively, which in turn causes their peers to avoid them. For example, Randy, when confronted with mildly frustrating events, would get very angry and lash out at the people and objects nearest him. The vast majority of children in this group are male.

The second group includes both males and females and shows a different pattern. Rather than driving peers away with their aggressive behavior, these children appear to have withdrawn as a result of not being liked by their peers (Coie et al., 1990). Reasons for this initial rejection reflect a number of individual and social characteristics. Some children demonstrate "contact incompetence" in which they do not seem to know how to act even when they are approached in a positive way (Hatch, 1986). For example, when a classmate approached Helen playfully and pretended to hit her with a pencil, she drew herself up and said stiffly, "You know you're not supposed to hit!" Some children may also be rejected because they are different in some way or are considered to be incompetent. Asher and Gabriel (1989) described conversations in which mildly retarded children were being taunted by their nonretarded peers, reflecting the frequent rejection of mainstreamed children. Sometimes children are rejected because of other attributes such as their race, culture, or class background. In these cases, unfamiliarity may create a discomfort and a distance that evolve into personal rejection. Helen's rejection may have initially stemmed from her "differentness," although her interpersonal awkwardness also contributed.

Whatever the reasons for the initial rejection, withdrawn children internalize their feelings and perceive themselves in a more negative way than do
their aggressive peers, even though the latter group is more disliked by their
classmates (Crick & Dodge, 1989).

Withdrawal may not always be an outcome of rejection. Some children
may start by being very socially anxious and avoid social activities and thus
begin a cycle of isolation (Rubin, LeMare, Lollis, 1990). They may not be
overtly rejected by peers, but simply unnoticed. Rubin (1985) raised some
questions about whether these withdrawn children were at risk as much as
overtly rejected children. In a longitudinal study, he found that children
who had been withdrawn in kindergarten were not necessarily at risk for
being rejected by the time they came to second grade. In young children,
withdrawn behavior may reflect a lack of social skills and a tentativeness
that children overcome as they gain more experience. However, withdrawn
behavior that persists into middle childhood is a sign of more serious adjustment problems (Rubin, 1985). These children are often inhibited from
exploring their social and material environments, which leads to deficits in
their impersonal and interpersonal problem-solving skills and subsequently
to negative social comparisons and low self-esteem (Rubin, Hymel, &
Mills, 1989). In their work with shy children and adults, Zimbardo and
Radl (1981) have recorded personal histories that show how these patterns
develop and the emotional toll they take. Thus, although withdrawn-
rejected children are less visible and disruptive than their aggressive-
rejected peers, we should monitor them closely to ascertain the nature and
extent of their withdrawn behavior.

When children are aggressive, they tend to pick on certain children as
targets, often referred to as "victims." Some of these children are also
aggressive and provoke attacks, but others are targets because they submit
too easily and will not stand up for themselves (Perry & Williard, 1989).
Interestingly, although the victims do not like their tormentors, they do not
avoid interactions with them and often imitate them (Dodge & Coie,
1988). Thus, bully–victim relationships can become entrenched rather easily and may impair the development of both parties—the one who is learning s/he can hit with impunity, and the other who is learning to accept and
perhaps imitate aggressive behavior. Children who are provocative victims
are more highly rejected than are bullies or passive victims (Olewus, 1990).
These children are disliked because they are aggressive, yet scorned because
they are victims.

Rejected children, in contrast to their popular peers, lack many social
skills. In response to conflicts, they practice techniques of avoidance and
angry retaliation more than their peers (Bryant, 1989). They also have a
hard time adjusting their behavior when the situation requires a different

response. For example, rejected boys (but not rejected girls) keep competing even when they are clearly ahead in a game, whereas nonrejected boys cooperate under the same circumstances (Taylor & Gabriel, 1989). Moreover, rejected children cannot (or do not) make the distinction between appropriate and inappropriate times to socialize; they make more overtures to peers during class time than they do during recess (Coie & Koeppl, 1990). As a result, rejected children are perceived as disruptive by both teachers and peers. Alternatively, unpopular children may flout the rules deliberately in order to form an alliance with peers (secondary adjustment), but they do it in such a way that their peers see their overtures only as unwelcome disruptions.

Rejected children's attempts to enter groups reflect both a lack awareness of others and limited social repertoires (Hazen et al., 1984). Their comments are often nondirected so that their communicative intent is unclear and unsuccessful. They also tend to initiate interactions in an inflexible and stereotypic way and do not adjust them to the demands of the current situation. For example, they may continue to insist that they be allowed to join a group even though it is obvious that there is no room for them. The following observation also illustrates this disfunctional repetition.

> Carmen (a rejected child) is sitting next to Eliana at circle time. She keeps glancing at Eliana trying to get her attention, each time leaning closer to Eliana. After a few failed attempts, Carmen begins to make faces as she looks over. Eliana stares straight ahead, her eyes fixed on the teacher. When Carmen sticks her face with her eyes popping and her tongue hanging out right in front of Eliana's, Eliana finally protests, and the teacher reprimands Carmen.

In terms of specific entry strategies, rejected children vary between being overly tentative and too intrusive. Putallaz and Gottman (1981) found that rejected children were more likely to make comments about themselves (e.g., "Guess what I just did!"), express a feeling comment (e.g., "I'm mad at Tony."), disagree with what the host children were doing (e.g., "You're doing that the wrong way!"), or ask an informational question unrelated to the ongoing activity (e.g., "Why is that red thing there?"). All of these approaches reflect the child's preoccupation with his or her own feelings, experiences, or needs and, in contrast to the entries of popular children, none show any sensitivity to the perspectives of the group members. Prolonged periods of hovering and the self-oriented entries have a high probability of being ignored or rejected. Unlike their popular peers, unpopular children act in ways to maximize the likelihood that they will be rejected or at least ignored.

In their interactions, unpopular children, in comparison with their pop-ular peers, are more disagreeable and less constructive when they are criti-cizing a peer and engage in longer and more intense disagreements (Ladd, 1983; Putallaz & Gottman, 1981). Negative exchanges between unpopular children usually deteriorate and become increasingly combative, whereas popular children often neutralize negative initiations (Asarnow, 1983). Thus, not only are rejected children's entries less effective, but, over time, their peers begin to realize that they do not enjoy interactions with these children and begin to reject them on the basis of their past experience or history. This tendency to reject on the basis of reputation increases during the early childhood years. Three-year-old children's acceptance or rejection of peers is related primarily to the strategy that the entering child uses, but 4-year-olds begin to show a relation between the status of the entering child and the success of the entry attempt (Ramsey, 1989c). Reputation is a strong factor in early elementary school (Hymel et al., 1990) and becomes increasingly salient from grades one to five (Rogosch & Newcomb, 1989). Thus, as children gain experience and the ability to think about long-term behavior of peers, their reputations make it increasingly difficult for rejected children to become part of their social group.

Emotionally, rejected children are either more likely to be out of con-trol or to show very little emotion (Sroufe et al., 1984). In the first case, children find the volatile child unpredictable and perhaps frightening. For young children who are just learning how to control their own emotions, the sight of a child who is out of control can be very disturbing. Children who show almost no emotion are also disconcerting. Their peers have a hard time "reading" them and, in the absence of emotional responses, do not know how to continue the interaction. Also, these children are less fun, as their interactions lack emotional vitality. When they do express their feelings, rejected children are more likely to express negative ones, which also makes them irritating work and play partners. In terms of their inner feelings, rejected children often feel more lonely than their peers (Asher, Parkhurst, Hymel, Williams, 1990). The intensity of this feeling varies among rejected children which may reflect the degree of rejection, the duration of the rejection (chronic versus situational), whether or not the rejected child has at least one friend, and the child's awareness and interpretation of the rejection. Their self-perceptions also vary, with some rejected children underestimating their competence in academic, social, and athletic areas and showing evidence of low self-esteem, and others overestimating their abilities (Boivin & Begin, 1989). Possibly, the aggres-sive children overestimate their abilities and the withdrawn ones, who tend to internalize their feelings, underestimate themselves.

Rejection by peers evolves over the course of numerous social interactions. In an ethnographic account of this process, Hatch (1988) describes how, over time, a child's inappropriate aggression and incompetence in peer contacts begin to elicit exclusionary responses from his peers. As his reputation develops, children refuse to accept him even when he is acting appropriately. Another dynamic that exacerbates this process is that, when a child is disliked, peers often approach that child provocatively, which leads to more aggressive events that further solidify the rejection (Olson, 1989). In short, once a cycle of negative interactions is established, it is maintained not only by the rejected child, but by the peer group as well.

Neglected Children

Erin is quiet and very interested in art activities. She rarely initiates contact with other children, but is agreeable when they join her at an activity. At the beginning of the year, several girls tried to get Erin to join them in the housekeeping corner. She would go over, but quickly would lose interest and return to the art area. When she is working, she is very absorbed in her projects and is oblivious to the classroom around her. Sometimes she wanders around the classroom and looks at groups of children somewhat wistfully, but rarely makes an effort to join.

Children who do not receive any high or low ratings from their peers are classified as neglected children. They appear to have little positive or negative impact on the social life of the classroom. They may be somewhat shy, as suggested by Dodge et al.'s findings (1983) that neglected children use more waiting and hovering entries. Although these children often receive negative responses to their entry attempts (Dodge et al., 1983), they are not consistently rejected as are their unpopular peers. Neglected boys are much less aggressive than their average male peers and appear to avoid aggressive interactions (Coie & Dodge, 1988). When children were asked to rate classmates on a number of behavioral attributes, neglected children had profiles similar to those of their popular and average peers (Rogosch & Newcomb, 1989). However, in another study they were rated lower on all dimensions, suggesting that their peers rarely thought of them (Coie & Dodge, 1988). These children are not disliked, but rather unnoticed. When children are forced to think about them, they see them relatively positively, but do not go out of their way to include them. Given their tendency to use passive entry strategies, they may often be ignored simply because their presence is not that visible when compared with more socially active children.

Neglected children appear to be uncomfortable and perhaps reluctant to join peer groups (Hazen et al., 1984). They both make and receive fewer initiations than members of the other status groups. Their attempts to initiate are often preceded by prolonged periods of watching. If they do finally try to join, their entries are quiet and not clearly directed towards any particular child and therefore are often ignored.

From the neglected child's perspective, the social life of the classroom may be somewhat distant. When shown videotaped vignettes of popular, rejected, and neglected children, the neglected subjects (elementary), in contrast to their peers, were unable to distinguish which children belonged to which status group. They may be more involved in particular activities and spend less time observing the social interactions and the social hierarchy of the classroom. Erin's absorption in her art activities illustrates this pattern. The social life of the classroom was not that salient or interesting to her. According to teacher ratings, neglected boys spend more time on-task than their male peers do, suggesting that they choose to engage in socially acceptable but more isolated activities that do not offend anyone (Coie & Dodge, 1988).

One question that teachers and researchers share is whether or not being a neglected child is an indicator or cause of poor social adjustment. At this point, there is not a definitive answer, but, unlike rejected children, neglected children do not describe themselves as lonely (Asher & Wheeler, 1985), and their self-ratings of competence are similar to those of their average peers (Boivin & Begin, 1989). However, they do see themselves as being more vulnerable in social relationships (Shannon & Kafer, 1984), so perhaps they are aware of their lack of experience and the fact that they are not in the social mainstream. Overall, however, these children do not present a picture of poor social adjustment. They are more likely to be the loners or the quiet children who are content in their roles as minor players in the social arena. Withdrawn and shy children, who were discussed in the previous section on rejection, may show up on sociometric measures as neglected. However, they are distinct from this group because they are uncomfortable with their relations with their peer group; they feel anxious about their peers and perhaps assume they are rejected.

Controversial Children

Jorge is a very active, curious, and friendly boy. His enthusiasm, however, often gets him into trouble, as he races into areas where children are already playing and disrupts their play, knocking over block buildings and children as he rushes by. He enjoys playful aggression and often instigates rough-and-tumble play and chase games. At circle time, he often makes faces and gets the other children laughing. He is a leader in making up aggressive fantasies. For example, he instigated a game in the housekeeping corner which consisted of putting the babies in the stove and "cooking them"; now he has several enthusiastic partners in this enterprise. Usually he is cheerful and often very funny, but he is also quick to lose his temper and to strike out, both verbally and physically. He is a leader among the boys, whereas the girls think he is "bad."

In many ways, controversial children are diametrically opposite to neglected children. These children have a major impact on the social life of the classroom, but their peers do not agree about what that effect is. Not only are their classmates divided in their opinions, but teachers and children often disagree about the nature of these children. Sociometrically, these are the children that are well-liked by some children and disliked by others. Typically they are socially, intellectually, and athletically talented, but more active than other children and prone to anger and rule breaking (Coie & Dodge, 1988). In many ways, their behaviors and the reactions to them are contradictory (Price, 1989). Both teachers and classmates see them as angry and aggressive, but at the same time they resemble popular children in their success at entering groups.

Despite their ability to enter groups, however, they spend less time in cooperative activities than do popular children, and, when they enter unfamiliar groups, they are not initially well-liked. Coie and Dodge (1988) also described several ways in which controversial boys engaged in divergent behaviors. They spend more time off-task, but, unlike their rejected peers, they do not have academic problems. Often they emerge as group leaders and facilitators, yet they also engage in a lot of aggression. Of all the children, they are reprimanded most often by teachers, yet spend the most time engaged in positive social behavior. Teachers tend to rate these children as more isolated than they appear to be from observational data and peer ratings. Perhaps because teachers see the effects of the aggression, they underestimate the more positive role that these children also play (Coie & Dodge, 1988). Their fellow students may also enjoy the rule breaking whereas their teachers interpret this behavior more negatively. Overall, the image that emerges is one of active, enthusiastic children who are humorous and volatile and often choose to ignore the rules or needs of others in order to pursue their own goals. Their high activity level, humor, and creativity, however, make them appealing to at least some of their peers. Interestingly, these children tend to have low self-esteem and negative self-perceptions (Boivin & Begin, 1989), which contradicts the image of the active and somewhat heedless child. One explanation may be that these children, who are in tune with their social environment, are aware of the anger they often evoke in both teachers and peers and may, in turn, judge themselves harshly.

FACTORS CONTRIBUTING TO INDIVIDUAL DIFFERENCES

The question of what makes some children more socially successful than others is obviously a major one in the minds of parents, teachers, and clinicians. Clearly, the behaviors of children that were described in the previous sections contribute a great deal to children's levels of acceptance. The question is, then, are there individual or environmental factors that predispose children to act in particular ways? Although we cannot assume causal relations, the following personal and environmental factors appear to be related to different levels of peer acceptance.

Personal Attributes

As mentioned previously, physical attractiveness is related to children's popularity (Coie, 1990; Langlois & Stephan, 1981). Physical attraction alone probably does not determine status, but adults and peers may treat attractive and unattractive children differently, which then influences the types of social expectations and behaviors that children learn. Attractive children may be accustomed to spontaneous admiration and therefore grow up seeing the social world as more responsive and friendly. Unattractive children, on the other hand, may learn to expect disinterest and approach interpersonal contacts with more wariness or distrust.

Motoric proficiency has also been associated with levels of peer participation (Hops & Finch, 1985). Withdrawn children (both boys and girls) tend to be less skilled motorically than their more socially active peers. For boys, motoric proficiency is particularly important and more related to social status than are social skills.

Children's names appear to contribute to social acceptance (Asher, Oden, & Gottman, 1977). Unpopular children are more likely to have unusual names (e.g., Herbert, Ursula). Possibly children react initially to unfamiliar names with avoidance that may, in turn, make the social world seem less attractive to the child with the unusual name. This factor may contribute to divisions among ethnic groups as children may avoid peers with unfamiliar names.

Characteristic Behaviors

Besides responding to the specific social behaviors described in the profiles of the status groups, peers also react to a child's personality and the compatibility between themselves and that individual. They may not consciously make these evaluations, but, at some level, they probably ask themselves the following questions (as delineated by Steve Asher, 1985):

- Is this child fun to be with?
- Is this child trustworthy?
- Can we influence each other in ways that I like?
- Does this child facilitate, and not undermine, my goals?
- Is this person similar to me?

Social Information Processing

Popular children are often described as "more socially aware" or "more tuned in to their peers." To explain how these differences in social awareness actually influence behavior, the following model of social information processing has been developed by Dodge et al. (1986). According to these authors, children's responses to social events can be divided into five steps. Children vary in the ways in which they respond at each point, and these responses then influence the subsequent ones. Thus, the same event may spark very divergent responses in children:

> Kim is a rejected child and Alberto is popular. They are both sitting in the reading corner, when Chai rushes in and grabs a book.

In the following description of the five social information processing steps, Kim and Alberto's reactions will be described.

1. *The child encodes the presented social cues.* Children may differ in terms of the cues that they focus on. Some may look at facial expressions, and others at less relevant cues such as clothing. Kim sees Chai taking a book. Alberto notices the arrival of a well-liked peer.
2. *The child interprets the encoded cues and gives them meaning.* Children's rules for this process may differ. For example a particular action may appear hostile to one child and friendly to another one. Kim immediately fears that Chai will either take the book she wants to read next or may demand her book. Alberto assumes that Chai is joining them in their activity.
3. *The child generates one or more potential responses to the interpreted cues.* Here the techniques that children have learned from parents and peers may make a difference in the responses children consider employing. Furthermore, what children have gleaned from steps 1 and 2 influences the choices of the responses. Kim considers holding more closely to her book, blocking Chai's access to the bookshelf, or ordering him to leave. Alberto thinks of something about his book he would like to show Chai.
4. *The child evaluates and decides which response to make.* In this step children consider their efficacy and the possible consequences of the possible actions. Aggressive children are more likely to think that aggressive

actions will be easy and effective (Perry, Perry, & Rasmussen, 1986). Moreover, aggressive boys (but not aggressive girls) do not expect any social sanctions for their aggressive actions. Thus, aggressive boys see aggressive actions as effective and low risk, so it is not surprising that they use these tactics quite readily. In this case, Kim realizes that she cannot effectively block the book shelf, but can at least hold on to her book and order Chai to leave. Alberto decides to show Chai the picture of the shark in his fish book.

5. *Finally the child enacts the the chosen response in accordance with her verbal and motor skills; a social reaction is elicited from the peer, and the whole cycle repeats itself.* Kim, clutching her book to her stomach, yells, "We were here first! Get out!" Alberto greets Chai and shows him the picture. Chai is now faced with the question of how to respond to his two peers. He goes through the same process of taking note of the information, interpreting the cues, and deciding what to do. In this case, he decides to ignore Kim, after giving her a dirty look, and joins Alberto to look at his book.

Although this whole process occurs in microseconds, early elementary students have been able to describe their reactions at each step (Dodge et al. 1986). As can be seen in the preceding example, children can focus on different kinds of information and interpret and respond to similar events in a variety of ways. These differences obviously have an effect on their social interactions and cumulative social standing in the classroom. As we will see in Chapter 6, this model of social information processing has several implications for helping rejected children learn how to respond more positively to their peers.

Family Relations and Environment

Teachers often speculate about the effects of families on particular children's social styles and development. Is Caleb shy because his parents are very quiet and reserved? Ashanda's exuberant social interactions are mystifying given how timid her mother is. Is the clinginess that Ali shows when his parents drop him off related to his reluctance to enter into peer activities? A number of recent studies have analyzed potential factors in children's families that may be linked to different social behaviors in the classroom. Obviously none of these factors can be assumed to be causative, as all the findings are based on correlational analysis. Also, when children and parents interact, the traits of the children influence the behavior of the family members as well as the reverse. For example, a difficult child may evoke harsher discipline from her parents than her more even-tempered sibling does. Thus, we cannot assume a one-way cause-and-effect relationship. However, knowing what family variables are related can give us some ideas of what questions to ask parents and how to work most effectively with parents on mutually supporting children's social development.

Parents potentially influence children's social behavior both directly and indirectly (Putallaz & Heflin, 1990). First, from watching their parents interact with others, children learn how to conduct social interactions. From this modeling, they acquire the cultural rules of interactions and the particular social styles of their parents. For example, children of mothers who use power assertive discipline techniques (threats or punishment to make a child obey) are more likely to use hostile strategies with their peers (Hart, Ladd, & Burleson, 1990).

Second, children may develop either generally positive or negative feelings about social interactions based on their interactions with their parents and siblings. If they enjoy these engagements, they are then more likely to approach other social interactions with more positive expectations. Mothers of popular children are more positive, focus on feelings, and are less demanding and disagreeable than mothers of rejected children (Putallaz, 1987). Conversely, mothers' tendencies to expect hostility in ambiguous situations and to endorse aggression as a solution to interpersonal problems are associated with their children's poor social problem-solving skills (Pettit, Dodge, & Brown, 1988).

Third, children are rewarded or punished for different social actions and, in this way, learn what behaviors are appropriate. Some parents also explicitly coach their offspring on strategies for different social situations. For example, a father might help his child devise a tactful way to decline an unwanted invitation. Finally, parents may indirectly influence children's social development by creating opportunities for children to have peer contacts. Their resources and willingness to arrange peer visits and play groups and to facilitate their children's participation in extracurricular activities affect their children's range of contacts. Parents' decisions also influence many aspects of children's social environment, from the type of neighborhood they live in to the frequency of out-of-home experiences. In all these dimensions, parents' interactions and relations with children are, in turn, affected by their immediate and larger social environments. A divorce, unemployment, or financial problems inevitably have an impact on the ways in which children and parents interact.

One important aspect of parental influence is the quality of the relation between the child and parents. In general, securely attached infants tend to be more successful in their later peer relationships (Waters, Wippman, & Sroufe, 1979), although this connection may be stronger for girls than for boys (LaFreniere & Sroufe, 1985). In the latter study, girls who were anxious-avoidant with their mothers at 12–18 months were assertive, but highly rejected by their peers in preschool. Their peers who were classified as anxious-resistant at 12–18 months were passive, withdrawn, submissive, and neglected by their preschool peers. The children who had been securely attached were characterized as warm, open, and positive in their interactions and were highly rated by both teachers and children. As one would expect, infants and toddlers who learn to trust their social environment and to enjoy interpersonal contacts become children who approach peers with positive expectations.

Another line of research has examined the relation between childrearing practices and peer acceptance. Erikson (1963) identified two dimensions of parenting that are relevant during the early childhood years: control and warmth. The control dimension is a continuum between permissive and restrictive, which describes the range between parents who make few demands on their children and allow them a great deal of latitude, and parents who impose many demands and greatly curtail children's freedom of expression. Baumrind (1967) identified three different styles of parenting that illustrate how different levels of control influence children's social adaptation. First, authoritarian parents tend to be restrictive and expect strict obedience. Their offspring, according to Baumrind, are more likely to be unhappy, fearful, passive, aggressive, and unfriendly. Second, permissive parents place few restrictions on their children who tend to be impulsive and aggressive and have low self-reliance and low self-control and a need to dominate groups. Third, authoritative parents fall between restrictive and permissive. They are flexible, but clear about important behavioral expectations. Their children tend to be energetic and friendly. The warmth dimension includes the range from highly affectionate, nurturant, and warm to hostile, cold, and rejecting. When parents are hostile, the effects of being either overly permissive or restrictive are exaggerated (Shaffer, 1988). Children of restrictive and rejecting parents are often extremely withdrawn and inhibited (Becker 1964); children of permissive and rejecting parents tend to be very hostile, and often engage in delinquent acts (Patterson & Stouthamer-Loeber, 1984).

Because most studies of parental effects were done in white middle-class populations, we need to be cautious about applying these findings to other groups. A number of studies have shown evidence of social class differences in childrearing styles and have concluded that low-income parents are deficient. Ogbu (1983) disputes this interpretation and points out that childrearing styles reflect the social skills appropriate for the future roles and expectations for children from that particular group. Authoritarian controls that might be considered too restrictive for children being prepared to work as professionals and managers might be very appropriate for children who

will grow up to work in more routine jobs that require unquestioning con-
formity. In his review, Shaffer (1988) states that warmth, sensitivity, and
responsive caregiving are the only universal positives of childrearing. As
teachers, we must be careful not to judge parents negatively because their
childrearing patterns do not match our expectations. Instead, each family
should be seen within their own social, economic, and community context.

STABILITY OF PEER STATUS

One concern teachers and parents have about children's social status is
whether and how children's status can be changed. For example, we might
hope that a shy child will become more socially active as s/he develops
more skills. Alternatively, if their daughter is not getting along with her
peers in school, parents may enroll her in some extracurricular groups in
the hope that she will find a more compatible group of peers. Some children, however, seem to recreate their position in their peer group over and
over again. In this section we will review the research on the stability of
peer status.

Status groups vary in their stability (Coie & Dodge, 1983). Rejected
children, particularly aggressive-rejected children, tend to be disliked year
after year and in a wide range of group situations. For these children, their
status may depend largely on their behavior, and, quite understandably,
most children do not like aggressive peers. Popularity is less stable than
rejection, but children who are generally well-liked in one situation are
often popular in other ones. Here again the behavior of the children may be
a major factor in their level of peer acceptance. Children who are socially
skilled and interested in others are usually well-received by peers. However,
the extent of popularity may also be influenced by the other children in the
group. A child who is very popular in one group may not be quite such a
star in a new group that contains many socially skilled children. Neither
neglected nor controversial status is as stable as rejection or popularity.
Neglected children may become more socially active as they learn social
skills or when they are in a smaller group. Because they are often interested
in particular activities, they are often more outgoing when they are with
peers who share their particular interest. Controversial children tend to
evoke quite contradictory reactions from their peers, so a change in group
composition may have an effect on their status, shifting them to either
more popular or more rejected status.

Children's behaviors are often predictive of their later status. Putallaz
(1983) found that she could predict children's status in the first grade on
the basis of their entry strategies, which she observed in a study during the

summer prior to their entrance to first grade. Children who were rated by their preschool teachers as cooperative players were described as more sociable by their kindergarten teachers a year later, and children who were more aggressive as preschoolers were more likely to be rejected in kindergarten (Ladd & Price, 1987).

Unfortunately for parents and teachers who hope that a change in group will make a difference, children often reestablish the same status that they had in their previous group. Coie and Kupersmidt (1983) found that fourth graders who were put in unfamiliar play groups reestablished the same status that they had in their classrooms by the end of the third session. The rapidity of this establishment suggests that children's behavior is consistent across situations and plays a large role in their level of peer acceptance.

Status, however, is not simply a function of children's behavior. Group dynamics often play a role, and, particularly for older children, reputation has a major impact on a child's social environment. How a child is treated and whom he gets to play with is often predetermined by peers' expectations and opinions (Rogosch & Newcomb, 1989). Furthermore, once status is established, children tend to play primarily with children of their own status group, which, in turn, influences the type of social experience children have. Ladd (1983) identified networks of popular and unpopular third and fourth graders and observed that they were characterized by different types of play. The popular girls spent more time in social conversation, whereas their unpopular counterparts spent more time arguing. Among the boys, the popular ones engaged in more cooperative organized play, but the unpopular ones were more often involved in conflicts or rough-and-tumble play. Thus, the division between the two status groups becomes more rigid as members develop their own interactive repertoires.

EFFECTS OF SOCIAL SKILLS TRAINING

The consistent connections between children's social behaviors and their level of peer acceptance have led researchers and practitioners to develop a number of social skills training programs. These interventions are designed to teach children specific social behaviors that help them have more positive peer encounters and, subsequently, gain more peer acceptance. In this section, the types of programs and their outcomes will be reviewed. Specific classroom applications will be discussed in Chapter 6.

The earliest intervention programs reflected a social learning orientation and were designed to model and reinforce specific behaviors. In one study, O'Connor (1969) demonstrated that withdrawn preschool children became more interactive after watching a film that depicted a range of social interactions among children (from a pair quietly sharing a book to a large group gleefully tossing a ball). Later, O'Connor (1972) compared the effects of modeling versus shaping behavior on the social interactions of isolated children. He found that modeling was the most effective approach; children seemed to change more after watching films of successful social interactions than they did when they were rewarded for specific social behaviors. O'Connor concluded that by watching the films, children learned how and why social skills were effective, whereas in the shaping conditions, they only changed their surface behaviors, which reverted to their former patterns as soon as the rewards were ended.

Spivak and Shure (1974) designed a more cognitively oriented program in which preschoolers were taught how to think about social problems by analyzing their causes and generating many possible solutions. The program involved daily instruction sessions (between 5 and 20 minutes long) over a period of 9–10 weeks and was divided into two parts. The initial training focused on the prerequisite cognitive and language skills (e.g., understanding and using correctly such words as "and,' "or," and "not") that underlie children's abilities to generate and evaluate a range of social strategies. In the second part, children responded to pictures depicting various social situations. They expanded their social problem-solving skills by learning to generate alternative solutions, to anticipate a range of consequences that might follow a particular action, and to see the connection between potential solutions and their consequences (e.g., "How might the boy feel if the girl hits him when she's mad?"). The evaluation of this program revealed that children's improvement in thinking and solving social problems had a positive effect on their classroom behavior. Not only did the children learn to inhibit antisocial impulses, they also began to use more adaptive and assertive social behaviors.

More recently, researchers have developed coaching techniques in which children are explicitly taught specific social behaviors. Typically, these techniques are designed for children in grades 2–6 and include instructing children about specific behaviors, discussing why they might work, giving them opportunities to practice these skills, and evaluating their performance in the practice sessions. One of the earliest of these programs (Oden & Asher, 1977) consisted of five sessions, four of which were used to teach different types of social skills: communication, cooperation, participation, and validation/support of peers. In each session, children were taught the skill and then given an opportunity to practice it in a play session with a peer and to review their performance with the instructor. The final session was used for review. Subsequent programs elaborated this coaching model in several ways. One model included efforts to individualize instructions so that they focused on specific skills that individuals lacked

(Hymel & Asher, 1977, cited in Ladd & Asher, 1985). In another study, researchers compared the effectiveness of coaching and modeling and found that coaching resulted in a decrease in negative social behaviors and that modeling (with films) led to an increase in positive social behaviors (Gresham & Nagel, 1980). La Greca and Santogrossi (1980) worked with groups of children who watched films of the targeted behaviors, received coaching, practiced their new skills with each other, and reviewed videotapes of these sessions to critique their performances and to generate new strategies. They were also given homework assignments in which they used their new skills with peers not in their training group. Another method included two extra sessions at the end of the training that were devoted to fostering the maintenance and generalization of the newly acquired skills (Ladd, 1981).

Ladd and Mize (1983) expanded the cognitive aspects of the coaching model. Instructors using this model begin by discussing the concept of the social skill being learned (e.g., turn taking). Children clarify what a particular skill is and is not by generating relevant examples. Then they receive feedback from the social skill instructor about how well their own concepts correspond to those taught in the session. In the second part of the training, children translate the concepts into behaviors by practicing the skill under instructor supervision. The child continues to practice in a variety of contexts with a decreasing amount of supervision in order to generalize the skill and become more independent in using it. In the final phases of instruction, children learn to evaluate their skills realistically and to assess whether or not they are gaining the desired responses from others (e.g., smiles, nods of agreement) and to adjust their actions accordingly. More recently, Mize and Ladd (1990) adapted this technique for use with preschool children. They used puppets to enact dramatic vignettes that illustrated various social problems (e.g., a child taking a toy) and possible solutions to those problems (e.g., finding ways of sharing the disputed toy).

The results of most of these coaching studies show that participating children usually modify their social behavior and become more well-liked among their peers. They are not necessarily chosen as best friends in the sociometric ratings, but they are less likely to be either completely ignored or rejected by their peers. These findings suggest that children's behaviors are malleable and that children can learn new ways of interacting with their peers, and, in turn, become more accepted by their peers.

Most of the recent social skills training programs have used some variation on the coaching model. However, other approaches have also been developed during the last decade. One intervention takes a social cognitive approach and emphasizes children's ability to see another person's perspectives (Urbain and Kendall, 1980). This approach is aimed at stimulating more positive social behavior by increasing children's understanding of the perspectives of others. Another intervention emphasizes learning to control anger (Lochman, 1985). Used with aggressive-rejected children, these techniques include teaching children how to stay calm in the face of frustration and provocation and how to recognize and control aggressive impulses. Because rejection is often associated with poor academic and physical skills, Hops and Finch (1985) have advocated concentrating on coaching or tutoring and training children in areas such as motoric proficiency. Coie (1985) conducted a study in which low-achieving rejected children received academic tutoring as well as social skills training. The ones who had the tutoring showed more long-term social status change than those who had only the social skills training. Comprehensive social skills training can also include teaching children how to recognize and express emotions, training them in relaxation techniques, and helping them identify and change self-defeating belief systems and self-statements (Cartledge, 1986b). For a comprehensive review of a number of methods and more explicit information on how they are implemented, readers may want to consult Cartledge's 1986 book, *Teaching Social Skills to Children.*

Many of the social skills training models can be adapted to classroom uses. This range of options is helpful because rejected children present a number of different behavioral and psychological profiles, and the method that might work for one child may not be appropriate for another. When teachers, parents and mental health professionals consider possible interventions, they need to identify the relevant factors for each child and to decide on both the content and approach of the model that seems most appropriate for that child's needs and strengths.

Social skills training can be implemented by parents, teachers, or mental health professionals (Ladd & Asher, 1985). Parents have the advantage of providing long-term involvement and advice. In a number of studies, they have been successful in either doing the actual training or supporting sessions that occur outside the home (Budd, 1985). Parents, however, are at some disadvantage as social skills trainers because children often balk at accepting this kind of help from their parents. Parents also might find it difficult to create situations in which their children could practice new skills with peers. Furthermore, children who are having social problems often have poor or problematic relations with their families; their parents may not recognize the problem or may actively resist their children's changes. Although parents may not be the ideal trainers, their involvement in the planning and implementation of any intervention is critical to its success. Without the support of the parents, most intervention programs will fail to have a long-term effect. Moreover, parents' involvement in the intervention may help them change negative cycles at home.

Teachers are often in an excellent position to provide social skills training. They see children for long periods of time and in situations where they can observe and support peer interactions. However, a teacher's impact is often diluted because he has to divide his attention among a number of children and cannot concentrate enough on one child to provide comprehensive social skills training. Ideally, children receive the more formal training from the school counselor or another mental health professional, and teachers support these efforts by reinforcing children for practicing their new skills and by arranging the classroom to maximize social opportunities and support.

Many mental health professionals occupy the appropriate role and have the expertise to conduct this kind of training. Most of the social skills models described in this section require someone outside of the classroom to implement the actual training. When a school counselor or social worker is available, she is the optimal person to provide the training to the children and to give follow up support and suggestions to parents and teachers. However, many schools do not have counselors, or, if they are available, they are too busy to provide the long-term training and support that many children need. In the real world, teachers are most likely to do the interventions; adaptations for classrooms will be discussed in Chapter 6.

5

Fostering Peer Relationships: Teaching Practices and Classroom Structures

Teaching always requires a balance between group and individual needs and a dual awareness of children's actual behavior and the context in which it is occurring. Often when a child is having a social problem, teachers and parents focus on the child's behavior without analyzing ways in which the environment may be contributing to the problem. Alternatively, sometimes we become engrossed in making changes in the classroom or curriculum and fail to recognize ways in which individual children are being affected. In short, when we consider ways of fostering the social development of individuals or creating a more positive social climate in the classroom, we need to think in terms of both the individuals and the environment of the classroom, school, and community. In the following chapters, this dual perspective underlies the guidelines and suggestions that are offered for providing optimal social experiences for children.

This chapter and the next two are organized around three complementary approaches to promoting positive peer relationships. First, in this chapter we focus on the general teaching practices and the overall organizational structure of the classroom that contribute to a positive social environment. Chapter 6 is a discussion about social intervention, the analysis of problems that involve specific individuals or social dynamics and the design and implementation of remedial strategies and interventions. Finally, Chapter 7 is a review of curriculum activities and materials that support the development of social skills and peer relationships.

AWARENESS OF CLASSROOM DYNAMICS AND INDIVIDUAL NEEDS

To support individual development and positive classroom dynamics, we as teachers need to be aware of current and potential individual and group needs and have a fairly accurate sense about how specific dynamics are evolving. For example, to plan an effective intervention, we need to know whether the isolation of a particular child is a function of poor social skills or a mismatch between the child and the social environment that prevents him from using the skills he has. With a clear understanding of the nature of the problem, we can set more precise and feasible goals and plan specific interventions that are easier to implement and evaluate.

Several methods of assessing classroom dynamics and individual needs have already been described in Chapters 3 and 4, respectively. In this section I will provide an overview of the observation procedures and ways they can be adapted for classroom use. For a more detailed description of specific methods, readers may want to consult Cartledge's chapter "Assessment and Evaluation of Social Skills" (1986a). The suggestions in this chapter are examples, not prescriptions; teachers can adapt these methods to suit their particular issues and classroom resources.

The most common and available tool for teachers is observation, which can be performed in a variety of ways, from simply counting the frequency of particular behaviors to taking detailed notes or using video or audio recordings. Teachers may find that some methods suit their styles more than others. For example, in our laboratory school one teacher uses maps of the classroom to make quick records of contact patterns, dominance events, and patterns of positive and negative social behavior. Another teacher prefers to carry a small notebook and jot down anecdotal records. A third teacher uses a list of the children's names and, at the end of the day, jots down each child's activities and the types of interactions she had observed. All three teachers have similar philosophies and classrooms, but differ in the medium that they find to be most convenient and informative.

Observations of Classroom Dynamics

Monitoring classroom dynamics requires a lot of attention to subtle detail, an option not available to most teachers who are busy organizing and overseeing 20–30 children and numerous activities. Administrators and teachers should try to enlist the help of teacher aids, students from local colleges, and parent volunteers, either to relieve teachers who then can observe or to help record information. When available, electronic record-keeping devices can facilitate this process. For example, programming the classroom computer so that children have to sign on will provide a record of the children who have worked together on the computer. Keeping records on the computer also will help. Spending 15 minutes a day or every two or three days entering observations and updating records of children's interactions will create a usable record and eliminate scraps of paper and scribbled notes that are quickly lost or rendered meaningless. If a camera is available, videotaping is another valuable data source. Even a few minutes of tape will often capture some of the subtle nuances of children's social interactions that may not be obvious at a cursory glance. Also, because young children quickly get used to videocameras, they often display the behaviors that they try to hide from teachers.

The following suggestions are organized according to the major concepts discussed in Chapter 3. However, each question does not require separate observations because a single observation can yield information relevant to many aspects of the classroom social scene.

1. *Children's Social Concerns*. Keeping in mind the types of social concerns that children of this particular age might be experiencing, teachers can keep anecdotal records of new themes in children's fantasies or conversations. They can also record events that highlight children's views regarding their peer relationships (e.g., concerns about friendships, lack of companions, efforts to initiate, competition over school work). As mentioned in Chapter 4, interviewing children informally about friends and who plays with whom also provides insights into how children are experiencing their social environment.

2. *Individual and Intergroup Contact Patterns*. Using maps of the classroom, preschool teachers can quickly write down the location of each child and indicate which peers are actually interacting. In elementary schools, teachers can note the groupings at recess or at lunch. By doing this once a day or every other day, teachers can begin to see what specific groups are forming or dissolving and which children are more isolated. These records also provide information on the kinds of group segregation that may be occurring. Are the groups homogeneous in terms of sex? race? social class? ethnic background? ability groups? With whom do the special-needs children play? If a pattern of segregation emerges, then teachers might want to watch more closely to see why that might be occurring. By keeping these records, teachers also get a sense of how groups are changing over time. As mentioned in Chapter 4, teachers can also observe children's play with "classroom friends" dolls (made using photographs of the children in the class) to see children's perceptions about who plays with whom.

3. *Dominance Hierarchies*. When observing and/or helping children settle disputes, teachers can note which children appear to be more consistently dominant and which ones usually end up in submissive roles. By keeping a record of these outcomes, teachers can begin to see if there is a clear dominance hierarchy in their particular group of children. Anecdotal records might also be used to record the types of persuasion strategies children are using and whether they reflect agonistic dominance or positive leadership.

4. *Peer Culture*. With anecdotal records teachers can monitor the themes of children's play and conversations. When the same routine, joke, entry gambit, etc., is heard or observed several times, then it has become part of the group culture. On a few occasions when children break rules, teachers might want to watch instead of immediately intervening to get a sense of how and why the children are violating particular strictures. What systems have they developed for communicating amongst themselves, for evading adult detection, for subtly transforming transgressions into acceptable activities? These actions can be viewed not simply as misbehaviors, but rather as clues to how children are developing their identity and gaining independence from adults.

5. *Classroom Environments*. On the maps (mentioned previously) teachers can record the type of play that is occurring in the different areas so that they can get an idea of how the different physical settings of the classroom influence the children's levels of interactions.

If an aide or volunteer is available, that person might be able to record children's reactions to various routines. How many interactions are interrupted? What happens when the schedule is changed? If free play is extended by 10 minutes does the quality of play become more complex or does it begin to deteriorate? If a group project period is scheduled right before recess, do children extend their interactions to the playground or do they spend their group time discussing plans for recess?

Observe the children's reactions to adults in the classroom. Is there less interactive play and work when adults are present? What occurs after you have intervened in a social situation? Are children able to build on your suggestions or do they simply leave the area or resume the dispute?

Observations Related to Specific Problems

Often we are concerned about a particular classroom dynamic or an individual child. To understand what factors are contributing to the problem, we need to design specific observational strategies to acquire the appropriate information. Forms such as those presented in Appendix 2 may be of use in recording one's observations. For example, let us suppose that the teachers in a preschool classroom have noticed an increasing amount of aggression during the last few weeks. They want to know whether or not their impressions are correct and, if so, which children or environmental factors are contributing to this trend. First, they might assess how frequently children are engaging in aggression and where it is occurring. To get this information, they can keep track of aggressive events and where and when they occur by recording each event on a Times and Locations form as shown in Appendix 2. Simple counting mechanisms such as moving small objects from one pocket to another, putting tallies on a map of the classroom, or recording with a wrist golf counter can aid in this process.

Once the teachers have established the frequency and location of aggressive events, they may notice that particular children always seem to be involved. To understand why and how these children keep getting drawn in, they might observe them more closely and note potential factors such as timing, issues, and companions to see what is likely to trigger an aggressive event. These observations can be recorded very efficiently by using the Individual Record form. To capture some of the subtle dynamics of these events, teachers may also want to write actual descriptions of aggressive episodes. These observations can be recorded on an Anecdotal Record form. Teachers may notice that some children seem to be able to end aggressive events quickly while others seem to get into protracted struggles. To understand these differences, they might want to know more about how long conflicts last. Teachers can use stopwatches to time these episodes and record the information on a Duration form as shown in Appendix 2.

These forms and checklists organize information so that teachers can compare behavior across children (e.g., an aggressive and a nonaggressive child), in different physical environments (e.g., does aggression occur more in the science area or the block corner? when there are many materials or just a few?) and at different times of the day (e.g., is aggression most common in the morning or afternoon? right before lunch? at departure time?). These comparisons, in turn, can provide clues as to why a certain pattern is occurring. With this information, teachers can consider changes in the physical environment (e.g., better supplies of a particular material if scarcity seems to be a factor) or the scheduling (e.g., moving lunch up by 15 minutes if timing appears to be an issue. Alternatively, teachers may decide to separate two particular children if they tend to initiate most of the aggression when they are together.

Sometimes the focus of concern is a behavior that rarely occurs. In this case, teachers can set up contrived situations that will evoke the target behavior. For example, if a teacher is concerned about why a particular child always seems to control the materials at a particular activity, the teacher might present a new and attractive toy to the class and observe how the child in question operates and how the other children respond. To observe a child's entering skills, a teacher could direct the youngster to join a particular group (e.g., "Take your book over to that library table and sit there with...") and see what happens. Teachers can also learn a lot by using role play in various forms. A first-grade teacher knew that some children were dominating the use of the jungle gym and not letting others have any access to it. The dominance was well established, and the teacher could not observe how the nondominant children were rebuffed because they rarely, if ever, tried to play on the jungle gym. She used some pipe cleaners to make a jungle gym and enacted with some puppets what she thought was happening. As she played out the scene, several children spontaneously talked about how they were not allowed on the jungle gym. The enactment brought the issue out into the open, which enabled the teacher and children to explore the reasons why it was happening and what children might do about it. The dominating children also saw and heard how their actions looked from the outside and how they affected their classmates.

Interviewing Children, Parents, and Colleagues

Interviewing children can also provide some insights into the nature of a problem. As discussed in Chapter 4, peers can rate each other and, under some circumstances, provide insightful behavioral descriptions of fellow classmates. If there is a problem in the classroom, the children often have good insights into what is happening, why it is happening, who is involved, and possible solutions. In one second-grade classroom, the teacher was concerned about the extreme territoriality that the children displayed on the playground. The yard was divided among different groups and outsiders were not "allowed" to enter certain areas. Not only did children spend most of their time preoccupied with excluding peers, but they also did not have access to a range of equipment and activities. When the teacher asked some individuals about why they felt so strongly about their turf, she learned that one group of boys were threatening to attack anyone who came into their area and so in defense, the other children had established their own territories. Armed with this information, the teacher was able to work with the boys to alleviate their defensiveness and to set up activities that would entice children to go into all areas of the playground.

Teachers can also talk to other teachers. In the foregoing example, these boys had a history of staking out their territory so their previous teacher was able to provide some useful insights into the nature of the problem. Parents are another good source of information, as they often hear their child's version of what is going on in the classroom. They can also let teachers know whether the same dynamic is being played out at home or in the neighborhood.

ROUTINES AND SCHEDULES

The organization of the day and the routines that mark the transition from one type of activity to another affect the social dynamics of the classroom in numerous ways. First, the allocation of time for different kinds of activities reflects and conveys teachers' social priorities. If the greater part of the day is devoted to individual seat work, then clearly peer interaction is a low priority. In classrooms in which children spend a lot of time in teacher-directed group activities, peer contact, but not peer interaction, is valued. Emphasis on small group activities, on the other hand, reflects a priority for peer collaboration and autonomy from direct adult control. Second, the rigidity of the structure has an impact on social interactions. In classrooms where transitions occur according to a fixed schedule, the socializing of children will be more regimented. If teachers, on the other hand, build in some flexibility so that they can lengthen or shorten the time spent in a particular activity, they will be able to accommodate the varying social rhythms of the classroom. Third, all classrooms have a number of routines and rituals that mark the beginning and end of the day and the introduction and conclusion of specific activities. The organization and substance of these routines also influence the types of social interactions that are likely to result. For example, if boys and girls are always told to line up separately, as is the case in many schools (Thorne, 1986), then the tendency for children to segregate themselves by gender is reinforced. Fourth, routines also vary in terms of the type of social behavior they reinforce. If the opening group time is devoted to the teacher telling the children what they are to do, then children are learning to depend on the teacher for direction. However, a morning ritual in which children and teachers share news and ideas conveys the message that everyone has a voice in the classroom.

To increase the children's opportunities for having positive social interactions and to develop these contacts to their best advantage, the following guidelines are suggested.

GUIDELINES FOR ROUTINES AND SCHEDULES

1. Allow times for a variety of social interactions: small groups, partners, all-class discussions and activities, and independent projects.
2. Provide enough time for these activities so that children can develop their interactions and shared ideas.
3. Organize the schedule with enough flexibility so that positive group interactions can be prolonged and negative ones shortened.
4. Develop routines that highlight individual children's skills and interests and bring children into contact with a wide variety of peers.
5. Give children a considerable amount of responsibility for conducting routines and taking care of the classroom. Many classroom tasks can be done cooperatively and in ways that help children develop a sense of social responsibility.

Because preschool and elementary classrooms have different constraints and possibilities in terms of schedules and routines, guidelines that are specific to these different settings will be discussed below.

Preschool Classrooms

In preschools, schedules are often quite flexible and fluid, and teachers have considerable control over how they plan their day. In full-day programs, staff rotations, meals, and naps sometimes pose constraints, but still leave large blocks of time that can be used for a range of activities, as described in the first guideline. The greater challenge is to keep adapting the classroom schedule to the changing needs and capabilities of the children. Because children are developing so rapidly at this age, teachers must be sensitive to group and individual nuances that signal a need for change. One teacher of 3-year-olds describes how initially, her children cannot sustain long interactions; after about half an hour, they begin to wander aimlessly and seek out the teacher. During the year, they gain more experience and begin to develop relations, and their play becomes more elaborate and sustained. Accordingly, the teacher gradually increases the free-play time, but carefully scrutinizes the reactions to each change in schedule. Because children at this age are easily excited and often lose control, the shift between productive interactions and mayhem can occur in a split second. Teachers, somewhat like orchestra conductors, have to have a feel for the optimal moment when to shift to another activity, begin to clean-up, or end circle time.

The routines at preschools provide a predictable regularity and a concrete signal that the focus or activity is changing. Circle time may invariably come between clean-up and snack; a particular song or other auditory or visual cue may signal the beginning of clean-up or the end of circle. Children find this regularity a reassuring way to keep track of the day and predict what will happen next. Many preschool routines potentially involve social awareness or interactions. Greeting songs often have verses in which particular children are "featured"; dismissing children at the end of circle can be done in ways to draw attention to their attributes or accomplishments; getting dressed to go outside can involve a great deal of peer assistance (especially in the wintertime in cold climates). Because preschool children are only beginning to be aware of others, drawing their attention to classmates helps increase interest in their peers, particularly at the beginning of the year or when a new child is entering the class. Emphasizing children's names and attributes and encouraging children to be interested in each other and look after each other can be woven into almost any routine. Hap Palmer's song "What's My Name?" is one of many songs that help children learn each others' names. When children are choosing activities, teachers can talk about who else is going to that particular area and even suggest ways in which they might make contact. "Ellen is going with you to the porch. She likes to play 'ocean' with the boat and blocks and so do you."

As children end their day, teachers often have a time when children talk about what they did. These occasions can also be used to draw children's attention to their classmates' interests and individual accomplishments.

Elementary Classrooms

In elementary schools teachers usually have less control over their schedules. Not only are days regulated by the timing of lunch and recess, but they are often interrupted with special activities such as gym, art, music, library, and computer time. Many teachers also have to follow guidelines that prescribe the amount of time they spend each week on certain curriculum areas. Thus, in their efforts to provide an environment conducive to positive social growth and peer interactions, elementary school teachers have to work with more constraints. They can, however, work with the administration to get a schedule that is most compatible with their goals. One second-grade teacher asked the principal to put all her specials on Tuesday and Thursday so that she could have more unbroken time on the other three days. She planned her group work for Monday, Wednesday, and Friday and used the other two days for individual work and conferencing with students.

To maximize children's social growth, teachers can use their existing curriculum to vary the children's social involvement. For example, if on a particular day the reading activity involves independent seat work, then the math activity should be done in partners or groups. The content of the curriculum remains the same, but the process by which it is taught is adapted to meet a variety of social needs. Specific suggestions for these adaptations will be discussed later in this chapter.

The fragmentation of the day can often disrupt efforts to involve the children in group activities. Elementary school teachers sometimes complain that they will "just get something started" when it is time to send the children to gym, music, or a special assembly. To avoid interruptions as much as possible, group and partner work should be scheduled for the times of the day when there are the largest blocks of uninterrupted time. This caution is particularly germane when groups are just starting. Children working in groups or with partners need time to develop their rapport and their ideas. Teachers also might consider staggering the beginning of these groups so they are not trying to get everyone started on the same day. One advantage that elementary school teachers have over their preschool colleagues is that the children can work quite independently. Thus, at one time, some children might be working on their own in individual projects and others might be working in groups that are well established, while the teacher is helping a new group get started.

Routines in elementary schools often involve moving from one room to another and frequently require that children walk sedately and quietly. The age-old battle over talking in the hall is familiar to every elementary school teacher and child. Teachers can shift the focus from trying to suppress children's desire to interact to channeling it in a more positive way. For example, children on the way to the gym can form pairs and be given a math problem to solve before getting to the gym. Alternatively, partners might be challenged to count the number of right hand turns or to identify a "secret" object based on a few clues. One teacher has her children develop walking patterns (e.g., one long step, two short ones) as part of their math curriculum. When using these activities, teachers should organize them so that the partnerships keep changing and children do not get involved in cross-pair competition. The pushing and shoving that often accompanies lining up to go to lunch or recess may be reduced if children are challenged to line up in different ways such as by the month of their birth or by the second letter of their middle name, without speaking. Instead of focusing only on being the first out of the door, children are exchanging information about themselves and learning to "read" nonverbal cues more accurately.

Other routines such as show-and-tell or sharing often become dry and listless. By changing the nature of social interactions during these routines, teachers can often enliven them. For example, "sharing" is usually done with one child talking and others listening, often restlessly. The format might be changed by having children interview each other about what they want to share. Teachers might have children talk in small groups and have each group come up with a story or event they want to talk about. Ongoing cooperative groups may be challenged to come up with an interesting item from their current project to share with the whole class. As with their preschool peers, elementary children need times to learn each others' names and become aware of their classmates' interests. The suggestions in the previous section can be adapted for these older children.

PHYSICAL ENVIRONMENTS

Ms. L. was discouraged about the lackluster quality of the discussions her third-grade class was having. Their written work indicated that the children had strong opinions and good ideas, but when she tried to generate group discussions, the participation was sporadic and the children seemed shy and reluctant to talk. She asked some of her students why they did not share their ideas in class and learned that one worry was that people in the back rows, who were not visible to the speaker, might be making fun of their comments. When she next attempted a discussion, Ms. L. had the children arrange their chairs in a circle and witnessed a dramatic change as children more freely talked and often argued with or supported each others' comments.

This very simple change in physical structure is a common technique of educators who are trying to generate more interpersonal contact and group discussion. Participants in a conversation rely heavily on eye contact and nonverbal cues to know when to talk and when to pause, when listeners understand and when they are confused. People at all ages, but especially children who are just becoming aware that they are the object of others' thoughts and opinions, find it difficult to talk to people they cannot see. Children who are sitting in rows or around separate tables do not feel this sense of connectedness with others and are therefore more wary about contributing their ideas. Also these arrangements allow children to conduct side conversations either verbally or nonverbally, which keep them from focusing on the group, and create a more risky environment for classmates who are addressing the group. Often very simple physical changes can dramatically affect the quality and quantity of social interactions.

A great deal of research has been done on the effects of physical space, and several books and articles have been written that deal exclusively with these questions. Readers who wish to get more detailed guidance in this area are encouraged to consult the resources mentioned in this chapter. In this section a few guidelines specifically related to children's peer interactions will be presented and are followed by examples of how they might be implemented in preschool and elementary school classrooms. Because classrooms come in all sizes and shapes, from barnlike church basements and large open-space classrooms to small rooms in old houses, the adaptations of these ideas will vary greatly according to the range of resources and needs. The starting point should be the following questions: "What do I want to have happen in this space? What functions do we want the space to fulfill?" By thinking about goals rather than the existing constraints, teachers often invent creative ways of using their space.

Guidelines for Physical Environments

1. The physical environment should provide a variety of spaces in order to support a range of social interactions and types of play and work. Children should have comfortable areas to work alone, in pairs, and in groups. Space should allow for a range of play, from sedentary to highly active.
2. These areas should have visible boundaries and be arranged to reduce the chances for conflict and to convey clear behavioral expectations.

3. The space should be adequate, but not too large. If the space is too big, children do not have enough contact; when areas are too crowded, children tend to get more aggressive.
4. The noise level should be moderate so that both children and teachers can be responsive to each others' social cues.
5. The physical environment should be aesthetically pleasing and convey a sense of order.
6. All children and teachers in the classroom should view the care of the classroom environment as their shared responsibility.

Preschool Classrooms

Preschool classrooms usually have a number of distinct areas that are used for different types of activities (e.g., role play area, block corner, art area). These spaces and their activities usually encourage different types of social interactions and play as discussed in Chapter 3. However, sometimes the social behavior and the type of activity are in conflict. For example, an art area that is in a wide open space may create a conflict between children trying to focus on their projects and their peers who are using the open area to play monster games. The quiet corner that is designed for more intimate and quiet conversations, but which is next to a noisy block area, may lead to conflict between two groups of children. Often, a particular area is too big or too small. In one classroom, the teachers constructed a large gross motor area with a slide and climbing structures. The area was attractive to the children, but was too large, and children's play often got out of control and then impinged on the quieter play in the rest of the classroom. When the teachers moved the barriers and reoriented the gross motor structures to provide a more contained space, the children were able to control their play. For ideas on types of changes and the process of deciding on them, readers may want to look at Susanne Wichert's book *Keeping the Peace*.

As children develop over the year, the size and structures of different areas might need to change. The small housekeeping corner that worked well in the fall for quiet enactments such as putting babies to sleep may be too confining for the more rambunctious and complicated family scenarios enacted in the spring. Teachers can create new spaces as they feel children's social needs evolve. One teacher felt that her children needed more opportunities to "get away" from the busy classroom and be with friends in some more private ways. She created a "hidey-hole" with a sheet thrown over a table. This more intimate space was very popular for several weeks. The change in seasons also influences the pressures on the physical environment. In cold and wet weather, when children are mostly indoors, teachers often need to expand the opportunities for noisier and more active play. At one school, teachers often put gym mats in the large hallways outside of the classrooms so that children could engage in more active play without disrupting the quieter activities in the classroom.

In preschools, 30–50 square feet per child appears to be optimal for maintaining a high level of involvement (Ramsey & Reid, 1987). If the classroom is too large, then teachers can block off some of the space with shelves or curtains in order to create a more intimate atmosphere. If it is too small, lofts, covered porches, and creative uses of the outside area may alleviate the effects of crowding. Because size is an absolute, it can often become an excuse for not making other physical modifications. "If only we had more space..." sometimes becomes a refrain when teachers are trying to organize their classroom. Size does pose some limitations, but it should not be seen as defining the program or limiting creative solutions.

High noise levels are often a problem in preschools because young children tend to go about their business noisily (e.g., crashing block buildings). Area rugs and curtains can absorb some sounds, and low barriers can contain the overflow of noise from one area to another. Arranging areas so that loud activities are not next to quiet ones can mitigate the effects of loud sounds. When noise is a problem, teachers can keep track of the activities and areas that are the loudest and try to modify them. For example, if the block corner is the site of crashes and other loud events, then a rug and even some carpeting on the shelves and walls may help reduce the impact of the noise in that area. In one classroom, the housekeeping corner had a stove and sink on the classroom edge of the area so that children standing at the stove often called out to children in the classroom and could be heard all over the classroom. The teacher experimented with a number of different arrangements and found that, by having the stove and sink face the windows, the children still played with them, but their voices added less to the overall classroom din. Moreover, the children were less distracted by external classroom events and seemed to concentrate on their current playmates more. Most preschool equipment is moveable and flexible and allows for considerable experimentation and creative problem solving.

Having an aesthetically pleasing and orderly classroom and involving children in caring for it go hand-in-hand. Children feel more comfortable and are able to interact with materials and each other more effectively if there is a sense of order, and if they can see each other and find materials to support their play. They are also likely to feel more satisfaction if their clean-up efforts result in a pleasant classroom than if they have simply removed the most immediate mess. Keeping clutter at a minimum and taking care to remove materials and pictures that have been around for a long time and have long since become "invisible" to the teachers and children is one way of maintaining a sense of order. Adequate storage and accessible space for materials is essential and should be considered in any physical renovations. One way of reducing the clutter without making the task overwhelming is to have one day a week in which children and teachers do a thorough clean up of one area, including removing materials that are not being used, wiping down shelves, and setting out new things. This activity not only helps teachers and children become more aware of what is available, but is also a meaningful way to involve children in caring for the physical environment.

Elementary Classrooms

Elementary classrooms pose some different challenges in their physical design. Although a number of "open space" classrooms were constructed in the 1970s, most of them have been either formally or haphazardly redesigned as self-contained classrooms. Most elementary classrooms are quite filled with either tables and chairs or desks, with little space left for less sedentary or small group activities. These limitations make it harder for teachers to respond to the constantly evolving social needs of their children. I have been impressed, however, by the creative ways that teachers have used even the most limited space and equipment to provide a wider range of social environment. Corners of rooms, areas behind large pieces of furniture, and even closets have been pressed into service as learning centers, conversation corners, role play areas, and group meeting sites. In some schools children can go to the school library to have group discussions and work on collaborative projects. Obviously, issues such as clear boundaries between areas and carefully planned arrangements are somewhat moot if space is extremely tight. Fortunately, these older children are usually engaged in more sedentary activities and are less distractible than their younger peers, so these issues are less critical at this age. Another advantage of the elementary students is that they can assume more responsibility for creating appropriate spaces. They can move chairs and tables and make impromptu barriers with notebooks in order to gain the space and privacy they need. In one classroom, I watched two second graders lying under a table as they worked on their math problems together. Children often enjoy rearranging the classroom as interests and topics change and require different kinds of spaces. At this age they are often quite creative at solving space problems in collaboration with the teacher. When doing this kind of planning teachers and children should start by brainstorming and fantasizing about possibilities in order to get beyond the constraints of the space as it currently exists. For new ideas and some inspiration, readers may want to consult *School Zone, Learning Environments for Children*, by Taylor and Vlastos (1975), and "Designing Play Environments for Elementary-Age Children" by Bergen and Oden (1988).

Noise level is not usually as much of a problem in elementary class-rooms, especially in self-contained classrooms. Because of the children's age and the nature of most activities, the noise levels are considerably lower than those in most preschools. Also, many elementary classrooms have wall-to-wall carpeting which helps reduce the noise. However, if a number of different groups are working at the same time, teachers may need to con-sider ways to help groups not disturb each other. For example, half-screens made out of three pieces of large cardboard can be used to provide both a visual and auditory screen between groups. A quiet corner can be desig-nated for children who need to concentrate on individual work. Small groups can meet out in the hall.

In terms of the aesthetics and care of the classroom, elementary school students can often participate in organizing and decorating the classroom so that they can influence how it looks and functions and feel a sense of responsibility for its care. This joint responsibility also enhances the sense of group identity. Although their choices of posters and bulletin board displays may not always agree with the teacher's taste, the students' involvement gives them a sense of ownership and insures that the classroom reflects their lives and values. Teachers obviously need to exercise a considerable amount of discretionary control, but can see children as partners in this process. Children often have creative solutions for displaying and storing materials and organizing the physical environment. These activities also provide occa-sions for children to work cooperatively and engage in collaborative problem solving and decision making. Decorating bulletin boards or the wall outside of the classroom can be the culminating event of a group project.

MATERIALS

The type, content, quantity, and availability of materials influence the quality of children's social interactions and attitudes in a number of ways. First, they affect children's autonomy to access and use materials. When materials are hard to reach or difficult to use without adult guidance, chil-dren are more dependent on the teachers' assistance. Second, design of materials can inhibit or encourage different types of peer interactions. If materials can be used by only one person, they may stimulate more solitary play; if they are also scarce, more antagonism may occur. More open-ended materials such as blocks encourage children's collaborations and shared ideas. Third, the level of challenge can either frustrate or encourage chil-dren in their efforts to interact and to learn. Materials that are develop-mentally appropriate and flexible can provide success experiences and enable children of different ability levels to play together. Fourth, the social and cultural content of materials influence children's awareness and appreciation for people from diverse backgrounds and can foster an appreciation of their own background. Almost all books, games, props, and pictures convey social values and an image of life, often at a very subtle level. Cumulatively, they create an environment that is more supportive of some lifestyles and attitudes than of others. For example, if the pictures illustrating the steps in a science experiment show the boys in active roles and girls in passive ones, children's gender stereotypes and self-expectations are being reinforced. Math problems that depict trips to middle-class grocery and toy stores often convey the underlying assumption that everyone has enough money to buy what they want. This limitation may alienate some children and reinforce the limited perspectives of others. One alternative is to have children make up math problems for each other. The process of inventing problems helps children understand math concepts and allows them to apply mathematics to issues that are relevant to them. A more detailed discussion of this issue and ways of counteracting pervasive stereotypes in many school materials can be found in an earlier book of mine, *Teaching and Learning in a Diverse World: Multicultural Education for Young Children*, published by Teachers College Press in 1987, and in Louise Derman-Sparks' book, *Anti-Bias Curriculum: Tools for Empowering Young Children*.

Classroom materials usually are analyzed in terms of the type of play they inspire or the specific concepts that they teach (e.g., Bergen, 1988; Day, 1983). These aspects are extremely important and should not be overlooked. In keeping with the main themes of this book, however, the following guidelines and discussions focus primarily on the effects of materials on social interactions. Because the kinds of available materials often differ across preschools and elementary schools, these two environments will be discussed separately. However, many materials can be successfully used in both settings.

GUIDELINES FOR SELECTING MATERIALS

1. Materials should be selected to support a wide range of social and independent play.
2. They should be developmentally appropriate and flexible so that they do not require constant teacher direction and can be used by children at different ability levels.
3. The selection of materials should include many open-ended ones that enable children to invent their own games and collaborative projects.
4. Materials should be easily accessible to encourage the children to use them autonomously and with peers rather than relying on adult direction.
5. Cumulatively, the materials in the classroom should reflect a wide variety of racial, cultural, and class backgrounds, and abilities. They should convey respect for all people, and reflect a sensitivity to the particular social and economic history and circumstances of children in the classroom.

Preschool Classrooms

Preschool materials usually support a wide range of social activities, as discussed in the section on physical areas of the classroom. Sometimes, however, children get into ruts in which they play with the same materials and children over and over again. If a teacher feels that this play is no longer productive, changing the materials can broaden children's social contacts and play styles by inducing them to try new kinds of activities. Simply moving materials to a new location can also stimulate new contacts and play. In one classroom the bristle blocks in the block corner had been continuously used by three boys to make media-based aggressive toys. When they were moved to the housekeeping area, however, the bristle blocks became cleaning brushes, medicines, and CB radios. The children who had been involved in the media play were initially very unhappy about this change, but then moved on to several different kinds of activities and a more varied group of playmates.

One important starting point is to be sure that enough materials are available. If they are scarce, children are more likely to fight over them, and children's interactions may be disrupted if they are constantly having to defend the materials they have. At the same time, an overabundance can make children feel overwhelmed and may entice children to spend all their time trying out new things rather than becoming involved in more elaborate play with a particular material and playmate(s). One framework that is often used to analyze the availability of materials in preschool classrooms is Kritchevsky, Prescott, and Walling's (1977) analysis of available play spaces. They make the following distinctions among play equipment and materials. Simple materials usually can be used by only one player at a time (e.g., a puzzle, a trike). Complex areas usually can accommodate four children (e.g., housekeeping area, sandbox with toys). Super areas can absorb up to eight children and provide for a wide range of the types of play (e.g., large climber with multiple entries and levels, a well-equipped block corner that is connected to the role-play area). By using this system, teachers can analyze the number of play spaces available for children. In general, 2.5 play spaces per child is optimal in terms of children's quality of play and their social involvement (Kritchevsky et al., 1977). As teachers analyze the number and type of play spaces, they can also assess the available materials for the kinds of social interactions that they can facilitate in order to insure a wide range of social experiences and opportunities for children.

Teachers can watch children's interactions with materials to assess the effects they are having on grouping patterns and type of play. Often small changes can make a difference. One teacher found that two telephones in the role-play area stimulated more play conversations than did a single phone. Alternatively, teachers can make telephones with which children can actually talk to each other (two cans connected by a string are the most primitive version; more sophisticated ones can be purchased). The inclusion of items such as cardboard tubes through which children can look at each other, and large floor puzzles that allow for more collaboration may facilitate more interaction and cooperative play.

For young children who are easily disorganized and overwhelmed, materials should be visibly displayed in an uncluttered fashion and in meaningful clusters. Low, open shelves allow children to get their own materials, which increases their autonomy and peer cooperation (Day, 1983). If they are not spending their time finding a teacher to help them, they have that much more time to enjoy the materials and each other. Also, once a teacher is present, children are more likely to rely on him for ideas and to initiate the activity, even though the children are fully capable of doing it.

The social content and values of materials should be scrutinized carefully. For preschool children, concrete materials with which they can interact have the potential for broadening their social perspectives. As teachers we should consider the range of lifestyles represented by the dolls, posters, household furniture and props, construction materials, play houses, types of vehicles, and books. Teachers often have to consider the balance of familiarity and unfamiliarity when working with young children. For very young children who are feeling scared at being in school, we need to provide a gradual transition by using materials and props that children are familiar with at home. For example, in a school in a Hispanic community, the housekeeping corner initially had boxes and cans that came from the local bodega, and utensils that were common in the children's homes. Later in the year, the teacher introduced unfamiliar utensils and props to expand children's cultural knowledge base.

Elementary Classrooms

In some elementary classrooms, many materials are designed to be used by individuals working alone (e.g., workbooks, guided reading series, problem sheets). Thus, teachers often have to be creative to adapt materials for collaborative use. Unfortunately, one common adaptation is to have children simply do their individual work in groups and then combine their scores for a group score. This adaptation does not really change the structure of the activity and, in fact, can create antagonisms among group members who do not want to be penalized by others' poor performances. More successful are games and projects that are constructed to require the collaboration of peers. Math problems that require several different calculations and graphic displays or social studies projects in which children have to create a whole city government are examples of ways to involve children in meaningful cooperative projects. Competitive board games can be adapted into cooperative ones by having children predict and monitor the cumulative score of the whole group.

Elementary teachers sometimes express concern that games and other collaborative activities will detract from children's more serious work. However, active and social involvement with materials has been shown to promote children's learning in both mathematics and reading (Bergen & Oden, 1988). For example, mathematics performance can be improved by having children play math games with each other (Rogers & Miller, 1984).

Some activities (such as reading) often are segregated into ability groups which often have negative social consequences, as described by Rizzo (1989). Games and group projects can help counteract this segregation by providing a vehicle for children with a range of interests and abilities to work together. Writing and illustrating a story, observing the growth in a plant, noting the seasonal change of where the sun comes in the window, planning how to make a dam that will not cause erosion, and quizzing each other on spelling words, are a few examples of activities that children can do together, even if they have different levels of ability. In implementing these activities, teachers need to monitor children's involvement and set up systems of accountability and provide support when needed. Sometimes very able children learn to "work the system" and take advantage of the flexibility to avoid putting in the effort. Children who are developmentally delayed often need some coaching and practice in specific skills to feel that they can be equal contributors to the group.

Children in elementary school are very aware of different racial and cultural groups, and, although their understanding of the economic system is rudimentary, they are aware of social class differences. They are also beginning to form attitudes and judge people as insiders or outsiders and are becoming less tolerant of their handicapped peers. Many materials can be used to introduce children to unfamiliar groups in meaningful ways. Biographies of famous people such as Martin Luther King and Harriet Tubman, and accounts of not-so-famous people (e.g., Aylette Jenness' *Families: A Celebration of Diversity, Commitment, and Love*), and fiction that depicts other ways of life and the conflicts that occur between groups of people (e.g., Virginia Sorensen's *Plain Girl*) can help children relate to unfamiliar people in a more personal way and provide a foil for discussing cross-group attitudes and feelings. Stories, crafts, dance, and music from many cultures may help children learn to appreciate the contributions of many people. Involving children in projects that relate to issues of poverty and unequal distribution of wealth, such as collecting food for a local shelter, can heighten their awareness of social problems and help them see themselves as part of a larger social environment. Local issues that directly affect children and their families (e.g., a local plant closing) can be used to create numerous math, reading, and social studies projects.

In the past decade, computers have become commonplace in elementary school classrooms and, to some extent, in preschool and kindergarten classrooms. Their advent has been controversial; concerns have ranged from the type of learning computers will induce, to their effects on children's interactions with other materials and their impact on the social dynamics in the classroom. This brief discussion will focus on this last point.

Initially, many early childhood educators warned that computers would cause children to become isolated; they painted the image of the preschool computer nerd, the already socially marginal child who spends hour after hour at the computer. Another fear was that computers would replace teachers and that children would spend their days interacting with machines instead of people. Teachers also worried that children would gravitate to the computers because of their attractive "magical" properties and not play with the other available materials that had more social potential. Overall, these fears have not been realized. Children do enjoy working with computers, but, after the initial novelty wears off, they resume their former play patterns (Fein, 1985). Computers are rarely used in isolation. Children often collaborate on mastering programs and frequently share their computer experiences and questions with peers. In one kindergarten classroom, the teachers observed that children seemed to argue more when they were working at the computer than when they were in other areas. However, the arguments were usually in the service of problem solving and rarely became angry. As long as the arguments remain reasonably amicable and no one is too frustrated, working together in this way may help children learn how to manage conflicts and how to collaboratively solve problems. One particular source of conflict with the computer is that usually one child controls the keyboard and, although verbal suggestions are accepted, the attempts of the second child to control the keyboard often lead to hands being pushed away and to some mutual annoyance. Teachers may want to investigate the possibility of having double keyboards or using other peripherals such as joy sticks and Koala Pads if conflicts over the keyboard seem to be undermining the quality of experience. When selecting both hardware and software, teachers can follow the guidelines for selecting materials that are listed at the beginning of this section. Computers potentially provide novel opportunities for joint problem solving and collaborative learning, both of which support children's social development. At the same time, teachers should avoid relying too much on computers to teach concepts and should ensure that some children are not using computers to avoid social contact.

STRUCTURE OF GROUPS AND PARTNERSHIPS

Adapting activities to promote different kinds of social interactions has been mentioned several times in this chapter. In this section specific guidelines and examples will illustrate how these modifications can be made. To provide an optimal environment for positive peer interactions, teachers should keep the following general principles in mind.

GUIDELINES FOR STRUCTURING GROUPS

1. Teachers, not children, should determine the membership of long-term and/or formal groups or partners (e.g.; classroom seating arrangements, group projects, lunchroom tables, and field trip partners) in order to avoid popularity contests and social anxiety and to use these opportunities to expand children's breadth of contacts. In particular, groups can be used to break down classroom divisions, such as sex, race, ethnic, and social class segregation.
2. Structure groups so that all members can participate equally.
3. Before groups begin to meet, teachers should help children develop skills in communication, collaboration, and conflict resolution.
4. Provide activities that enable groups to develop a sense of cohesiveness and communal effort.
5. Use a number of different group formats and sizes. For some children, pairs may be most comfortable; for others, working with three or four peers may be preferred. Also, different academic goals lend themselves to a range of group sizes and structures.
6. Provide tasks that are challenging and complex enough to keep all members involved. If there is too little to do, children will lose interest. (When people are members of groups that are "undermanned," they participate at a higher level and more readily include marginal members [Willems, 1967].) When appropriate, establish an accountability system that emphasizes participation and effort.
7. Be sure that the larger context of the classroom supports the group structures. For example, comparing children's academic competence in displays of work and reward systems may undermine efforts to integrate children from different ability levels.

Preschool Classrooms

Preschool groups are often quite fluid, and children move in and out of interactions almost continuously during the school day. Teachers, therefore, are often responding to groups that are already formed rather than planning the composition of groups. However, in their suggestions to children, they can try to insure the equal participation of all members, help the group work toward a common goal, and enrich the activity so that all the children can have a meaningful role. For example, when helping children resolve a conflict about whether or not there can be two "mothers" in the house-keeping corner, the teacher can point out how much work parents (both mothers and fathers) do with specific reference to tasks that need to be done. He can also point out that most parents have to do work outside of the home and encourage an extension of the dramatic play into some enactments of "going to work." Obviously these suggestions should be offered with a light touch with questions and observations, not direct instructions (e.g., "It looks as though there is a lot of work to do taking care of the baby and cleaning the house and making dinner...." "What happens when one parent has to go to work? What is she going to do? What will the other one do?"). In this role as observer–consultant, teachers can help children develop their group experiences and learn how to function in a more inclusive and egalitarian way.

For some activities, preschool teachers may want to predetermine group composition in order to alleviate children's social anxiety and encourage a broader range of contacts. In one 3-year-old classroom, children were very concerned about who their friends were; every circle and snack time turned into a small melee as the children rushed to sit down next to the two or three most popular children. The anxiety about who was going to sit next to whom began to permeate the whole day and absorb an inordinate amount of the children's attention. In response, the teacher introduced a game in which she placed children's pictures around the circle and snack tables and they had to find their picture and sit at those places. After a while, the children learned how to play the system by surreptitiously moving the pictures to again jockey for positions near one of the popular children (a good example of secondary adjustment). The teacher then made the procedure more challenging so that the children were assigned in pairs to find a particular color, animal, or some other object. As soon as the teacher assumed control of who was going to sit next to whom, the children were visibly relieved and the friendship claims became less urgent. One other advantage of this strategy was that children had a common task that they could talk about as they looked for their particular animal, shape, flower, etc. Field trips and special projects are also occasions when teachers can break up the usual groupings and try out some new combinations. If one child seems to be eager to make contact with another, but has not been able to accomplish this goal, a cooking project or woodworking project may be an opportunity to pair them up and see what happens. Sometimes teach-ers simply want to keep the social dynamics fluid and so will set aside a time in the day when children are all expected to find a new playmate, someone that they have not played with on that day.

When teachers form groups, the activities should be designed to promote equal and active participation by all members and a sense of shared purpose. For example, one preschool teacher wanted to help some very domineering children learn how to work as members of a group. She formed a group that included these children and some other capable, but more easygoing classmates and had them plan and then construct a town with blocks. The project was complicated and involved a lot of group decision making. Children had to compromise and negotiate at all stages. The teacher began the project by enacting and discussing various situations in which children might disagree. In this way, the children had a chance to think about how they might handle conflicts before they happened. During the project, the interactions were often quite vociferous and, at times, the group almost disintegrated At the end, however, all the children had contributed and even cheerfully cooperated in cleaning up the materials they had used. The common and challenging goal of planning and constructing a town gave the children who were not usually friends a space for getting to know each other and learning how to manage and resolve conflicts.

Teachers can construct a number of different groups and social situations in order to meet the academic and social needs of their children. Children can work in pairs, groups of three, four, or larger and can play a variety of roles, depending on their social need. In one classroom, the teacher wanted to help a very isolated and shy 4-year-old develop more self-confidence and a more positive image with his peers She gave him the job of teaching his classmates how to make "animal sandwiches." Although his power was momentary and contrived, he did gain a little visibility and seemed more confident in his subsequent interactions with others.

Elementary Classrooms

In elementary schools, classroom work groups are likely to be more formal and meet over a period of time. Children may be in project groups for social studies, partnerships for science experiments, tutoring partners in math, and ability groups for reading. Aside from the social clustering at recess and other free times, children's groups are not spontaneously formed. Thus, elementary teachers can plan and structure the groups with more precision than their preschool colleagues can. By placing children in a number of different groups, teachers can keep changing the mix of children to prevent segregation by ability, gender, race, and any other traits that children use to divide themselves. If there is a clear and challenging focus for each group, the members of the group may get so absorbed in the project that they forget that they are not with their best friends. Teachers can use groups to reduce tensions among different classmates or to "bring out" more isolated children. Careful planning is required, and even then some combinations may prove to be disastrous. However, if children are in a number of different groups, an unhappy combination will not have a huge impact on any one child. Moreover, children can learn a lot about how people work together when they are in a situation where that is not happening. In Chapter 6, ways of using groups with specific children and social dynamics will be discussed in more detail.

A number of cooperative group models have been developed for elementary school classrooms. All of them explicitly require equal contribution of all members and encourage a sense of group cohesiveness. As summarized by Slavin (1988) and Furman and Gavin (1989), the ones that are most appropriate for young elementary school children include the following formats:

Student teams–achievement divisions in which students teach each other the material that the teacher has presented to the class. Students are quizzed on the material individually. The scores that they contribute to the teams are based on the degree they have improved over the last quiz, so children at all ability levels can contribute to the teams' success.

Teams–games–tournaments has a similar structure, but instead of individual quizzes, the teams compete in class tournaments in which students compete against others of comparable ability.

Jigsaw in which each group member becomes an expert on a particular aspect of a shared study topic. The members then teach each other about their area of expertise. All students are tested on all areas of information and so are interdependent.

Group investigation in which teams are formed around student interests in specific topics. Students choose goals, work on an open-ended project, and present their findings to the rest of the class. They are graded as a group on their project.

Learning Together is similar to the Group Investigation model, but the students are not graded on the project, although they do receive comments on their project.

Traditionally, academic progress has been measured by students' independent mastery of material and demonstrated competency on tests. As a result, some teachers and school administrators are concerned about whether cooperative groups will impair children's achievement. A great deal of research has shown that cooperative groups, if they are carefully planned and well run, can increase academic achievement as well as foster positive social relationships (e.g., Sapon-Shevin, 1986; Slavin, 1983, 1988).

Cooperative learning is also associated with a rise in self-esteem, increased interpersonal cooperation and altruism, and more skilled perspective taking (Furman & Gavin, 1989). A series of studies using different cooperative models also showed that cross-race friendships and the integration of main-streamed children increased among children who participated in mixed-race and mixed-ability cooperative groups (Slavin, 1983, 1988).

Some of the models mentioned here use intergroup competition as a way of promoting group cohesion and motivating children to work in their groups. Competition between groups can contribute to the building of intragroup affiliation, but should be used judiciously to avoid intergroup antagonism. Teachers need to develop some systems of accountability (e.g., a skit or report presented to the class, a final paper), but should be careful not to overuse competition and scores when using the teams–games–tournament and student teams–achievement divisions models. The larger social context of children should also be considered in the use of competition; some cultural groups are more comfortable with competition than others (Zahn, Kagan, Widaman, 1986).

The issue of grading often comes up when children are working in groups. Teachers wonder if they should give group or individual grades. If everyone in the group is given the same grade, it might be unfair to members who worked a lot harder than others. On the other hand, teasing out individual efforts from the group performance is almost impossible. If possible, teachers should avoid giving letter grades and, instead, engage the group in evaluating its own work and how it might have been better. Grades can interfere with the group's functioning by making children more critical of their own and their peers' efforts. Moreover, if a teacher has to be constantly evaluating and comparing children's work, she will be less effective in helping children develop mutual respect and appreciation. One teacher described how she had children work in groups to present different news items to the whole class. She did not grade them on these projects, but challenged them to make their presentations lively and interesting to their classmates. They tackled these assignments with a great deal of enthusiasm as they were highly motivated to make their classmates interested.

To help children function well in groups, teachers need to introduce group assignments with discussions about group process and ways of resolving potential problems. For example, a teacher might have the children role play a hypothetical situation in which one group member is always talking and never listening. Teachers can also role play these situations (often to the delight of their children). In the follow-up discussions, class members can generate solutions to the problem. In this way, issues can be raised and strategies practiced without individuals being put on the spot. If children have had little previous cooperative group experience, they should begin in groups that are highly structured and carefully monitored to help children gain skills in a safe environment. At the beginning of the year, teachers may want to try out a lot of short-term groups to assess how various combinations of children work together and the overall skill level of the class before setting up more long-term and involved groups.

Once groups have started, teachers need to monitor them very carefully, particularly at the beginning. They may need to provide ongoing support for children who lack certain academic skills so that all group members can maintain their level of contribution. Meeting frequently with each group and asking about how people are working together and how decisions are made may help diffuse potential conflicts. Older children can keep a journal or record their reactions and turn them in. Assigning group process roles such as a "facilitator" is another way of assisting the group in its social processes. The facilitator usually makes sure that everyone is getting a chance to talk and reminds people that they need to listen. This person may also summarize the discussion and help move the conversation on to the next part of the project. Another person may be responsible for making sure that group members are comfortable. For example, if one child has had his idea voted down, this member might ask him how he feels and make sure that he does not feel devastated and is not taking the decision personally. Other roles such as secretary or scribe can be used if the group needs to record information from their meetings. By rotating through these roles, children become much more attuned to group processes, others' points of view, and their own impact on the group. Sometimes children, in their efforts to circumvent adult instructions, manipulate assignments so that they can avoid the work (Holloway, 1991). They may spend their time trying to figure out ways of doing the work in the fastest way or choose the easiest tasks, rather than actually thinking about the topic. Teachers need to find an effective balance between giving the groups adequate autonomy, yet monitoring them enough to discourage children from "working the system" to the detriment of the group and the academic goals.

One type of group often used with young elementary children is the "author's circle" in which children read excerpts from their recent writing and get comments from their peers. Prior to the meetings of these groups, teachers typically describe ways in which children can give each other compliments and criticisms. Teachers and children also discuss how it feels when someone makes a negative comment and how to accept these criticisms as helpful suggestions. One teacher presents these issues in a very dramatic and humorous way that invariably makes the children feel more relaxed and open to the process.

> "How do I feel when Laurita says that she doesn't like the ending of my story? I feel horrrrible!!!" wails Ms. S. as she clasps her hands to her

chest. The second graders laugh, and Henri pipes up "That's how I feel!" Ms. S. then begins to lead a discussion about how hard it is to hear criticism, yet why people's suggestions can make our writing better. The children chime in with lots of ideas and suggestions.

Before and during group work, teachers may have to coach children on resolving conflicts. Group interactions provide excellent opportunities for children to learn how to manage controversy (Johnson, 1981). When managed constructively, conflicts over ideas can motivate students to seek new information, question old assumptions, and use their reasoning to come to new conclusions. In terms of social goals, controversy helps students become more aware of others' perspectives and learn how to disagree without becoming angry or defensive. However, children often need guidance and support to use these conflicts positively. In one third-grade class, the children were working in groups to make commercials that they were to present as skits to the class. In several groups, boys and girls argued vehemently over which products to use. There was also a fair amount of disagreement over the the styles of the commercials (e.g., special effects versus more human interest). The teacher held a class meeting, and she and her student teacher enacted a typical argument. The children thought it was uproariously funny, but did recognize themselves and came up with some creative solutions (e.g., if the boys choose the product, then the girls choose the style of commercial; put all the options on pieces of paper and draw one from a hat). Conflicts within groups can sometimes be worrisome, but if teachers and children can approach them as useful learning experiences, they can lead to positive rather than negative outcomes.

TEACHER ROLES

Aside from setting up the environment and managing the program, we as teachers profoundly influence the social climate of the classroom in our day-to-day interactions with children, parents, and fellow staff members. In this section three specific teacher roles will be considered: supporting and facilitating social interactions and relations, setting and maintaining behavioral expectations and limits, and modeling social behavior.

GUIDELINES FOR TEACHER ROLES

1. Teachers should be genuine in their interactions with children and not feel that they have to feign emotions. At the same time, they need to protect themselves from becoming too entangled or consumed by children's emotional issues.

2. In supporting children's social interactions, teachers should be available, but not intrusive or overbearing.

3. In establishing and setting limits, teachers should maintain an authoritative role by establishing and enforcing clear expectations, yet involving children in discussions about rules and consequences.

4. Consequences for misbehavior should be based on restitution to the victim(s) rather than retribution against the miscreant.

5. Teachers should model caring and respect for all people in their interactions with children, parents, and colleagues.

Supporting and Facilitating Peer Interactions

Teachers vary in both their personal styles and philosophical orientations about how closely involved they should be with the children in their classroom (Day, 1983). Some maintain a fair amount of distance from the children and stay away from children's activities unless they perceive a need to assist or redirect behavior; others like to direct all aspects of children's play; and others are attentive to the activities that children are doing, but move in and out and adapt their roles depending on the situation and the needs of the children. The third orientation is related to children's higher involvement with the activities and with each other. Knowing that adults are available, but are not overbearing, enables children to play and work together without relying on adult direction. In programs in which the adults were distant and more involved in nonchild-related activities (e.g., administrative tasks), children's interactions were more disruptive. In short, the most effective teacher–child relationship is one in which teachers and children have come together in a spirit of cooperation and a joint responsibility for maintaining a pleasant milieu (Day, 1983).

As teachers we must be very aware of the nuances of classroom interactions and be able to shift roles smoothly. In a brief span of time a teacher might sternly redirect a misbehaving child, comfort a crying child, instruct a group on how to do something, observe two children arguing and decide not to intervene, offer suggestions to children who are having trouble using a piece of equipment, and praise someone who has just completed a difficult task. In other words, teachers are constantly shifting the focus and affective quality of their interactions with children. As teachers go through these shifts, they must also express their feelings in a genuine manner. If the teacher in the example above is still angry about the misbehavior of one child, her praise to the other one may sound forced. Children readily pick up on these nuances and may come to distrust the teacher's genuineness. In this case, the teacher would do better to stay a little distant until she has recovered her equilibrium. As teachers we also need to strike a balance by being attentive and involved, yet not becoming entangled in or debilitated by children's feelings or actions.

As teachers approach children who are having a problem, they often wonder at what point they should intervene. In general, first watching and trying to understand what is transpiring will help teachers make more timely and effective interventions. Obviously, if the children are in physical danger, then immediate action is necessary. However, disputes do not always become fights, and children are often resourceful in resolving minor conflicts. Too quick an intervention may interfere with the children's efforts to resolve the situation and undermine their confidence and motivation to do it on their own. Alternatively, the teacher might move physically closer in order to provide a reassuring and calming presence, but not directly address the children. This action also allows the teacher to watch more closely and learn what is happening in order to make a more effective intervention if it seems to be necessary. For example, a child who is frustrated because she is having trouble getting the blocks to stay where she wants them may react by yelling at her partner. If the teacher only sees the last event and reprimands the child for yelling, the problem will not be solved. However, if the teacher encourages the child to get her partner involved in the project, then the dispute may evolve into a cooperative interaction.

Not only is timing important, but so too is the degree of intervention. Many adults find it all too easy to simply take over an activity or group if it is not going well. If things have really fallen apart or time is short, this response may be appropriate. However, a lighter touch is usually more effective in terms of the children's learning. For example, if two children are fighting over the use of a toy, the teacher might first watch to see if they can resolve it. Then he could ask them to sit down and see if they can think of a way to resolve it. If they have no ideas, he might suggest a few alternatives. If they cannot select one, then he might make a specific suggestion. If all else fails, then directing them or removing the object of contention may be necessary. As illustrated here, the teacher gradually extends his influence from observer to consultant to coach, and finally to director.

As children gain more social skills, they need less adult supervision. In elementary schools, many peer interactions occur in areas that are not directly observed by the teacher (e.g., groups working in the hallways or playing in the corners of the school yard). Unless the problem erupts into a fight or overt scapegoating, teachers may not even know of its existence. The teacher, therefore, is less likely to intervene in specific interactions. However, she may act as a consultant if children are dealing with more persistent relationship problems (e.g., a child who refuses to do his part in a group, a threesome in which children are feeling insecure and competitive).

In these cases, the teacher might not intervene during a particular episode, but rather discuss it with the children afterwards and help them understand why a particular dynamic is occurring and how they might change it over a period of time.

Setting Limits

Teachers play a significant role in setting behavior expectations and enforcing limits. Children feel safer when they know what behaviors are expected and that they will be protected from others' misbehaviors. At the same time, they need to feel some control and a sense that the rules are meaningful. In a classic study (Lewin, Lippitt, & White, 1939), children were placed in groups that were directed by a series of leaders who used various leadership styles: authoritarian, democratic, and laissez-faire. When under the authoritarian or laissez-faire leaders, the same groups displayed more aggression than they did under the democratic leaders. With the authoritarian leader, the children were not aggressive while the leader was present, but as soon as she left, aggression rose sharply, as did scapegoating. Under the democratic leader, children were more cooperative. This study shows the profound effect that the limit-setting style of the teacher has on the social climate of the classroom.

To create a democratic environment, we need to involve children in establishing the behavioral rules and norms of the classroom. Obviously the extent to which they make these decisions depends on their developmental levels. Young preschoolers cannot anticipate the kinds of problems they might encounter over the year, but they can respond to the specific question of "What do we need to do to make people feel safe in the playhouse?" if that has been the scene of some rough play. Second and third graders, on the other hand, may have some very sophisticated ideas about how to establish classroom rules and the types of consequences that should be used to enforce them. Regardless of children's ages, we should approach limit-setting issues by first trying to see them from the children's perspective and, as mentioned previously, asking the children either in a group or individually what they think the problem is and how might it be solved. One first-grade teacher designed a lesson in which the children in groups had to share a set of information cards. Although cards were plentiful, the children kept fighting over particular ones. He gathered the class together and asked them to discuss the problem. The children pointed out that some cards were clearly more interesting than others (e.g., sharks versus codfish) and that all the children wanted to keep the best cards. With the teacher's guidance, the children developed a set of rules about how long a person could use a particular card and ways of making sure that each group member had equal access to the popular cards. After this discussion, the class resumed their work in a very amicable fashion.

When confronted with limit breaking, teachers often need to impose consequences before children learn to adhere to the rule. Usually misbehavior is punished with the intent of making miscreants feel uncomfortable. Subsequently, they often feel victimized or angry and may try to relieve these feelings by repeating the act. An alternative method is to emphasize restitution rather than retribution (Schaffer & Sinicrope, 1983). Designing consequences around restitution forces the offender to think about the effects of his or her actions on others and to consider positive steps to ameliorate them. Viewed in this manner, these rule infractions can be used to help children develop their awareness of others, their social reasoning skills, and their social problem-solving skills. Obviously, this technique cannot always be used, but since most rules are based on being considerate of others, infractions usually involve another's injury that can become the focus of discussion. Property damage is the easiest situation in which to use this method because the nature of the injury is concrete, and often the remedy is clear-cut. The aggressor can help rebuild the block tower or assist in remaking the picture. If the victim has been personally injured, restitution may be a little harder to design since, obviously, the act cannot be undone. In this case, the aggressor can be encouraged to find a way to make her victim feel better; a funny card, an apology, or some assistance with math homework are a few examples. Teachers should not force children to apologize, as we have all seen the ineffectiveness of the reluctantly muttered "Imsorry" as the child turns away. The child may decide that an apology is the best way to make the victim feel better, but in that case it is the child's decision.

When children do things that are annoying, but do not cause any specific damage, such as disrupting group time, the form of restitution is also a little less clear. The usual method is to separate the child from the group. However, time-outs often have negative consequences if they further humiliate or isolate a child who is already socially marginal (Rizzo, 1989). Practically speaking, time-outs sometimes escalate the level of conflict as the excluded child often rises to the challenge by disrupting the group from afar. Teachers know all too well how effectively the excluded child can still distract his peers by making "raspberry" noises in the hall or pressing his face in the window in the door. In a restitution approach, the disrupting child might collaborate with the teacher to choose the story, the topic for discussion, or the song and, in this way, contribute positively to circle time. If the child feels some responsibility for the success of the activity, she may feel less inclined to disrupt it. Moreover, this participation gives her some positive attention, the need for which may underlie the disruptive behavior in the first place.

Chronic misbehavior may be indicative of more serious problems related either to the children involved or to the environment. If a child continuously disrupts circle, teachers may want to consider whether or not the child is ready for an activity with that kind of structure. Likewise, if particular children are always involved in fights or property damage, a longer and deeper examination of the problem may reveal either some psychological problems or some ways in which the social environment is working against those individuals.

Teachers as Social Models

Teachers greatly influence children's social orientations and skills by modeling positive social behaviors with children and with colleagues and parents. A teacher who yells at the children to "Shut up!" is not in a very good position to encourage or enforce more positive social problem-solving strategies. Obviously, teachers do not have endless patience and inevitably will feel angry and frustrated sometimes, but if the overall approach is one of respect and caring, then children will reflect that in their interactions with their peers and the teacher. Not only do children observe and learn specific skills, but a harmonious climate usually reduces the level of tension and the potential for antagonistic interactions.

Children are acute observers of adult interactions. The ways in which co-teachers and teachers and other school staff members interact are noticed by children. The principal who stands at the door frowning at the nervous first-year teacher is teaching the children about intimidation. The teacher who patronizes her classroom aide is teaching the children that all people are not worthy of respect. In one second grade the teacher realized that the children took the school staff for granted and were often inconsiderate. She invited the custodian, the school secretary, and a cafeteria worker to come and talk to her class about their jobs and what they liked and did not like about them. Afterwards, the children made a list of all the things they could do to make the staff's jobs easier, and from that point on were more considerate of the school staff. They cleaned up the room more carefully, made sure that they had the right change for lunch, and tried to be more prompt in bringing back school forms. By putting these kinds of chores into the context of helping other people, the teacher made them more meaningful, while also providing a model of respect and consideration for others. Interactions between teachers and parents are also observed by children. If a teacher dismisses a parent's concern, children learn that they do not have to listen. If parents disparage teachers, children learn they do not have to respect them. Positive teacher–parent relations create a more harmonious environment and demonstrate to children how people who do not know each other well can find ways to get along.

To help children appreciate and respect diversity, school staff should be comprised of people from a wide range of backgrounds and abilities. Participating in a setting in which people from diverse backgrounds work together successfully is one of the best ways for children to grow up feeling comfortable in a diverse society. Also, seeing people in roles other than their stereotypic ones helps breakdown the assumptions that children have. One of my students described how having a teacher who was in a wheelchair had helped her overcome a lot of her negative attitudes about handicapped people in particular and differences in general. Her teacher also provided an excellent model of someone who has overcome difficulties. Unfortunately, because of location and availability of teachers representing some ethnic groups, many schools are staffed by a relatively homogeneous group of people. Obviously, hiring practices should be examined and modified to improve the situation. In the meantime, teachers can invite members of the local community who represent a wide range of occupations, interests, and ethnic groups to visit the classroom. With these experiences, children will become familiar with a wider range of people and see that each person is an expert about a particular job or avocation. If children have negative stereotypes about particular people (e.g., "garbage collectors"), visiting these people's work places and having them talk about their lives and their work may begin to challenge these negative assumptions.

6

Social Intervention: When? To Whom? How? And How Much?

As teachers we influence children's social behavior in a variety of ways. The previous chapter explored how decisions about the physical environment, the daily schedule, the organization of activities, and types and enforcement of limits all affect the social climate and the peer and teacher–child interactions that occur in the classroom. This chapter focuses on ways in which teachers influence the outcomes of particular individual and classroom problems by designing and implementing strategies to remediate them. Many of the suggestions in this chapter are based on the research on intervention programs that was described in Chapter 4 and will address issues raised about classroom dynamics in Chapter 3 and individual differences in Chapter 4.

DECIDING WHEN AND HOW TO INTERVENE

The dilemma of when and how much to intervene is familiar to most teachers. We have all had the experience of watching social episodes in which at least one child is unhappy and have wondered whether or not to go over and rectify the situation. Likewise, we have all worried about what to do when we see a child who is chronically engaged in negative social encounters. "If I intervene and support her, then she might be seen as a teacher's pet on top of everything else...if I try to give her some suggestions, then she may feel that I'm against her too...but at the same time, if I stand back and do nothing, the situation may just get worse...." These ruminations are familiar to all of us, whether we are simply debating in our minds about a course of action or discussing these questions with colleagues and supervisors. This first section offers some possible approaches to making these decisions.

132

When confronted by these decisions, teachers know that there are some clear "bottom line" rules. The classroom must be a safe environment for all children; if someone is getting physically or psychologically hurt, an intervention is imperative. When parents report that a situation is making their child very tense or unhappy, then teachers need to intervene. If a child or a situation appears to be deteriorating, the teacher must act quickly to reverse that trend. The decision about what to do and when to do it, however, must be based on a number of factors including the teacher's resources and skills, the type and the extent of the problem, the particular needs of the children involved, and the larger social issues that may be influencing the dynamics of the classroom.

To be effective, we need to plan strategies that are most compatible with our personal styles. Some teachers act more like stage managers in that they set up the environment and watch carefully what is going on and discretely and sparingly direct the children; others may be more directive. When asked what they would do if a child appeared to want to join a group, but was hesitant, three teachers offered different answers. The first teacher said that she often makes an indirect comment such as "There's lots of room here, perhaps someone would like to join...." within the hearing of both the entering child and the on-going group. In this way she is obliquely supporting the newcomer, letting the group know that she expects him to be allowed to join, and attempting to prevent a conflict or failed entry. In responding to the same situation, another teacher said that he preferred to let the interaction unfold without any intervention and then, if a conflict occurred, guide the children through a discussion about how they felt and help them arrive at a solution. A third teacher said she would probably help the onlooking child find another activity rather than try to force a social interaction and risk the chance of rejection. Although each teacher had a preferred style, they all said that their actions would depend largely on the particular children involved. Thus, interventions and strategies develop from a convergence of teachers' styles and children's needs.

GUIDELINES FOR DECIDING WHEN AND HOW TO INTERVENE

1. Observe the situation carefully and determine the extent and seriousness of the problem.
2. Analyze the problem and desired outcomes from the *children's* perspectives.
3. Clarify ideas and generate possible strategies in discussions with colleagues and, if appropriate, outside consultants.
4. Discuss the problem and possible strategies with parents.
5. Consider possible external pressures that might be contributing to the problem.
6. Define the goals of the intervention.

7. Evaluate possible strategies to insure that they are developmentally appropriate and oriented to promoting children's growth, not simply suppressing behavior.
8. Define the adults' roles to provide the optimal balance between children's autonomy and adequate guidance.
9. Approach implementation with alternative plans and great flexibility.

As an initial step, we need to identify the extent and seriousness of the problem. Many of the assessment procedures discussed in the previous chapters can be adapted to be used in this process. Teachers should also trust their intuitions. If they sense something is wrong, systematic observations or discussions with the children often confirm their perceptions and clarify the nature of the problem. Sometimes we are not fully aware that a problem exists until we find ourselves thinking "Oh no, not again!" and realize that a particular event is part of a larger and more persistent pattern. The seriousness of the problem is usually evident in the children's reactions. If the children involved are clearly unhappy, tense, or frustrated for more than a few days, then the situation warrants attention. Another clue is how the situation affects the rest of the classroom. When it begins to affect other children and the overall social atmosphere of the classroom, then teachers need to decide if this person or dynamic have that much control. One second-grade teacher described how the competition among a group of five girls for the attention of the two most popular members resulted in a prolonged discussion every day about who was going to be whose friend that day. "They were unable to get involved in any activities until this issue was decided and then we could all get on with the day." Because this competition was dominating the school lives of the children involved and to some extent the rest of the classroom, the teacher felt that some intervention was necessary to limit this competition.

The decision-making process about what to do includes observations, discussions with children and with colleagues, and a lot of trial and error. When teachers notice something is wrong, the first step is to observe and try to learn as much as possible about the nature of the problem and to try to understand it *from the children's perspectives*. The latter point is most important; intervention attempts often fail because teachers do not understand the children's purposes and therefore make a change that the children subvert. For example, in confronting the problem of the competition among the five girls, the teacher initially told the children that they could no longer have these discussions and tried to get them involved in activities right away. The girls simply "went underground" and played out the competition with constant fights throughout the day, which were even more disruptive. Discussions with colleagues and supervisors can be very helpful to clarify one's own impressions, generate ideas for solutions, and think through the implications of various strategies. School administrators must insure that trained personnel are available to come and observe the child and the classroom to provide a more objective and fresh perspective on the problem. School counselors, social workers, special education personnel, fellow teachers, or administrators can participate in this observation and decision-making process. In small schools that do not have these resources, the administrator should contact the local colleges, mental health agencies, and early childhood resource programs and develop a list of local professionals who are qualified and willing to act as consultants.

Designing strategies involves creativity, flexibility, and a certain amount of risk taking. We often have to rethink the way we do things and invent novel approaches. The development and implementation of strategies involve many trials and many errors, sometimes planned and sometimes spontaneous. When opportunities present themselves, teachers can take advantage of them to try out potential strategies. For example, if two children are absolutely inseparable, then the absence of one partner may provide an unexpected opportunity to try pairing the partner with other classmates to see what will happen. Because individuals and the dynamics among them are fairly unpredictable, all interventions should be designed with some flexibility so that teachers can shift to another approach if their initial ideas are either not working or are causing unintended negative effects.

As teachers consider their goals and strategies, they need to decide how they will measure the effectiveness of the outcome. Because children's behavior is always unpredictable, having multiple outcome measures is preferable. When the second-grade teacher began to analyze the problem of the five competitive girls, he listed several outcomes that would indicate a reduction in their anxiety about the competition: less time spent vying for the attention of the popular children, more interest in peers other than the two popular girls, and more interest and involvement in activities. Sometimes outcomes are not obvious in the classroom, but parents may report that their children are less anxious about coming to school, or that they seem more confident in their neighborhood group, or less aggressive at home. Children may demonstrate their changes in places other than the classroom, and so monitoring their behavior in other settings is valuable.

Whenever possible, parents or another adult who is significant to the child should be involved in analyzing the problem and developing strategies. Often behavior that is troublesome to a teacher is also worrisome to family members. Parents can also report about the child's behavior in other settings to provide more clues as to possible causes of the problem. Most important, teachers and parents often can support each others' efforts. In dealing with the competition among the five girls, the teacher and parents worked together to get the children involved in more activities and other peers both inside and outside of school, and monitored at-home visits and contacts to minimize the children's concerns about being excluded by particular subgroups. Sometimes problems reflect conflicts in values between home and school that can often be resolved with clearer and more consistent communication between parents and teachers.

In some communities, parents may have a difficult time participating in this process. Their work schedules may preclude contact with teachers; they may speak another language and feel intimidated about coming into the school; they may feel alienated by schools and distrust any overtures by the teacher. Teachers can reach out by arranging home visits and evening and weekend conferences and by having a community member whom the parents know and trust available as an advocate and, if necessary, as an interpreter. If the child is being cared for by other family members, such as a grandmother, an aunt, or an older brother, they should be involved in any discussions and plans. Several programs designed to prevent and alleviate children's social problems include family involvement in schools, Saturday programs for families and extensive use of home visitors/consultants (e.g., Comer, 1985; Dodge, 1991; Evans, Engler, & Okifuji, 1991). To build trust, we need to maintain contact with family members on an ongoing basis, not only when a problem arises. If a good rapport has been established, then discussions of difficulties will be easier. In cases in which the child's problem is related to some disruption or abuse at home, teachers should learn as much as they can and work with the school social worker or local social service agency to find ways of providing as much stability and support as possible for the child.

Throughout the process of analyzing the problem and designing strategies, five general principles should be kept in mind. First, all behavior is purposeful and makes sense to the children doing it, so any individual or group pattern or intervention plan should be analyzed from the children's perspective. Second, the distinction between intervention and interference should be clear. Both "intervention" and "interference" refer to an outsider entering the situation with the intention of changing the course of events. However, in the former, the intent is to facilitate or protect; in the latter, it is to hinder or thwart the actions of others. Our actions should be geared to promoting the growth and meeting the needs of children that the children are expressing, not simply stopping an action or repressing a behavior. Third, teachers need to balance the goals of fostering children's autonomy with providing adult guidance to facilitate their development in social skills. Fourth, the immediate and larger social context of a specific behavior or situation should be considered; often children are reacting to external pressures. Fifth, for any serious problem, strategies should include some family involvement. Finally, each situation and each child is unique, and interventions will vary with the particular problems and resources of each child and situation. Strategies should be developmentally appropriate and designed to emphasize children's strengths as well as to remediate their problems.

The next sections of this chapter illustrate the ways that teachers can intervene by presenting a number of different types of problems and possible solutions. These examples do not cover all potential problems, and the solutions are not prescriptive answers. They are offered simply as examples to help teachers identify their own questions and arrive at their own solutions. The first section will focus on ways to work with individual children with issues related to peer acceptance. As discussed in Chapter 4, some children are popular, others are rejected, some have controversial roles in the class, and others are ignored and perhaps neglected by their peers. Many children do not fit any of these categories and are usually referred to as "average." However, they may share some characteristics with their peers that fit these more defined categories, so aspects of the following discussions are applicable to them as well. Although most research and intervention programs have focused on rejected children, we need to keep in mind that all children need support in order to fulfill their social potential. Second, teachers are often faced with relationships that are troublesome for various reasons. Perhaps two children have a very close but very unequal relationship; group members may be encouraging each other to defy the teacher and avoid work. Strategies for helping children extricate themselves from unsatisfactory or counterproductive relationships is the topic of this section. Third, as discussed in Chapter 3, children often divide themselves by sex, race, social class, culture, and abilities. Strategies to make these boundaries more permeable and to encourage children to expand their range of playmates and appreciate their diversity will be described. The final section of this chapter will focus on teaching children strategies for managing and resolving conflicts.

INDIVIDUAL DIFFERENCES IN PEER ACCEPTANCE

Individual differences in peer acceptance may reflect a number of factors, as discussed in Chapter 4. Children's behaviors have a great influence on their peer acceptance. However, classmates' interpretation of behavior may be biased by the child's physical appearance, social class, race, culture, and abilities. Moreover, the social dynamics of a classroom have an impact on the role of each individual. For example, one child who was a well-liked "tomboy" as a kindergartener became an outcast in her first-grade class. The teacher initially was puzzled by this shift, but after some thought realized that the other first-grade girls were quite sophisticated and very concerned about clothes and hair, and this more tomboyish child suddenly did not have any common ground with them. The boys, meanwhile, were in the throes of "hating all girls" so that this child could not ally herself with them either. In a less gender-polarized group, she might have been less isolated. Teachers' attitudes are also important; their preferences for children are a predictive factor in children's sociometric status (Taylor & Trickett, 1989). The rejected child has been the primary focus of most intervention studies, but other children, even popular ones, often face social pressures or create a problematic dynamic in the group. Therefore, the following sections include discussions about a range of individual problems and ways in which they might be approached.

GUIDELINES FOR INTERVENTIONS RELATED TO PEER ACCEPTANCE

1. Assess the individual's behavior and how that is contributing to the problem.
2. Try to see from the child's point of view what purposes lie behind her or his behaviors.
3. Analyze the role of the peer group in establishing or maintaining the problematic situation.
4. Examine our own attitudes toward the child(ren) involved to be sure that we are not conveying positively or negatively biased messages about particular children.
5. Consult parents about home and community factors that may be contributing to the problem.
6. Design strategies that—
   a. help children get their needs met in more productive ways
   b. teach children needed social and academic skills
   c. involve peers and help them change their images of and reactions to the affected child(ren)
   d. involve parents in a positive and collaborative way.

Popular Children

Children who are popular are generally well-adjusted, likable, and successful in forming positive relations with peers. Thus, they are rarely viewed as problems. However, sometimes their popularity itself becomes a problem. Because many children want to play with them, they often feel pressured to try to keep everyone happy. One mother of a very popular kindergarten child reported that her daughter worried all the way to school about how she was going to make sure that everyone felt alright. This concern about others' feelings probably contributed to her peers' affection for her, but also meant that her popularity had become a burden. Teachers can alleviate these pressures by assigning children to groups and areas for part of the day or, in the case of elementary classrooms, organizing games during recess, until classmates break the habit of relying on the popular child to make these decisions. In the case of this kindergarten girl, her teacher got her involved in several different projects in which children were assigned to groups. For these periods of time, the girl did not have to feel responsible for the well-being of her classmates. Her friends, meanwhile, momentarily stopped clamoring for her attention and learned to enjoy the company of other children which helped diffuse their need for the popular child's attention.

Teachers sometimes unwittingly pressure popular children by relying on them to help less popular children and intervene in negative classroom dynamics. For example, isolated children may be paired with popular ones in order to help them feel more a part of the mainstream. Sometimes, popular children will be asked to take leadership positions to reverse a particular dynamic (e.g., to help stop the scapegoating of another child). In many respects, these strategies make a great deal of sense and are examples of using children's culture and peer structure to initiate change. At the same time, teachers need to be aware that popular children are not invincible and are susceptible to peer and adult pressures because they tend to be more socially aware.

Sometimes popular children use their status in less desirable ways that cause dissension among their peers. One 3-year-old girl was sought after by her peers; every day she promised three or four classmates that they could sit next to her at snack. Since she only had two places next to her, this over-commitment caused many hurt feelings and small fights. She seemed to be fascinated by her power and often initiated these promises; her actions were not simply attempts to accommodate her peers. Because the child was too young to understand the negative consequences of her manipulations, the teacher alleviated the problem by assigning seats for snack so that snack seating was no longer an issue. A kindergarten teacher, faced with a similar problem, enacted a skit with his student teacher in which children were being excluded from the snack table. These older children recognized the problem that their behavior was creating and stopped the practice of saving seats. A popular first-grade boy presented a slightly different problem. He was very bright and had a lot of good ideas and social skills, yet he wanted to control his peers. When he entered a group, he was usually welcomed, but then would take over and dominate the ongoing activity. He sometimes belittled the game in progress or "accidentally" knocked over their project. The children were attracted to him, yet he undermined their confidence, work, and play. After she noticed this pattern, the teacher began to support the children in the group and let Alan know that she was aware of his actions and that she expected him to support others' play, not simply impose his own ideas (e.g., "Alan, these children are building a city. They have some very interesting plans that they can tell you about so that you will know how you can help.").

As children get older and peer groups become more rigidly formed, popular children often define who are the insiders and who are the outsiders. Keisha, a popular second grader, decided which shoes, which logos on shirts, and which hairstyles were in and which ones were out. Her group of high-status girls was inevitably correctly attired and adorned, whereas the other girls did not meet her exacting standards. Because she was highly desirable in the eyes of all the children, her judgments carried a lot of weight and were quite devastating. After observing this dynamic, the teacher realized that Keisha's exclusionary comments often followed the more challenging academic and physical activities in the classroom. Although Keisha did well in these activities, she seemed nervous, and the teacher surmised that she might be using her social status to alleviate her anxiety about her skills. The teacher gave her more positive support in her work to help her feel more confident so that she did not have to rely so much on her social power. Another reason for this dynamic was children's developmental concerns about who they were and what others thought of them. For this group, clothing and style composed the arena in which these concerns were being enacted. The teacher decided to develop a social studies curriculum around the issue of clothes and adornments both to use this interest to extend children's learning and to try to put their fashion concerns in a larger and more neutral context. She had groups of children (that included the "insiders" and "outsiders" and both genders) study clothing in other cultures and other historical times. By learning about what had been considered fashionable in earlier times, and how "funny" they looked now, the children began to see their own concerns in a larger and sometimes humorous perspective. Some also became fascinated by clothing in other countries and tried to replicate some of those items, which further diminished the importance of specific articles of clothing in their classroom. Needless to say, this curriculum also served as a good vehicle for broadening the children's knowledge and appreciation for unfamiliar groups of people.

Rejected Children

Interventions for rejected children have been developed and evaluated by many researchers during the past 15 years, and a number of consistent recommendations have emerged. Most studies, however, have been conducted in carefully controlled environments with extra staff to do the actual interventions. Thus, the current challenge is how to implement these interventions in the classrooms with fewer resources and less control.

Rejected children often have multiple problems that both contribute to and result from the rejection. Teachers can sometimes feel overwhelmed trying to provide support for a child who is caught in a negative cycle with his or her peers. Most interventions require some concentrated work with both the child and with his or her classmates, and teachers need to alert (adamantly!) their supervisors that they need additional support, if they are dealing with a chronically rejected child. In preschools, the administrative staff, fellow teachers, or outside consultant can sometimes provide assistance; in the elementary schools intervention plans should be developed with the school counselor, special education team, and other support staff. If there are rejected children from a number of classrooms, school counselors might want to consider some group intervention work to provide the most efficient allocation of resources. If no additional resources are available, teachers can still make some helpful changes and at least try to prevent the child from becoming more entrenched in the rejection cycle. Parent, student, or senior citizen volunteers might be able to offer assistance so that the teachers have more time to devote to the child who is having trouble. However, administrators need to know that, without timely intervention, rejected children are likely to become a much greater drain on resources as they go through the school system.

The first task when confronted with a rejected child is to identify as precisely as possible the factors that are contributing to the rejection. As discussed previously, rejection can stem from a number of sources both within the child and in the social environment. Effective interventions rest on an accurate analysis of the causes. If teachers are alert to a cycle of rejection that is beginning to occur, then intervention may be easier and more timely. For example, in one first grade, a girl who fit the profile of a controversial child became increasingly out of control. As the balance between positive social interactions and disruptions began to tilt toward the latter, she began to evoke increasingly negative responses from the other children. The teacher quickly focused on helping her control her behavior in order to stop the negative cycle from becoming too entrenched. In his observations, the teacher noticed that the disruptions often began during sustained work periods. The child appeared to get frustrated and restless and then tried to engage her peers by creating disturbances. Based on this pattern of the misbehavior, the teacher surmised that the work period was too long for the girl and had her break it up by going to the library for the last part of the time. He also involved her in some cooperative projects that involved a wide range of activities and an opportunity for her to interact positively with her peers. Her parents and the teacher developed a homework plan

that would provide her with some additional help and a chance to feel supported by her parents in her academic work. As her behavior calmed down,
her relationships improved. The teacher commented, however, that he had
to monitor her closely as she could slip easily into a more negative role.
This case illustrates how the quick and accurate identification of the causes
is optimal for developing effective strategies.

Potential goals for rejected children include learning to process social
information more accurately, developing specific social skills, controlling
aggression, increasing academic and physical skills, becoming motivated to
change, and gaining realistic social expectations. The choice of strategies
depends on the particular problems that the child is having. Many methods
have been developed in work with elementary school children. However, a
number have been adapted for preschool schldren. This section will discuss
adaptations in both settings.

Many rejected children misread the social cues; in particular, they
tend to assume that their peers are approaching them with hostile intentions and, in turn, respond with aggression. By placing the rejected child in
cooperative settings and closely monitoring the interactions, teachers (or
counselors) can intervene at crucial moments to challenge the child's
assumptions about the intentions of his partner(s) (Price & Dodge, 1989).
For example, Ray (rejected child) and Amal are working on a joint woodworking construction. When Amal accidentally knocks off the block that
Ray has placed on the structure, the teacher quickly asks Ray what he
thought happened and why it happened. If Ray is assuming that the act was
purposeful, the teacher can have Amal explain why it happened and be
sure that Ray understands. The teacher can then help Ray find an appropriate response to the incident, perhaps asking Amal to be more careful or
simply ignoring the incident and continuing with his work. By intervening
quickly whenever Ray begins to become angry or embroiled in a conflict,
the teacher can interrupt the familiar ways in which he processes information and challenge him with new information and alternative responses.

A second cognitive approach is to teach children specific social skills
that they lack as discussed in Chapter 4. The instructional methods include
teachers modeling and coaching children on ways to approach peers and
interact with them more effectively. To continue with the example of Ray
discussed in the previous paragraph, the teacher, in a separate session, might
do some explicit coaching on how to interpret social cues and how to
respond when feeling angry and how to resolve conflicts. Then, when the
block is accidentally knocked off, she can remind Ray of their previous discussions about ways to react when someone does something you do not like
(e.g., "Remember how we talked about how to tell people to stop doing
something that you don't like? What are some of those words that you could

use now?"). If a school counselor is conducting these coaching and modeling sessions outside of the classroom, teachers need to be kept well informed of their content, so that they can reinforce these concepts in the classroom.

In addition to doing the instructing and coaching, teachers can enlist classmates to support positive social behaviors (Furman & Gavin, 1989). Peers are constantly reinforcing and modeling behaviors, but not always in a positive way. For example, children who submit in the face of threats and attacks may be encouraging a child to be aggressive. Teachers can reverse this pattern by enlisting specific classmates to support the efforts of children who are trying to learn new behaviors. When setting up an activity in groups, teachers might ask the children to compliment each other when they observe a particular behavior (e.g., listening to another, supporting another's idea). In this way, everyone, including the target child, is reinforced for using the desired behaviors. In one study, researchers devised a way of getting children to focus on their social skills by having them make a film of children engaged in friendly conversation, which they would show to students at the local university (Bierman & Furman, 1984). Teachers might adapt this technique by having children make a videotape to show younger peers ways that children can get along with each other. Another technique is the buddy system (Osman, 1982) in which the target child is assigned a buddy who reinforces and models the desired behaviors and helps prevent or defuse negative social interactions. For example, if a child often gets into fights, his buddy can point out when peers are being provocative or can urge the target child to leave when tempers begin to flare.

Most of the methods for social skills training have been developed for elementary school children who are more able than preschoolers to think in hypothetical terms and monitor their own behavior. Some of these techniques have been adapted for preschool children (Mize & Ladd, 1990). For the younger children, puppets can be used to illustrate alternative ways in which children might react to difficult or provocative situations. The authors found that children who received this training became more accepted by peers over the long term. Puppets are a good vehicle for engaging young children, but Mize and Ladd point out that enacted aggression (e.g., hitting, kicking, and yelling) are highly attractive and stimulating to children and suggest that aggressive actions be depicted in a subdued fashion. Stories, flannel board enactments, and teacher enacted skits can also be used to help children develop a wider range of social skills.

In preschool classrooms, the most effective social skills training may be the spontaneous coaching and modeling that preschool teachers do almost continuously. Although puppets, flannel boards, and children's stories are useful in getting the children to consider new strategies, teachers can encourage new behaviors in the context of ongoing interactions. Because children are usually engaged or potentially engaged in peer interactions, preschool teachers have lots of opportunities to offer suggestions (e.g., "Can you tell Nona how you feel with words?" "Lewis, what is some way that you can help Allison, now that you have knocked over her block tower?"). When confronted with a child who is clearly lacking skills to interact successfully, teachers may want to focus their efforts a bit more specifically on that particular child and his or her behavior, but continue to provide ongoing coaching in the classroom.

Because many rejected preschool children lack effective communication skills, teachers often act as interpreters as they facilitate children's peer initiations and ongoing social interactions (Hazen, Black, & Fleming-Johnson, 1984). First, they can help children understand what is going on in a particular group before they try to enter (e.g., "Let's listen to what they're doing here. What are they playing? What could you do to help with that?" (Hazen et al., 1984, p. 34). Second, they can help the children consider alternative strategies for entering if their first attempt fails (e.g., "Kiera is already driving the truck, what could you do to make the truck go better?") If the child cannot think of any alternatives, then the teacher might suggest some specific strategies (e.g., "The truck may need to get some gas, perhaps you could set up a gas station…"). Third, teachers can draw children's attention to their peers' efforts to communicate with them (e.g., "I think that Ricardo is trying to tell you something when he pushes you away from the computer…what is he trying to tell you?" "Did you hear Sarah's question, Quan?"). Fourth, teachers can assist children in making their own communications clearer (e.g., "Clarence, you are making lots of good roaring sounds, but I don't think Pablo knows what you are. Can you tell him what you are playing? Maybe he would like to play too…"). Children often do not make the target of their communications clear, so teachers can remind them to address their comments more explicitly (e.g., "I don't think Jack knows you're talking to him. How can you let him know?") (Hazen et al., 1984, p. 34). In many subtle ways preschool teachers constantly provide social skills training. If teachers are trying to modify a particular child's behavior, they might want to keep track of these spontaneous interventions and assess whether or not they seem to be working.

Children who are rejected because they are aggressive need to learn how to control their aggressive impulses as well as find alternative ways of interacting (Coie & Koeppl, 1990). If children cannot control their anger, they will not have the presence of mind to consider alternative strategies. Coie and Koeppl describe two approaches that might be used alone or together. The first one involves analyzing the environment for all the ways in which children's aggressive actions are being reinforced and trying to eliminate their positive effects. For example, if classmates tend to yield in the face of the aggression, children learn that aggression works; it helps them gain the ends they desire and it gives them power. Sometimes parents or other family members directly or indirectly reinforce children's aggression. Although teachers cannot control all the environmental factors, they can try to organize the classroom and work with peers to minimize the reinforcement of a child's aggression at school. They can eliminate toys and games that seem to inspire his or her aggression and replace them with more neutral materials. Furthermore, teachers can coach peers to ignore or resist a child's aggression so that it is no longer being rewarded. If possible, teachers should work with the child's family to make changes at home that might help reduce a child's level of aggression. Often parents are eager for help, but, if the child's aggression is caused or encouraged by the parents' own behaviors or by their inability or unwillingness to cope, then it is unlikely that teacher's will be able to assist.

The second approach (Coie & Koeppl, 1990) focuses on the self-control of the children. In individual or group training sessions, children learn to recognize their body cues when they are becoming angry and to use self-control statements (e.g., "I know that I'm getting angry, I am going to sit still and take some deep breaths."). Along with learning control, they also receive social skills training so that they learn alternative strategies to replace their aggressive ones. Children can also receive "stress inoculation" in which they experience provocative situations in role-playing situations and practice controlling their angry responses. Behavior change can be transferred to the classroom by having children set weekly goals for themselves and reporting back to their group. This type of program has been effective in reducing aggressive and disruptive behavior in elementary classrooms, especially if it continues over a period of time (18 sessions or more) (Lochman, 1985). It also has resulted in less aggression at home and has helped raise children's self-esteem (Lochman, Burch, Curry, & Lampron, 1984). Because this intervention requires a considerable amount of work with the individual children, it might be done most effectively and efficiently in a group run by the school counselor. As members of a group, these children also can practice their new skills with each other and provide mutual support as they confront the difficulties of trying to change their roles in their respective classrooms.

Preschool children have a hard time anticipating their feelings and often react before they are aware of what they are doing. One 4-year-old boy who was being reprimanded for hitting a child defended himself by saying, "I didn't hit him! I didn't see my arm do anything!" Thus, training sessions which focus on more hypothetical situations are probably not appropriate for these younger children. However, preschool teachers frequently intervene when they see a child losing control and help the child find more acceptable ways of expressing her or his feelings. They encourage children to use words and take out their anger in nonhurtful ways, such as pounding and kneading clay. As part of their regular curriculum, preschool teachers also teach children how to control their bodies and actions with music, creative movement, and yoga. For children who are especially aggressive at this age, teachers can teach them concrete ways to calm themselves, such as breathing deeply or holding or rubbing their arms. When a child is beginning to lose control, the teacher can signal her to remind her to do one of these physical exercises to calm down.

The DUSO kit (Developing Understanding of Self and Others) is an excellent resource for both preschool and early elementary classrooms. With puppets and stories, it provides teachers with excellent tools to help children expand their social strategies and to learn how to manage conflict and help their peers who are having a difficult time in social situations.

Rejected children are often disruptive in the classroom and draw negative attention from both teachers and peers by interfering with everyone's efforts to get work done. Coie and Koeppl (1990) suggest two strategies for counteracting this behavior. First, explicitly rewarding children for on-task behavior may counteract the rewards of disruption and induce them to be more attentive. If children spend more time engaged in their academic work, they may experience more success, which, in turn, might reduce their disruptiveness.

A second strategy is to coach children on academic skills to diminish disruptiveness that has evolved from the fear of academic inadequacy. This training can be modeled after the social skills training in which the remediation focuses on the individual's particular needs. This kind of intervention may also work for children who are becoming isolated from their peers because their skills are less developed than those of their peers. In one kindergarten, the teachers noticed that a child who had been socially very active began to withdraw as her peers became more interested in academic work that she was not ready to do. Although children should not be pushed if they are not ready, some extra help may enable them to participate enough to stay in the social mainstream. If teachers notice that disparities in skill development are beginning to be obvious, they might want to adapt the structure of the classroom activities to mute the social consequences of these gaps. For example, projects might include a wider range of activities (e.g., drawings, acting out a situation, making a structure out of Legos) so that completing a project does not depend as heavily on a few cognitive and fine motor skills. In preschools, the academic work is less of an issue, but teachers may notice that children who have trouble with a particular activity may react by trying to disrupt it. One 3-year-old who was afraid of going down the slide often sat at the bottom of it and refused to let other children use it. The other children reacted by getting frustrated and angry at him. Once the teacher helped him master the slide, he no longer needed to prevent others from using it.

Rejected-withdrawn children who are too shy and anxious to join the social mainstream present a challenge different from that of aggressive-rejected children. They are distinguishable by their low self-esteem, their extreme anxiety, their deference to peers, and their reliance on teachers to solve social problems (Rubin, LeMare, & Lollis, 1990). They need to gain the skills and confidence to approach peers in order to make a positive social adjustment.

Several approaches have been suggested by Rubin et al. (1990). First, these children need experiences that help them to develop some self-confidence. As discussed in Chapter 5, all activities and aspects of the management of the classroom should be designed to promote children's positive self-images. With these very anxious children, however, teachers may want to be especially careful in how they judge their work and the kinds of demands they place on them in order to minimize the chance of these children feeling humiliated. Because rejected-withdrawn children already feel badly about themselves, they will readily believe the worst, so even the most careful criticism may be misinterpreted. Teachers may also identify these children's special interests or skills that might be introduced to their classmates to give these low-status children a chance to be in the advantaged position in the class. Obviously, this kind of intervention has to be carefully planned so that it does not become another humiliating experience. If a child is interested in rocks, but her peers have no interest in the subject, then having her bring in her rock collection would not be a good idea. However, if the class is studying rocks and the children are excited about different geological phenomena, then this child may enjoy being an expert and gain status and visibility in a positive way.

Second, rejected-withdrawn children need to learn how to be more assertive so that they do not feel overwhelmed by their peers and unable to control what occurs in an interaction. Participating in plays or puppet shows in which they might play assertive characters is one way to help these children feel their potential power. In one preschool classroom, the teacher had the quietest children play the monsters when the class enacted *The Wild Things*. These exercises should be done in small and informal groups, as it is unlikely that a withdrawn child would willingly perform in front of the class.

Third, withdrawn-rejected children can be paired with younger or less able children so that they have the opportunity to assert themselves and initiate social interactions without the likelihood of being rejected. In one study (Furman, Rahe, & Hartup, 1979), withdrawn preschool children dramatically increased their rate of interactions with classmates after only ten 20-minute play sessions when they were each paired with a peer who was one year younger. The children who were paired with age-mates also made moderate gains, suggesting that simply being in a protected situation in which rejected-withdrawn children are guaranteed a play partner and no disruptions may have some benefits. These interventions can be adapted easily in most classrooms. Children in the first, second, or third grades might help in the kindergarten a few hours each week. In preschools that have mixed age groups, children might be paired with their younger classmates for special projects. Teachers also might suggest to parents that they try to plan some afterschool activities with the younger children.

In their writings about shy children, Zimbardo and Radl (1981) suggest several classroom strategies that may help to make the environment a comfortable one for shy children. Teachers should be sensitive to children's potential discomfort for being singled out for any reason (including positive ones). These children feel safer if the teacher moves slowly and accepts their need to be on the periphery for a while, before gradually being eased into the social mainstream of the classroom. Teachers need to make the classroom a safe place for these children by clearly being in control of the class and preventing intimidating events such as fights. They also need to watch for potentially painful events such as party invitations and valentines being distributed to some (but not all) of the children in the class. Honig (1987) has reviewed the research on shy children and has added some other suggestions to those of Zimbardo and Radl. For shy children, the optimal classroom has predictable and consistent routines and activities that are organized so that children can interact in very small groups. These children also need teachers who are very warm, accepting, and encouraging and willing to provide support yet encourage independence. To accomplish these goals, teachers need to listen to shy children with great attention and make them feel important, attractive, and lovable. Honig also suggests that training shy children in relaxation exercises and encouraging them to develop a sense of humor may reduce their self consciousness. Coaching children on specific interactive skills, such as entering and leaving groups and asking appropriate questions, may further help these children join the social mainstream.

Extremely withdrawn children may be showing symptoms of severe psychological or family problems that may be beyond the reach of within-class interventions. If children do not seem to respond to some of these efforts, teachers should refer the child and the family for psychological evaluation and therapy.

Rejected children sometimes lack the motivation to change. As discussed previously, many of their behavior patterns are being reinforced and serve, in some ways, to make them feel intact. One approach is to help children reframe the event (Coie & Koeppl, 1990) so that the problem behavior is seen as counterproductive, not as a way of reaching one's goals. For example, Coie and Koeppl found that they could convince children to try to contain their aggressive reactions by pointing out that their peers were manipulating them to make them lose control.

Besides working with the rejected individual, teachers also should scrutinize the role that the peer group plays in causing and/or maintaining the child's rejected status. They may want to think about the peer culture and whether it is contributing in some way to this cycle. Are peers provoking a child to act aggressively? Is a particular child a favorite scapegoat? If so, why do the children need a scapegoat? Are classmates taking advantage of the overdeferent child? Do they treat a particular child as though she does not exist? Based on answers to questions such as these, teachers can consider strategies for working with the peer group that complement interventions focused on the individual. Strategies for intervening with the peer group include increasing the amount of positive contact between the rejected child and peers, nurturing a few positive relationships between the rejected child and his or her classmates, and helping classmates see positive attributes of the rejected child.

The cooperative structures that were described in Chapter 5 can provide ways of increasing positive peer contact among children. In one study with rejected elementary school children, the children who both received social skills training and participated in cooperative groups made more sustained improvement in both peer acceptance and social skills than did their peers who received only social skills training or only participated in a cooperative groups (Bierman & Furman, 1984). A second-grade teacher who used this technique reported that the groups that were most helpful for rejected children were those that were small and had been given clear objectives and procedures so that there were fewer potential disagreements. Another way of increasing peer contact is to enlist the help of some of the more prosocial children to make contact with the rejected child. They might be asked to involve a rejected child on a project or to be the child's "buddy" if a buddy system is in place. The converse of this technique can also be used. One preschool teacher often has the low-status children pick partners for special projects to insure that they have someone to play with and, in a sense, to use the lure of the activity to counterbalance the low status of the child. Teachers, however, need to be sure that children do not resent being with low-status peers, as that would simply increase the alienation. With very anxious children, the groups need to be constructed carefully to be sure that they are in situations in which they can succeed. Probably forming the children into pairs in which there is no possibility of two or more children excluding or overpowering the rejected child is the best format until the child becomes more assertive in his or her peer contacts.

In addition to increasing the amount of time rejected children spend in positive peer interactions, teachers may also want to try to foster more sustained relations with one or two potential friends. Rejected children are sometimes unrealistic about which classmates they can attract and may feel disappointed if they cannot play with the most popular classmates. One or two friends, even if they are low status, can reduce a child's isolation and create a positive environment for the child to develop his social skills. Teachers can watch children in their various contacts and play interests and try to promote relationships between rejected children and their classmates who may not necessarily be popular, but can have a beneficial effect on the rejected child.

Young children tend to see people in an all-or-none context and therefore find it hard to see anything good about a rejected child or to change their perceptions about a child whom they do not like. Teachers can help children see each other in a more differentiated way by using several methods. First, many behaviors of rejected children also are irritating to teachers who sometimes tacitly give classmates permission to scapegoat a rejected child (Osman, 1982). By conveying a positive attitude toward the child, teachers can often reverse the negative cycle of rejection and provocative behavior. As one teacher put it, "We need to find something about each child to like, in fact, to love, and to concentrate on that, but it's not always easy!" When redirecting a child's behavior, teachers should do it as quietly and privately as possible to avoid drawing classmates' attention and adding to their reasons to reject the child. Second, teachers can plan group activities that will make the rejected child's positive behaviors salient (Price & Dodge, 1989). These groups should be structured so that (a) the status of all members is equal; (b) positive attributes of the disliked child become evident during the sessions in order to challenge the preconceived images that the peers have; (c) children cooperate to achieve a shared goal; (d) the disliked children have an opportunity to communicate personal information about themselves and be seen as a distinctive and multifaceted individual; and (e) the social norms of the contact situation favor equality (Cook, 1985). Teachers should monitor these groups carefully to insure that the experience is positive. If they go well, these groups provide rejected children a chance to learn more positive ways of interacting and an opportunity to be seen as a valued group member. Teachers can also insure that children see the changes by making comments about how well the group is going and highlighting the rejected child's contribution.

Teachers might also need to address group attitudes that affect the rejected child's status. If the child is perceived as different from peers because of race, class, culture, family life, or abilities, then teachers need to address these issues in a variety of ways. A multicultural approach (Kendall, 1983; Ramsey, 1987) in which all aspects of the curriculum are infused with the goals of broadening children's perspectives and fostering their respect and appreciation for other ways of life offers many possibilities to approach this problem in a wide range of activities. These guidelines will be discussed in more detail in the later section on cross-group segregation.

In all efforts to intervene with a rejected child and her peer group, we need to maintain clear and realistic goals and help the child do the same. Everyone will be frustrated if the expectations are that this child will become popular. Instead we should think in terms of a "threshold of acceptance" (Oden, 1986) and try to interrupt the cycle of rejection enough to stop the actively negative interactions. Teachers may also look outside of the school for support in this process. Although children may not be able to transform their status in the classroom, they may be able to apply their new social skills with members of a new group, such as an afterschool program, a community art class, a church group, or a neighborhood group. Summer programs can be an excellent opportunity for children to "start fresh" and develop skills and confidence that may enable them to make a better start in the following year. If parents are willing and able to be involved, they can play a key role in facilitating this kind of development. By informing parents about potential problems before they become major ones, teachers can help the parents be most effective when their children are playing in the neighborhood or having friends come and visit. Teachers and parents can arrange visits with classmates that are realistic and may help support potential friendships. They can also collaborate on planning positive extracurricular activities in which children can experience some social success.

Neglected Children

One of the key questions about children who seem to be somewhat invisible to their peers is whether or not they are outside the social mainstream by choice. Those children who are too anxious and withdrawn to participate have already been discussed in the section on rejected children. In this section the focus will be on children who are not necessarily unhappy with their role as less visible players in the classroom. Some children simply prefer to play alone and like to do activities that do not require peers to make them fun. We should not force these children into the social mainstream, but we do need to insure that they are having enough experience so that they will not become isolated later because they lack the skills. Particularly in the preschool, some children are just not ready for a lot of peer involvement. As they develop, they may show more interest, and teachers can support their efforts to join the social life of the classroom. One way to promote their social contacts is to find other children who like to do the same activities and get them in at least physical proximity with each other. As they are involved with parallel play, some opportunities for conversation may arise, and children will have a chance to have some companionable moments even though they are basically working on their own. Teachers can sometimes facilitate these interactions by pointing out similarities in the kinds of projects they are making or encouraging them to help each other out if they need assistance. This kind of encouragement should be done carefully. One teacher tried to encourage a relationship between two very quiet 3-year-old girls. As a result, one girl begin to follow the other one around everywhere and was resoundingly rejected by her peer who was not ready to enter into a more sustained friendship. The goal is not to create best friends or to transform these children into gregarious class leaders, but simply to bring to their attention the fact that other children share their interests. Another goal is to help their classmates, who may be more attracted to their active and outgoing peers, appreciate the skills and presence of these quieter children. Teachers can draw children's attention to accomplishments of these children (e.g., block constructions, stories, art work) when children share their work.

In an effort to integrate neglected children into the classroom, one program was developed for elementary school children, in which popular children were trained to be student–peer facilitators. They worked with neglected children by greeting and praising them, initiating interactions with them, offering academic assistance and social support (during and after school), and modeling more effective behaviors when the neglected child acted in a self-defeating way (Middleton, Zollinger, & Keene, 1986). This program was efficient in terms of maximizing professional time and minimizing classroom disruptions and proved effective in raising the level of the neglected children's social impact and acceptance.

Controversial Children

Children who are controversial are typically active, somewhat heedless but likeable children. Surprisingly they often have low self-esteem, which suggests that they may be ambivalent about some of their disruptive behaviors and the negative consequences they sometimes cause. Sometimes children such as the class clown are "egged on" by their classmates to misbehave. They may feel that they have to comply with their classmates' requests because their position in the classroom rests on their bold behavior. Their classmates in turn reward the misbehavior by paying attention, laughing, and applauding. In these situations, teachers need to help the controversial child see that this attention is an attempt to control his or her behavior and is not necessarily a sign of popularity. The teacher, by being alert to this dynamic also can deflect classmates' provocative behavior when they see it coming and prevent yet another episode. One second grader liked to "dance" en route to the pencil sharpener, causing great delight and disruption among his peers. The teacher learned to move closer to him as soon as he got up from his seat in order to remind him nonverbally to stay in control. She also brought in some tapes and had the children dance during indoor recess so that all the children had time to show off their dancing and teach each other new steps. By interrupting this cycle, and helping the child find alternative outlets, the teacher helped this child avoid getting entangled in an unproductive cycle. Depending on the age and abilities of the child, teachers might want to use role playing, puppets, or small group discussions to help children expand their roles.

Another approach with these children is to help them feel more confident of themselves. Some of the behaviors may be an effort to gain group admiration because they do not feel very self-assured in other areas. One 4-year-old often became very rambunctious whenever his usual friends sat down to do any kind of manipulative activity. He would wheel around the classroom and clown around, trying to draw their attention away from the activity. The teacher realized that he was reacting to his fear of not being able to do these activities and found that when she made a place and time to work with him on these skills, his need to disrupt diminished somewhat.

Many controversial children may not require any particular interventions. They may not be conflicted by their role and instead may enjoy their visibility. However, if they are negatively affecting other children, or if they are dominating the class or galvanizing the children to reject the rules and roles of the teacher, then some efforts to redirect their behavior may be necessary.

PROBLEMATIC RELATIONSHIPS

Children form peer relationships for a variety of needs, some of which may be detrimental for their long-term personal, social, and academic adjustment. Some relationships also continue well after the original attraction wears off, but children do not know how to extricate themselves. An exhaustive account of the different types of relationships is impossible, given the enormous variability in group dynamics. However, a few prototypical situations and possible strategies will be discussed in this section to illustrate ways of analyzing and responding to these problems.

GUIDELINES FOR INTERVENTIONS WITH PROBLEMATIC RELATIONSHIPS

1. Identify the composition, roles, and dynamics of the relationship and why it is so important and compelling to the children involved.
2. Consult with colleagues and parents as appropriate.
3. Generate alternative ways for children to get their needs met outside of the current relationship.

4. Experiment with different group compositions and structures to see how children react to changes in roles and companions.
5. Based on the outcomes in number 4, set up a variety of group and partner activities that support the children to expand their range of contacts and social behaviors and roles.
6. Collaborate with parents on extending the child's friendship network outside of school.

When children are feeling insecure, they often gravitate to very close and exclusive relationships, which, in turn, become quite possessive. In one kindergarten two girls who came to school together played together continuously throughout the day. They always chose the same activity and, if the teachers assigned one of them to do a separate activity, the other one would hang around wistfully until her partner was finished. If one began to show interest in another child, the other one would become very demanding and adamantly exclude the other child. The teacher allowed this intense involvement to continue for a while, because the children clearly needed the security that this relation provided. However, as usually happens, the children began to show signs of feeling confined by the relationship. Their play became increasingly repetitive and their interactions were more listless, yet quarrelsome. The children did not seem to realize why they felt uncomfortable and reacted by becoming even more demanding and possessive of each other. The teacher took advantage of this restlessness to help the girls extricate themselves from this confining twosome. He created some group projects and put the girls on separate teams, but still allowed them time to be together if they wanted it. Gradually, the intensity of the relationship waned and the girls remained friends, but no longer in an exclusionary and possessive way.

Children also form relationships that are a reaction to the social dynamics and structures of the classroom. In a kindergarten classroom two quiet boys sought each other out, in part, the teachers surmised, to protect themselves from some very rambunctious peers. For the most part, the children seemed content, but the teachers were concerned that their social contacts were so limited. Interestingly, another child ended up being the catalyst for change. He also had become less enthralled with some of the more active play and began to play near the two quiet boys. Gradually the three children began to play together and slowly incorporated more classmates. The entry of the first child may have reassured the first two that they would not be overwhelmed or intimidated by the other children in their class.

Another partnership that can be restrictive is when a male and female child create a kind of "pseudomarriage." The children often declare themselves "in love" and widely announce their adult marriage plans. These relations do involve some cross-sex encounters, which is positive in terms of expanding children's range of contacts, but they are often more entangled and constraining than they are broadening. In one first-grade classroom, Felipe "fell in love" with Andrea and spent a great deal of time hovering around her and trying to control her every movement. Andrea initially liked the attention and the status it gave her among the girls, but soon it became irritating and restrictive, especially when she wanted to spend time with other children. She was also aware that her actions controlled Felipe's mood and felt burdened by this responsibility. The teacher was concerned because the relationship was confining, and the emphasis on "being in love" had some sexual overtones that were inappropriate for young children. Moreover, Felipe was starting to be teased by his male peers and seemed to be at risk for becoming rejected by them. The teacher began to separate the two children and often had the boy stay and talk with her for a few minutes as the children went out to recess in order to give Andrea a chance to find her own playmates and become established in a group. She paired Felipe up with other peers and gradually, he began to show interest in becoming part of other groups. He had to overcome some initial resistance because he was known for "wanting to be with the girls," but over time, he became part of a number of groups and no longer focused exclusively on Andrea.

Relationships in which one member is very dominant and the other(s) are submissive can also create problems. First, one child is learning that she can always have her own way, and the other(s) are becoming accustomed to giving in and perhaps setting aside their own priorities. These dynamics are difficult to change because they often meet complementary needs. For example, a submissive child may be relieved to have someone tell her or him what to do; the dominant child prefers to have a compliant partner. Not surprisingly, the dominant child is often more dependent on the submissive one than the other way around. A person cannot dominate unless she has a compliant peer, whereas a submissive child can usually find a group or person who is happy to have a deferent partner. In one pair of 4-year-olds, this pattern became clear when the submissive child was absent. The dominant child tried to draw some other children into his play, but as soon as he began to boss them around they left. On the other hand, when he was absent, his submissive partner readily found other playmates. In this case, the teachers focused their interventions on helping the dominant child feel more more relaxed about letting others take the lead. They put him in groups with more assertive peers; and whenever he started telling his companions what to do, the teachers helped the other child(ren) express their preferences and guided the group through a negotiation process. The teachers constantly reinforced the idea that all the children had good ideas and could contribute to the project at hand. The dominant child gradually became less insistent on having his own way, although he still sought out his more submissive peer whenever he could. By challenging children to change roles and by observing their reactions, teachers can learn more about why particular children need to be dominant, and they can help all the children develop more positive leadership skills. In one classroom, a child who was very dominating participated in a group in which each child had a turn to be "boss." As the children rotated through the boss role, each showed striking differences in their leadership styles and in their abilities to accept direction. The dominating child was very upset whenever he was not the boss, and the exercise failed in terms of helping him learn to be more flexible. However, the teachers gained insights into his need for being in charge that they could use in further interventions. They also realized that several of the other children had a hard time asserting themselves and giving directions. This realization led to some whole-class activities designed to help children develop positive leadership skills.

Submissiveness can also be a means of controlling another person. In one pair of girls, one child appeared to use her submissiveness to insure the loyalty of the dominant child. As she became more and more of a doormat, the dominant child took increasing advantage of her, often belittling her and threatening to find new friends. The submissive child then became more desperate to please and accepted this behavior, which inspired more of it, and so the cycle continued. To try to break this pattern, the teacher worked with the pair to help them equalize their roles under very controlled conditions. She set up a project that required their collaboration and had them take turns directing the project. She coached them on listening to each other and making requests in a polite way. Initially she had to intervene a lot as they frequently slipped back into their old ways of interacting. However, after a while, they began to have more balanced interactions. When they were not working on the project under her guidance, she kept them apart by assigning them to different activities so that they would not undermine their progress in her absence. Gradually the interactions on the project became more egalitarian, and both girls began to spend more time with other classmates. Their relationship did not get fully resolved, as they seemed to drift apart, and the submissive child clearly missed her dominant friend. However, the negative cycle was interrupted enough so that each child was able to develop some new relations and ways of interacting.

Similar to the dominant/submissive relationships are the entanglements that often bind bullies and victims. As discussed in Chapter 4, victims do not necessarily avoid their tormentors and may even provoke bullying behavior. They may have a need to feel victimized or feel that this attention is better than none. Children chronically in the victim/bully roles may need some outside counseling to address their motivations for these self-destructive behaviors. However, a comprehensive program for dealing with bullies and victims has been developed in Norway (Olewus, 1990) and has several features that could be applied in schools in this country. This program encompasses the involvement of the whole school, individual classrooms, and parents. A major feature is the consistently applied sanctions against bullying and the closer monitoring of times when it occurs. Olewus recommends that teachers and students make very explicit class rules against bullying and discuss how well these rules are being followed at regular class meetings. These sanctions should be accompanied by efforts to create a positive class and school social climate by emphasizing cooperative activities and group cohesion. At the individual level, teachers should have serious discussions with both the bullies and the victims and have conferences with their parents in order to understand why this behavior is occurring and to collaborate with the parents in trying to stop it. Teachers also need to support and protect the victims and help them gain more peer acceptance. Many of the ideas discussed in the section on rejected children are applicable to this effort.

Intense rivalry between two children can spur children to work hard at academic tasks or athletic skills, but may also have a deleterious effect on the classroom and the children involved. First, focusing only on outdoing a peer does not promote real learning or skill acquisition and can create a considerable amount of tension, not only between the protagonists but in the whole classroom. Children not directly involved in the rivalry often feel diminished because they are not doing as well as either of the rivals. It also sets a competitive tone which distracts everyone from the real educational goals of the classroom. When these rivalries emerge, teachers might first want ask themselves if there is anything about the structure of the classroom that might be fostering these feelings. The use of ability groups, the ways in which children's accomplishments are displayed and discussed, and the reward system for performance are a few of the factors that might inadvertently be setting a competitive tone. Sometimes the school environment promotes competition between classrooms and individuals in ways that convey the idea that winning is everything. Obviously, the messages that children are hearing from their parents are also germane. If a child has been told that she must always be the best in whatever she does, she may need to constantly reassure herself by outdoing her peers. Teachers can try to counteract this dynamic by setting up cooperative and collaborative activities that simply remove the possibility of "winning" and "being the best" so that the children do not have anything to be rivalrous over and can see peers as partners as opposed to opponents. For example, learning games can be structured so that children keep a cumulative group score rather than individual ones. In some activities, competition jeopardizes performance so children have to confront the negative effects of being overly competitive. For example, if children are putting on a play, they must work together, not compete with each other. Activities can also be structured to help children focus on improving their own performance and the intrinsic value of the activity instead of measuring success by outdoing others. Instead of having children do the same project which allows for easy comparison among peers, teachers can have children work in interest groups in which the topic of study is the most salient factor, not the comparative accomplishments of individuals.

Finally, teachers sometimes confront relationships in which the teacher is the common enemy, and children form a bond by resisting the work and rules of the classroom. Usually these dynamics do not emerge strongly until the children approach adolescence, but some early childhood teachers work with young children who already feel alienated from school and collaborate in avoiding work and creating disruptions. Sometimes this dynamic is caused by children's anxiety about their adequacy to do the work. In this case, teachers can try to help children feel more confident and provide training to increase children's chances of success. Often this alienation reflects a distance and disharmony between the children and the school which may mean that the program is not sensitive to the children's particular backgrounds and is not meeting their needs in some basic ways. Some ways of ameliorating this type of situation are discussed in the next section.

CROSS-GROUP SEGREGATION

Children often divide themselves by sex, race, social class, culture, and abilities, and these divisions are sometimes fairly rigid and hard to bridge. At the same time, our children must become more comfortable and effective in interacting in a diverse society and functioning in a variety of roles. Thus, reducing the distance between groups is an important part of fostering children's social development.

GUIDELINES FOR INTERVENTIONS IN CROSS-GROUP SEGREGATION

1. Assess the extent of the segregation; are there some children who "cross over" or are the groups totally separate.
2. Analyze the factors that functionally contribute to the segregation (e.g., behavior patterns, language differences, level of assertiveness).
3. Establish realistic goals of expanding children's range of friendships; do not expect to eliminate completely same-group preference.

4. Set up groups and partnerships where members of different groups can come together as equal participants.
5. Move materials and modify areas in the classroom to attract different people to particular activities and create new group constellations based on shared interests.

When we notice that children are dividing themselves along gender, racial, cultural, or class lines, we first need to observe in order to decipher why and how this separation is occurring. In the case of gender cleavage, the obvious factors are play style and activity preference. With other differences, the contributing factors may not be so obvious. As discussed in Chapter 3, subtle variations in verbal and nonverbal language, as well as more salient differences such as lack of a shared language can create a sense of unfamiliarity and discourage children from spending time together. Teachers can analyze how these differences work by observing what happens when children in the different groups are together. Do they fight? Do they seem bewildered by each other? Do they lack a common activity? One conversation overheard in a 4-year-old classroom illustrates how these divisions perpetuate themselves.

> Richard and Sarah are in the housekeeping area. They had previously made a big point about playing together. They are banging pots and pans around and Sarah suggests that they make a pizza and have a party. Richard looks puzzled but nods his head. As Sarah begins to "cook," Richard bangs his pan more and more loudly and begins to gesture wildly at Derrick across the classroom. "Look it's a monster! He's coming to get us!" He begins to toss pots and pans in the air as he continues yelling. Sarah looks exasperated, puts her hands on her hips and says slowly and deliberately "We are not playing monsters! We are making pizza!" Richard looks crestfallen and puts down his pans. He stands around watching Sarah for a few minutes and then mumbles something about needing to go to the bathroom and leaves the area.

If some children engage in cross-group contacts, teachers might watch them to see how they negotiate the differences. These "bridge" children may provide some clues about what activities and strategies might be effective in reducing the divisions. Teachers might also design classroom structures and grouping patterns in which these children can facilitate contacts between children who do not usually interact.

The immediate goal may not be to have people from different groups become best friends, but rather to be able to interact in a comfortable and productive way that may eventually lead to friendship. For example, close cross-sex friendships are rare in many preschool and most elementary classrooms. Given the gender differences in play style and interests, the peer pressure to remain in single-sex groups, and the salience of sex differences in the larger society (e.g., media roles, emphasis on sex-typed clothing, etc.), the chances of many cross-sex friendships actually developing are slim. However, boys and girls can interact in a relaxed and mutually supportive way when they are involved in absorbing projects in groups that the teacher has formed (Thorne, 1986). The distinction between work partners and friends discussed in Chapter 3 may be helpful when planning strategies to increase intergroup contact and relationships. Group collaboration provides opportunities for children, at least momentarily, to see each other as competent individuals and to develop some mutual respect, even if they do not become friends. Although children from racial or cultural groups initially may feel uncomfortable with each other, they may find, within the context of shared goals, that they have more in common than they had assumed. By creating situations in which children become familiar with each other, teachers can facilitate the development of potential friendships.

The formation of teams that are composed of children from the different groups is the most obvious way of integrating children who might not seek each other out on their own. The structure of these groups should insure that all members have equal status and a stake in accomplishing a shared goal. The guidelines discussed in Chapter 5 and in the section on rejected children in this chapter all apply to this method of increasing cross-group contacts and affiliation. When children are at different developmental levels, the challenge of creating equal status and opportunity within each group is considerable. One approach is to design projects that include a number of different types of tasks, so that a child's skill at drawing or role playing can compensate for poor writing or reading skills. Children who are delayed in all areas might be assigned special tasks that are within their reach, such as compiling and stapling the book that the group has composed together. However, these assignments should be made carefully so that children are not viewed as marginal members. Using a range of media, such as recording on tape or performing a skit, allows children who may have weaker academic skills to participate fully as group members.

In preschools where groups are more spontaneously formed, children can be encouraged to interact with a wider range of peers in a number of ways. One common technique is to arrange the room to bring children who usually play separately into closer proximity. For example, if the block and housekeeping areas are near each other, then the boys and girls may interact more. Often these encounters consist of the boys attacking the housekeeping area under the guise of being bad guys or monsters. These invasions are usually repelled by the girls, creating cross-group antagonisms. Teachers can help the children find ways to integrate both kinds of play. For example, Corsaro (1985) describes how he convinced the attacking male fire-breathing dragons to use their fire to help the girls cook dinner and keep the babies warm. Another teacher put a suitcase in the role-playing area that stimulated a great deal of travel play and then space travel which involved both boys and girls in a number of roles. A kindergarten/first-grade teacher said that the time she had the most gender-integrated play in her classroom was when she made the block and housekeeping areas into a farm. The blocks became the field, the house was the farm house, and she added an area that was the store. As children planted seeds, harvested vegetables, took them to the market, and prepared food, all the participants moved in and out of the areas and engaged in all of the related activities. In one preschool classroom, the teachers removed the barrier between the housekeeping and blocks and found that the frequency of cross-sex contacts among the younger children increased considerably (Kinsman & Berk, 1979). Two kindergarten teachers constructed an "Outer Space" center in what was formerly the housekeeping and block areas (Theokas, 1991). They found that the number of cross-sex contacts increased markedly during the period of time that the space center was available. Moreover, the rate of cross-sex cooperative play steadily increased during this period, suggesting that, as they spent more time together, the boys and girls learned how to interact with each other more effectively. Disappointingly, the number of cross-sex contacts plummeted as soon as the areas became housekeeping and blocks again. A month later, however, the rate of cross-sex contacts had gone up again, close to the level it was during the space center. Thus, the creation of an exciting, but relatively gender neutral area, seems to have had a long-term positive effect on children's willingness to play with opposite-sex peers.

A second technique is to move materials around so that areas become attractive both to boys and girls and to children who have different interests and abilities. One teacher had the children paint using matchbox cars and trucks to spread the paint. This activity lured a number of boys who usually resisted art activities and they happily joined the art regulars in making "truck paintings." Putting the dolls into the block corner and encouraging the children to create structures for the babies can attract new children into that area and provide a novel stimulus for those who are usually there.

A third strategy is to use some desirable activity to lure children into mixed group situations. In one classroom, the children were allowed to go in small groups on to the adjacent porch. It was a very popular activity, and the children were always clamoring to be allowed to go. To reduce the gender cleavage in the classroom, the teacher told children that if they wanted to go out on the porch, they had to invite a child of the opposite sex to go with them. Sometimes the children felt that the sacrifice was too great and chose not to use the porch, but most complied and, once they were outside, played well together. When trying to bring boys and girls together, teachers may want to form groups of four or five so that there are at least two members of each sex. Larger mixed-sex groups appear to have more cooperative and longer interactions than cross-sex dyads (Ramsey, 1990). The activity preferences of boys and girls are fairly predictable, but children from different ethnic backgrounds may divide themselves in a variety of ways. However, the same principle of using activities to attract children from different groups can be applied across numerous divisions.

Beyond bringing children from different groups in contact with each other, we also need to be sure that the content of the curriculum encourages children to respect and appreciate each other and each others' backgrounds and abilities. Reading material, topics in social studies and science, math problems, role-play props, pictures on the wall, and art projects should all be scrutinized for how equally and authentically they represent different gender, racial, cultural, economic, and ability groups. Underlying assumptions about family composition and sexual orientation should also be examined. Many families and groups are underrepresented in curriculum materials, pictures, and books, which contributes to some children's alienation from school and their invisibility to children who are members of overrepresented groups. To compensate for this disparity, teachers can develop curriculum around the specific backgrounds of children in their classrooms and involve family members in various projects to convey more explicitly the value of individuals' and families' experiences. For example, in the curriculum on clothing described in an earlier section on popular children, the teacher invited parents to bring in their old clothes and show the children styles that they used to wear. Also several parents recently had immigrated from Haiti and they brought in articles of Haitian clothing, which increased the interactions and mutual interest between the children whose parents were born in the United States and the children of recent arrivals. Almost all curriculum activities can be adapted in similar ways.

Children sometimes divide themselves along social class lines, partly because each group has different experiences in terms of access to materials. One kindergarten teacher noticed that her children from low-income families were sometimes left out of conversations that focused on the latest toy fads, be they mechanical gadgets or exotic dolls. She raised some money and bought a few of these toys for the classroom, so that all children could have access to them. Although this intervention did not address some of the more basic and long-lasting social class divisions, the teacher found that it did reduce the numbers of conversations that were divided by social class.

Reducing the separation between differently abled children poses some

challenges beyond those presented by gender, ethnic, and social class segregation. In the latter divisions, the children have the potential for becoming
familiar to each other and finding some common ground. When children
have different abilities, the range of shared activities and common experience and knowledge may be limited by actual physical differences. At the
same time, playing with same-age peers is the most effective way of teaching social skills to children with special needs (McHale, 1981). To be successful, programs for socially integrating children with disabilities must be
carefully planned and often require training of both the mainstreamed children and their peers. One second-grade teacher who had a hearing-
impaired child in her room set up a discussion in which the child and the
special education teacher described how people become deaf, demonstrated
how different hearing aids worked, and taught the children some sign language. The teacher reported that the children were fascinated by this information, and she felt that, as a result, the children were more comfortable
with their hearing-impaired classmate and more effective in communicating with him.

Sometimes teachers and parents are concerned that programs designed
to accommodate children with disabilities will not be challenging enough
for nondisabled children and may have a deleterious effect on their development. However, in one study of children in heterogeneous groups, the
only effects were a reduction of inappropriate play behaviors by severely
delayed children; no detrimental effects were observed for children at any
level (Guralnick, 1981). In fact, interacting with handicapped children
may increase children's awareness and appreciation of others' perspectives
and abilities to adapt to them. Children who participated in cooperative
groups with mildly retarded classmates revised their perceptions and
became more accepting of their retarded peers (Ballard, Corman, Gottlieb,
& Kaufman, 1977). In one program, peer facilitators were trained to support and accommodate to the restricted skills of autisticlike peers (Strain,
1985). They learned how to take more responsibility for interactions with
peers who were not responsive and to provide the physical support that
their autisticlike partners needed (e.g., placing the puzzle piece in that hand
of a child who did not respond to the suggestion to pick it up). This program was successful both in the development of social problem-solving
skills of the peer facilitators and in the increased level of positive social
behavior on the part of the autisticlike children. Thus, integrating children
with different abilities can facilitate the social development of all the children in a classroom group.

In many ways, methods of integrating children with disabilities are similar to those for integrating rejected children. Children with a range of abilities have been integrated successfully into group projects that are carefully

designed to incorporate a number of ability levels and are preceded by some social skills training for all members (Ballard et al., 1977). As with rejected children, some handicapped youngsters also benefit if the peer group experiences are supplemented by direct social skills instruction. (Odom, Jenkins, Speltz, & DeKlyen, 1982). Teachers and children should approach the integration of children with different abilities realistically. Particularly in the case of children with severe problems, gaining a high level of popularity is unlikely. However, for many children gaining some degree of acceptance and one or two peers that consider them as friends may be sufficient to make them feel comfortable in the classroom (Ballard et al., 1977). Teachers also need to be realistic about what they can do and be sure that they have adequate support from administrators, special education consultants, and guidance counselors to implement these programs.

CONFLICTS

Conflicts are an inevitable part of any classroom. Children have genuine conflicts of interest over the use and distribution of materials, the ascendency of different ideas, the adherence to particular rules, and the desire to control each others' behaviors. Although they can disrupt the classroom, conflicts should not simply be suppressed. To function in groups, children need to learn how to simultaneously meet their own needs and accommodate the needs of others. Conflicts are part of that process as children learn how to coordinate their own and others' perspectives and weigh their own needs against those of their peers. Because young children are only beginning to be aware of different perspectives, they have a difficult time resolving conflicts, but, at the same time, can benefit from the experience of trying. While engaged in a conflict, children are confronting the reality that their needs and perspectives are not necessarily shared by everyone. They also need to find a way of resolving the dispute that will satisfy all the protagonists. Thus, these episodes can be used to promote children's awareness of others' perspectives and their social problem-solving skills.

GUIDELINES FOR INTERVENING IN CONFLICTS

1. Analyze the conflict in terms of its seriousness and its potential to lead to harm. In particular, be aware of cultural differences in how children react to disputes, because the same behaviors may not signify the same level of intensity in all cultures.
2. Support children's efforts to manage conflicts, rather than rush to implement an expedient solution.

3. Teach children skills in talking through conflicts before they are asked to exercise these skills during a conflict.
4. Move in slowly when children are engaged in a conflict so that you are not shortcircuiting their efforts to negotiate.
5. Use conflicts to support children's developing ideas about how the social world works.
6. Watch conflict patterns to see if there are any particular areas, times of day, or types of activities that seem to be conducive to conflicts.
7. Analyze these patterns and make changes to prevent recurring conflicts.

Teachers often wonder about if and when they should intervene in children's disputes. Most agree that, if the conflict is momentary and the children are able to resolve it, they should be left alone. We also need to be aware of cultural differences in how children express frustration and anger. Loud voices and angry gestures may signal an imminent fight in some groups, but not in other groups. Conversely, quiet arguments are not necessarily less intense than noisy ones. However, if the situation is getting out of control, the children seem stuck, or one child is at an obvious disadvantage, then teachers should offer assistance. When making these decisions, teachers also should consider the individuals involved and their relationship. Some children are more likely to escalate conflict, others are able to manage it. Children who are friends are more likely to arrive at an amicable resolution than two nonfriends. On the other hand, some friendships are conflictual and every action becomes a point of contention.

When teachers have decided to intervene, they often try to get children to use words to express their feelings, to talk *to* each other, not *about* each other, to tell each other how the other's actions affected them, and to try to come to an equitable solution. Because children tend to resist this process, they often have to be guided through it very specifically (e.g., "Sondria, please tell Aletha what she did that bothered you....Now, Aletha, tell Sondria why you did that....It sounds as though the real problem is that you both want to play with the same doll....Can you think of any ways that you both can play with the doll?...Sondria, that's a good idea, one of you will be the mother and one of you will be the babysitter....Do you like that idea Aletha?...How are you going to decide which one will be the mother and which one will be the babysitter?...Now that you know what you will be doing, let's go back to the doll corner and you two can begin to play.").

One problem that teachers often encounter is that children are too angry to engage in this kind of conversation. Obviously the tears and active aggression have to be brought under control before children can begin to engage in this process. One teacher has her children "find a clear space" which is away from the contested objects and/or area. This action symbolizes the beginning of a new interaction and creates a neutral context for the discussion. Practically, this technique also prevents the protagonists from making a grab for the desired object and derailing the discussion. Teachers can also help children calm down by comforting them, having them take a few deep breaths, and getting them to relax for a few minutes. If the children are really upset, then efforts to resolve the conflict may have to wait until the protagonists have had a chance to get away and gain some distance from the conflict.

Most teachers agree that "talking through" the conflict is a good way of teaching conflict resolution, but many admit that they rarely implement this technique because it takes too much time. They find that it is more expedient to simply remove the contested object, separate the children, distract them with another activity or give them a time-out. Teaching children how to sit down and actively resolve conflicts requires that they learn a new way of interacting with each other, a new vocabulary, and some sophisticated social problem-solving skills. Teachers can prepare children to use this technique by demonstrating it with puppets, flannel board stories, and role plays so that the children have some idea of how to proceed before they are confronted with a specific conflict. The DUSO kit (mentioned previously) has several relevant stories and exercises. Several activities are also included in Wichert's book *Keeping the Peace* (1989) and Crary's book *Kids Can Cooperate* (1984). When teachers are setting up groups that will be working together, they can include specific instructions about conflict resolution. In one kindergarten, children were taught how to follow this procedure, first with puppet shows and stories, then with careful guidance when they were engaged in actual conflicts. As they became more adept at the process, the children were able to resolve their conflicts more and more independently. Thus, an initial investment in teaching this technique may end up saving time because the children can take care of many disputes without involving the teacher. Moreover, children who learn these skills one year can build on them the following year. When asked if she taught children conflict resolution skills, one first-grade teacher said that she no longer had to because the children mastered them in kindergarten.

Elementary school children who are more aware of each others' needs and feelings are able to use this awareness to make these discussions more meaningful. Preschoolers, on the other hand, are often simply unable to "see" another's perspective and so making this process meaningful for them requires that it be done in a very concrete way. One teacher of 3-year-old children described the process as "orchestrating" a conversation between two children. She found that, given her children's inability to describe (and in some cases recognize) their feelings, she often had to provide the words (e.g., "Evan, you look as though something is wrong...can you tell me what it is?...are you feeling sad?...angry....”), the reasons (e.g., “You seemed to get upset right after Kimberly came over to the blocks....Can you tell me what made you feel that way?...”), and the solutions (e.g., “Let’s go over and see if Kimberly can help you with your building....”). The teacher felt that, in some ways, she was walking the children through a process that they were not fully engaged in and did not quite understand. However, she concluded that it was useful, because the children were learning that they had to do something with each other after a conflict and that they could not simply leave or complain to a teacher. The teacher, by translating more sophisticated concepts into meaningful terms, is stretching children’s capabilities and helping them gain the necessary skills. In orchestrating children’s conflict resolutions, the teacher is working in the child’s zone of proximal development, her potential skills that are evident when she is being assisted or guided by an adult or more mature peer. In this kind of intervention, the teacher is initially quite directive, but gives the children more independence as they gain the required skills. Even when the teacher is directing the conversation, he is stimulating children to be aware of the the effects of their actions, not simply telling them what to do. For example, he might ask children “How do you think Eduardo is feeling after you hit him? What can you do to make him feel better?” as opposed to simply directing the child, “Tell Eduardo that you’re sorry.” Thus, at the preschool level, teachers may be helping children to recognize that conflicts must be followed by some procedure, giving them some vocabulary for describing their feelings, and fostering their early awareness of others’ perspectives, not necessarily expecting them to fully engage in the process of conflict resolution.

In one somewhat unexpected way this technique can reduce the level of conflict between the protagonists. When teachers tell children that they must sit together and not play with anything until they have come to a solution, the children sometimes react by quickly resolving the conflict so that they can get back to their play. In this case, the teacher and the method function as “the common enemy” that can create a cooperative bond directed towards fulfilling the conditions as quickly as possible. Some teachers have expressed concern that, under these conditions, the children may be going through the motions without really thinking about the process. However, even if they are not fully engaged in the process, children are learning that they must deal with their fellow protagonist and the source of conflict and cannot simply leave, fight, or rely on an adult.

7

Activities and Resources for Teaching About Social Relationships

Previous chapters of this book have focused on the social development and understanding of children in the context of their ongoing interactions with peers and adults in the classroom. This chapter will review activities and resources that enable children to consider various aspects of social relations from sources other than their own experiences. Activities such as stories, problem-solving tasks, enactments, and games often provide a space in which children can reflect on particular social dynamics that they may not be able to recognize or resolve within the context of their own interactions. Many of the resources and activities described in this chapter can be used to promote a number of the goals of this book. The first three sections reflect the cognitive and emotional aspects of social development and include materials related to understanding the distinct nature of different social relationships, recognizing the power and importance of relationships, and becoming aware of the effects of external events and pressures on relationships (e.g., a family moving away). The fourth and fifth sections address specific behaviors and attitudes that help children initiate and maintain friendships and cope with the lack of friends. The final two sections focus on the broader social context of relationships and emphasize the appreciation of diversity and the commitment to social responsibility.

Children's books are a primary vehicle for this kind of teaching. By engaging children in stories, we enable our young readers and listeners to empathize with different experiences and points of view and experience a wide range of social dilemmas. Every story is rife with possibilities. Besides reading the story, teachers can stimulate children's thinking by discussing various aspects of the plot and characters. Children can engage in problem-solving activities by predicting the outcome of the story when they are part way through or by making up new endings when they are finished. When children role play situations and characters in a book, they learn how to perceive situations from a variety of perspectives and literally be "in another person's shoes." Teachers can focus the children's attention on various aspects of a story by changing the plot a little and challenging children to imagine how that might affect the outcome—in other words, the original story can become a stimulus for a wide variety of activities. The books discussed in this chapter are listed in Appendix 3, and may be a valuable resource for teachers to use and adapt in ways that are appropriate for their particular class.

Children's stories can be used to develop curricula in a number of areas. Many projects are inspired by favorite stories. Children can make pictures, murals, collages, and sculptures to portray various characters and episodes. Also they enjoy making up songs to accompany a story and to dramatize some of the events. Children can hone their dramatic skills by enacting stories and perhaps putting on more formal plays and puppet shows for younger peers. Stories that take place in different historical times and regions of the country and the world often enliven social studies curricula by adding an element of human interest. Biographies of inventors and scientists can inject life into science curricula (e.g., the biographies of George Washington Carver, Thomas Edison, Marie Curie). Even math problems can be written to relate to a favorite classroom story. Elementary-school children can calculate how many miles Harriet Tubman had to travel in her various escape routes from the South; they can do endless math projects on the statistics of famous sports players such as Jackie Robinson. Younger children can focus on concepts of big and small with books such as *Amos and Boris*.

The major problem with children's books is the disproportionate number of stories about white middle-class children and the relative paucity of good stories that represent a wide range of lifestyles and social and economic circumstances. Despite efforts to counteract this imbalance, the distribution of stories included in this chapter is still weighted in favor of white middle-class experiences. Teachers may want to augment commercially available books by writing and illustrating their own stories using photographs of children in their classrooms and communities. Children and parents can participate in this process, often with wonderful results.

THE NATURE OF DIFFERENT SOCIAL RELATIONSHIPS

Children experience the fact that relationships differ; their interactions with their parents are distinct from those with their peers; some people are strangers, others are familiar. They encounter some people in very limited roles (e.g., the checker at the supermarket) and interact with others in more complex and ongoing ways (e.g., teachers at school). Their contacts with some people are friendly; with others, their encounters may be fairly cold or even hostile. In classroom stories, games, and discussions, children can make these distinctions more consciously and consider the sources and implications of these differences. By analyzing a range of social relations and how they differ, children expand their ideas about relationships and gain a context for looking at their own relationships more objectively.

Stories

Relationships within families offer a wide variety of interactions, problems, and vehicles for understanding social and emotional issues. Sibling relations are often a complex juxtaposition of intense rivalry and mutual devotion. Children learn that they can be extremely angry, yet deeply committed to each other. One book that illustrates this tension is *I Hate My Brother Harry* in which a little girl is tormented by her 7-year-old brother's incessant teasing (e.g., the green frosting is made of ground-up frogs). At the same time she sees some glimpses of his affection for her (e.g., bringing home library books for her when she is sick) and realizes that love and conflict can coexist. In *Timothy Too!* an older boy is annoyed by his younger brother's insistence on being with him all the time. However, when the little boy meets a child his own age and no longer is as interested, his older brother misses the attention and invites both boys to listen to him practice the saxophone. As often happens in sibling relations, children dislike each other, yet miss the sibling if s/he is no longer around. Both *Peter's Chair* and *She Come Home Bringing Me That Little Baby Girl* tell how a young boy's jealousy about the arrival of his new sister gives way to acceptance of his role as the big brother. Books with these themes can provide a way for children to talk about their sibling relations, especially if they find them troubling. They also illustrate the fact that relationships do not have to be destroyed by conflict and misunderstanding, which is a common assumption among young children. Other books show the affection and caring that can occur between siblings. *Do Like Kyla* portrays a warm relationship in which the younger sibling always imitates her older sister Kyla. In the last scene Kyla imitates her younger sister, suggesting that the relationship might become more reciprocal.

Stories about grandparents illustrate the range of relationships children can have with adults and help them differentiate the roles of different adults in their lives. In *I Dance in My Red Pajamas* a young girl delights in knowing her grandparents in a different way than her parents do. Despite her parents' instructions to be quiet while visiting her grandparents, the little girl and her grandparents enjoy a rambunctious evening of music and dancing. In *Grandma Is Somebody Special*, a young girl savors ways in which her relationship with her grandmother is different from her relationship with her parents.

Children's views of family relations can be expanded by reading stories about many different kinds of families. One excellent book is *Families: A Celebration of Diversity, Commitment, and Love*. It is a series of photographic essays that portray many different families—single parents, blended families, adopted families, gay families, multiracial families, and communal groups. The theme that families are people who love each other and take care of each other is illustrated in a number of vignettes. A number of books about divorce are also available. Some illustrate well the continuity of relationships and love despite the disruptions of parents' separating and moving.

A number of stories have been written about children and neighborhood friends of different ages. *A Special Trade* chronicles a child's relationship with an elderly neighbor. The older man takes Nelly for stroller rides when she is a baby, teaches her how to walk as a toddler, and joins her on many adventures as she grows into a young girl. When he becomes ill and is confined to a wheelchair, she reciprocates by taking him for walks and keeping him company. This story portrays a very special cross-age relationship and ways in which relationships change as people get older. It also demonstrates how people play reciprocal roles in each others' lives and the many ways in which they can show their caring for each other. *Hi Mrs. Mallory*, which is story of a friendship between a young African–American girl and an elderly impoverished white woman, illustrates how people of different ages and backgrounds can find a common ground and mutually enjoy each others' lives and skills. *Honey I Love* is a wonderful book of poems that describe how love is present in a range of relationships—when a child hugs her mother, admires her friend's ability to run, or wonders why her elderly aunt is so withdrawn.

These examples are a tiny sample of the vast literature about different social relationships. Almost all children's stories involve some kind of social dynamic. As teachers read these stories, they can use them to help children see the wide range of social relationships that exist and that are part of their lives. By asking children how the story might change if the characters were different (e.g., same-age friends instead of siblings), teachers can help children identify how relationships are unique, yet share many characteristics.

Activities

Thinking Games.   One way for children to expand and clarify their ideas about relationships is to participate in focused discussions with teachers and/or peers about specific social dilemmas that challenge their current assumptions. A technique called "thinking games," developed by Carolyn Edwards (1986) in her book *Promoting Moral and Social Development in Young Children: Creative Approaches for the Classroom*, can be adapted to numerous social relations issues. Briefly, thinking games, which can either be conducted in adult–child interviews or as whole-group discussions, consist of enacted story situations that conclude with a problem or dilemma which the children are encouraged to answer. The questions are designed not to elicit correct answers but to help children articulate their assumptions and recognize some of the contradictions in their own reasoning. For example, in one thinking game about friendship, a child is greeted by two friends; one gives her a toy and the other gives her a hug. The children are then asked which child is the best friend. In response to this dilemma, the children have to consider whether material gain or emotional support is a more valued aspect of friendship. As they hear each others' comments, children begin to question their own assumptions. Young children may initially feel that the toy, which is more concrete, is the more valued resource, but after hearing peers debate about how they feel about hugs versus toys, they may begin to question this belief. Thinking games are designed not to change children's minds, but rather to help children recognize their assumptions, play with alternative ones, and to stretch their understanding to incorporate new ideas.

Almost any peer issue can be cast in this framework and be portrayed with a variety of media. Adult enactments, puppets, small dolls, and video vignettes can be used to stimulate children's discussions. Teachers can use events and comments that occur in the classroom for ideas. For example, one first-grade teacher realized that the children were segregating themselves into very rigid groups and excluding outsiders. He invented a skit about two children who learn that they have some common interests and enjoy talking to each other. However, they belong to different groups, and, at lunch time, they have to make a decision about whether to sit with their respective groups or with each other. As the children discussed what the characters should do, they had to consider the relative merits and constraints of group loyalty versus interpersonal preferences. They did not come to any conclusions, but began to recognize the different perspectives and the dilemmas each presented. Subsequently, the teacher noticed some abatement in the rigidity of the groups and heard children refer to the skit in their discussions about group membership.

Adult–child relations and authority and moral issues can also be addressed with these activities. One of Edwards' skits involves the dilemma of a young child who has been told by her mother that she cannot go outside until she cleans up her room. Meanwhile, a circus parade is coming near her house, and she will miss it if she has to clean up her room first. As children discuss whether or not the child should sneak out of the house, and whether or not the mother is being fair, they are considering aspects of the authority relation between parents and children. Older children, who are beginning to realize that adults are not as omniscient and infallible as they once thought, might consider dilemmas such as whether an adult is bad if they mistakenly give the wrong instructions, or if they use "bad" language under duress. These situations encourage children to recognize their changing perceptions of adults and to discuss them in a challenging, yet safe context.

Teachers interested in implementing this type of curriculum should read Carolyn Edwards' book for more detailed instructions on developing and implementing these activities. The activities in the book are designed specifically for preschool children, but, as seen in some of the previous examples, the format can be adapted for use with older children.

Role Playing. Children often spontaneously role play different characters including parents and children, media figures, and community workers. In this context they portray many social relationships, and we can challenge children's assumptions by suggesting slightly different conditions or simply raising questions. When children are enacting various superhero roles, teachers might question the assumptions about why certain characters get to do certain things and have particular powers and what would happen if these change. If the police are arresting the robber, the teacher might want to raise the question about whether that would be right if the person had not really robbed the house, but it only had looked as though he had. Young children often enact "Good Guys and Bad Guys" themes; teachers might ask children about these categories and see if the children can define attributes that characterize these two groups. These suggestions do not imply that teachers should start imposing story lines on children's dramatic play. If a group of children, however, has been playing a theme over and over again, teachers can challenge the children to look at their assumptions and generate some new scripts and situations that stretch their ideas about social relations.

Older children often enjoy putting on plays. Most of these have issues related to social relations as their themes. For example, the story of Goldilocks is about access to resources and the protection of private property. Teachers may change the standard script to present new dilemmas and see if children can generate novel solutions. For example, Goldilocks might be portrayed as a poor homeless person who is hungry and tired and has no place to go. Instead of seeing her only as an intruder, the children will have to think about what is fair in terms of distribution of property and whether there are times when it is alright for someone to take things from another. The class can be challenged to create a new ending in which everyone is given an equal share of the resources. This project may stimulate a lot of discussion about property rights versus fair distribution of resources, which can also contribute to children's moral reasoning.

THE POWER AND IMPORTANCE OF RELATIONSHIPS

Young children are beginning to appreciate the ways in which relationships influence all aspects of our lives. With stories and activities, we can help them understand that a relationship is greater than the "sum of its parts," that two people can accomplish what a single person cannot, and that groups can affect the outcome of an event more than an individual can. Older children can begin to understand how, cumulatively, relationships affect the social fabric of communities and the larger society, and, in some cases, the course of historical events.

In group times, teachers can incorporate songs such as "A Very Good Friend of Mine" or "Won't You Be My Friend?" (published in Patty Zeitlin's song book, A Song Is a Rainbow) that celebrate the pleasures and recognize some of the difficulties of close friendships.

Stories

Many stories for young children demonstrate the ways in which two or more people (often depicted as animals) can accomplish more by collaborating. One classic example is the book Amos and Boris, the story of a mouse and a whale who, because of their different sizes and skills, are able to rescue each other from death. The story of Ton and Pon humorously illustrates the difficulties as well as the advantages of working together. Another account of people working together for a common goal is a recent book A Chair for My Mother. Here a single mother, her mother, and her daughter work to save money for a comfortable chair after they lose all of their furniture in a fire. The story also shows a community pitching in to help families in need. Amoko and Efua Bear illustrates the need for friends to take care of each other. Amoko, a young Ghanaian girl, loves her bear, but is often careless and almost loses him as a result.

For older children, biographies of famous people and accounts of history are rife with examples of how people's relationships with parents, teachers, friends, and enemies changed the course of their lives and, in some cases, of the course of history. One classic example is the famous relationship between Helen Keller and her teacher Annie Sullivan as depicted in Helen

Keller. Many biographies of Martin Luther King (e.g., *Meet Martin Luther King, Jr.*, and *Martin Luther King, Jr.: A Biography for Young Children*) show how his childhood experiences of being excluded by white people inspired him to want to change the rules of society so that black children would no longer have to experience that kind of pain. *The Story of Jackie Robinson: Bravest Man in Baseball* portrays several different relations that show the contrast between the harsh cruelties of racism and the supportive relations among team members. Teachers can draw children's attention to this facet of a story by having children imagine how the plot might have turned out if two particular characters had not known each other.

Activities

Cooperative Games.   One way for children to experience more con-cretely the power of working together is to adapt activity structures so that children experience a shift from individual goals to cooperative ones. As children experience these modifications, they can consider how their rela-tions with their peers changed. For example, children might paint separate pictures of a field trip and then be organized into groups to collaborate on a set of murals. Afterwards, the teacher could ask the children what they remember from the two activities and if they did things differently. The children may not necessarily feel that the cooperative activity was better (e.g., they say "we fought more"), but they may still recognize that the murals are more elaborate than their individual projects. Regardless of their reactions, they have an experience that gives them some insight into the ways in which goals affect relationships and interactions. Teachers can also modify games so that children experience a shift from competitive goals to cooperative ones and vice versa. Preschool children might partici-pate in two rounds of musical chairs, one that has the traditional elimina-tion and another that is the cooperative nonelimination version. For older children, teachers might shift from competitive tag to cooperative tag, in which the children who are caught join the chaser, holding hands, so that soon there is a large line of children running together. After these games, teachers can ask the students which one was more fun and why. They can probe students about how they felt about each other in each game to see if children can articulate the effects of cooperation and competition on their feelings and perceptions about their peers. Preschool children cannot stand back and compare their two experiences as well as their older peers can, but they might be able to say which game they preferred and felt hap-pier playing. Terry Orlick's two books on cooperative games provide excel-lent guidelines and examples for restructuring games to be more coopera-tive. An earlier article of mine also outlines ways of adapting activities to be more cooperative (Ramsey, 1980). Crary's book *Kids Can Cooperate*, the Luvmours' book *Everybody Wins*, and Wichert's book *Keeping the Peace* are other good sources for activities.

THE EFFECTS OF EXTERNAL EVENTS AND PRESSURES ON RELATIONSHIPS

Relationships are often affected by events and dynamics in children's environments. Children need to understand this phenomenon so that they can recover from disruptions and changes that inevitably occur in their relationships. Young children may be able to understand only that when a family moves, friends miss each other. Older children can begin to comprehend the fact that lack of jobs may force families to move, which, in turn, disrupts social relations.

Stories

Moving and having to make new friends or being left behind and mourning the loss of the departed friend are common themes in children's books. *We Are Best Friends* is a story about two boys who are best friends and have to adjust when one of them moves away. Each one writes to the other affirming their best friendship, yet also describing new friends that they have met. This story illustrates the initial devastation that children experience, yet also their resilience in finding new friends and continuing to enjoy their social lives. A similar story line is found in *My Friend William Moved Away*. The narrative and pictures poignantly describe the children's feelings as they watch the house being emptied of furniture and say their final goodbyes. The child who is left feels lost, but begins to make friends with a little girl on the street who tells him that she has felt lonely watching his friendship with William. In a slightly more complex story, *My Best Friend Moved Away*, the child who is left behind tries to thwart the move by destroying the "For Sale" sign on his friend Nick's house. After the move has occurred, the two children have a reunion which does not go well because Nick appears to prefer his new friends and no longer likes the activities that he and his friend had shared before. In a way this ending affirms children's worst fears, but the protagonist makes plans to play with some other friends in the neighborhood, which supports the idea that while children are hurt by these events, they also can survive them. *Lonely Lula Cat* illustrates the loneliness of the child who moves. Lula Cat misses her friends and tries to enlist the aid of the Star, the Moon, and the Owl to return her to her old home and former friends. Instead the owl helps her write to her former friends, and Lula Cat begins to appreciate her new friends instead of simply missing her old ones. Unfortunately, most books about moving are set in white middle-class suburban settings and so offer a limited perspective on this kind of disruption. One exception is *Blue Willow*, which is the story of a migrant worker family and the painful disruptions that their young daughter experiences every time they move. Another story, *Jyoti's Journey*, portrays the frightening, yet exciting transition from Jyoti's family and home in India to a new apartment and way of life in London.

Death is another type of loss which, fortunately, occurs less frequently among children's friends and is the subject of fewer books for children. Most books about death have focused on grandparents or pets. One in which a friend dies (although he is an elderly friend) is called *Badger's Parting Gifts*. The animal friends of the badger mourn his death, but soon realize that their friend has left each of them a special ability that they can pass on to others. In this way, the badger remains with them in a special way. In *I Had a Friend Named Peter*, Betsy learns that her friend Peter has been hit by a car and killed. She has to confront the finality of death and the painful realization that recently in anger she had told Peter she never wanted to see him again. In her grief, she begins to find ways of positively remembering Peter by comforting Peter's parents and making a picture that captures her friendship and images of Peter to help herself and others remember her friend. This book is an excellent resource for children who are dealing with issues about dying and also illustrates that our appreciation and caring for others do not have to end when they die.

Differences in lifestyles, resources, and values also affect relationships. In one story, *Sam Comes to Dinner*, Seymour the cat, who is an expert cook, is preparing a meal for his gourmet friends, when Sam the dog from next door, who does not fit in with Seymour's friends, tries to get invited to the dinner party. In the ensuing conflict between the meticulous Seymour and the messy Sam, the dinner is ruined and Seymour's friends leave in a huff. Sam stays and helps Seymour who comes to appreciate Sam's good nature and loyalty more than the elegance of his snobbish friends. In the end, Seymour even condescends to prepare hamburgers for Sam. In *A Country Tale*, Cleo and Lucy are two cats who enjoy each other's company and life in the country. However, their friendship is disrupted when a visiting wealthy cat favors Cleo and excludes Lucy. As Cleo tries harder and harder to fit into the wealthy lifestyle she becomes more distant from her former friend. When she realizes how little her wealthy patron really cares about her, she returns with chagrin and some relief to her former friendship and simpler way of life. In both these stories, one partner wishes to identify him or herself with a more prestigious group and ignores the more enduring qualities of loyalty and friendship in the process. Often, due to the influence of media advertisements, children are infatuated with the expensive clothes or toys of their peers which may blind them to more important qualities and cause them to exclude children who do not have the same material advantage. These stories also provide a challenge to our society's emphasis on commercialism and material wealth that children adopt all too readily.

Biographies often provide vivid examples of how people's relationships have been affected by their economic, political, and historical environment. Biographies of people such as Martin Luther King, Florence Nightingale, George Washington Carver, Jackie Robinson, Harriet Tubman, Thomas Jefferson, Jane Addams, and Amelia Earhart illustrate how people's lives and relations are affected by their sociohistorical context. They also show how people can affect those circumstances.

Activities

Thinking Games.   One way children can consider the effects of outside circumstances is to engage in thinking games about whether or not relationships continue to exist when two people are separated. One common event in our society is that families relocate for new jobs. Because young children often assume that friendships depend on proximity, they often feel concerned about whether friendships will endure once they no longer see each other on a daily basis. For older children, these situations could include stories about immigration, either for political or economic reasons, and the subsequent impact on families and friendships. Teachers could also include stories about children who are friends, but their relationship is not approved by their parents because of differences in economic, racial, ethnic, or religious backgrounds. Although they have only a limited understanding of social class, children could talk about what happens when one friend can afford more toys and activities than the other one. Teachers might develop a dilemma might about a child who has to decide whether or not to engage in an activity (e.g., dancing or gymnastic lessons) that her friend cannot afford to do.

LEARNING TO BE A GOOD FRIEND

As teachers guide children in their social interactions, they are constantly giving advice about how to nurture relationships and resolve interactional and relational problems. Numerous games and stories provide situations and models to heighten children's awareness of the nature of friendships and their limitations and the skills required to maintain these relationships. This learning can be facilitated if children see the benefits of these skills by looking at other people's experience as well as their own. Teachers can also incorporate songs such as "There Is Always Something You Can Do" by Sarah Pirtle, which can be found in her book *Discovery Sessions*.

Stories

Many stories describe children's friendships in which some kind of disruption or misunderstanding occurs. The protagonists usually assume that the friendship is over forever, which is what many young children feel. In most stories the friends are reunited in a way that helps them become more aware of others' perspectives and more accepting of the limitations of a particular friend and the friendship itself. Teachers can emphasize these aspects of the stories by asking children to identify what the protagonists did to cause the disruption and by having the class think about what other ways the characters might have handled the situation to prevent or ameliorate the problem. Children can also identify skills and understanding that the characters demonstrate as they attempt to resolve the conflict. When pointing out these possibilities, teachers should avoid being "preachy" and maintain a more inquiring tone in which they and the children together try to identify the social problems and their causes and consider alternative solutions. One group of teachers and researchers combined several books about friendship to create a curriculum unit on story comprehension and social learning (Moss & Oden, 1983).

Some books depict the day-to-day ups and downs of friendships and can be used to help children see that friendships can continue even if there are fights and misunderstandings. For young children, who often assume that a fight will end a relationship, these books can be used to challenge that assumption and encourage them to resolve problems that arise. *Rosie and Michael* and *Oliver and Allison's Week* are good examples of this plot, as they describe the disputes, exchanges, and most of all the trust that exist between two friends. The fact that they depict cross-gender relationships may also be useful for teachers who are trying to encourage children to cross the gender divide. *Frog and Toad Are Friends* is another story which describes multiple encounters between two friends, some positive and some negative. Throughout the book, it is clear that the relationship is stable and not jeopardized by the vicissitudes of the daily interactions.

A number of books about children's friendships focus on events that occur when one partner is gone for a while. These disruptions often, for a time, appear fatal to the friendships. The resolution usually involves both parties becoming more aware and appreciative of each other and, in some cases, able to allow more flexibility and independence in the relationships. In *Best Friends* (by Steven Kellogg) Kathy's best friend Louise goes away to camp and, to Kathy's dismay, has a wonderful time. The book describes

Kathy's jealous fantasies which may help children recognize their jealousies and possessiveness. The crisis is resolved when Louise admits how much she missed Kathy and the two girls agree to share in the care of a newborn puppy. *Maude and Sally* is the story about two best friends who share everything from sandwiches to dress-up clothes. When Sally goes to camp for the summer, Maude has to accept the fact that Sally is making new friends, and learns that she can enjoy other children as well. When Sally returns, their tight twosome is expanded to include Maude's new friend. *Patrick and Ted* has a similar plot, told in a more simplified way and suitable for younger children. Here the friends are depicted as bears. One leaves for the summer, and their reunion in the fall is rocky because each one has changed and has added new interests that they do not always share. The resolution involves a recommitment to the friendship as well as a recognition that they also will be more independent. In *Jealousy*, Rosalie is quarantined with the mumps for two weeks, during which time her best friend Victor becomes friends with Sophie. In the ensuing struggle over Victor, the two girls realize that they can enjoy being part of a threesome.

Several books depict misunderstandings that cause hurt feelings and fears that the friendship is over. In *Best Friends* (by Miriam Cohen), two preschool boys illustrate the fragileness of early friendships. In a typical preschool exchange, children are talking about who is friends with whom and one of the pair is named as someone else's best friend, which causes a rupture in the friendship. They are reconciled when they collaborate to save some baby chicks from dying of the cold. In a similar plot about older children, Happy *Birthday, Ronald Morgan* depicts a conflict between two friends who each feel that the other one has failed to support him during Show and Tell. The conflict is resolved when one friend plans a surprise birthday party for the other.

Other books describe the effects of missed appointments on partners' mutual trust. In *Rollo and Juliet Forever* two cats who are fast friends make plans to spend the afternoon together. When Rollo fails to show up, Juliet is infuriated and retaliates by pouring tomato juice over Rollo's head. He responds in kind, and the battle is on. They enjoy hating each other for a few weeks and then make tentative and halting efforts towards reconciliation. Eventually they do reunite and accept the fact that fights are an inevitable part of a relationship, but need not mar their closeness. With a similar plot, *Not at Home* is the story of Sally's disappointment when she goes to spend the night at her friend Lorraine's house only to discover that she is not at home. An older neighbor helps Sally to cheer up, but she is still furious and so is Lorraine, who thinks that Sally never came. After avoiding each other for a week, the two children finally have a showdown in which they learn of the misunderstanding and then make up and plan a new weekend together. This book concretely illustrates how people can interpret the same event in two different ways, which may help children grasp the idea that each person has his or her own perspective. A misunderstanding is also the cause of a dispute in the *Hating Book* which focuses on a child's hurt feelings when her best friend is clearly avoiding her. When she finally goes to talk with her friend, she learns that the source of the problem is a misreporting of her comment about her friend's new dress. *I'm Not Oscar's Friend Anymore* illustrates how quickly friendships can disintegrate when the partners misunderstand and hurt each other. The narrator imagines all the terrible things that his former friend Oscar must be feeling as a result of their destroyed friendship, which of course describes how he himself is feeling. However, when he approaches Oscar, the latter does not even remember the fight, which is another good illustration of the differences in people's interpretations of events. *Three Wishes* is a story of young girl Nobie who finds a lucky penny and begins to make wishes. After a fight with her good friend Victor, she wishes he would leave, and he does. She then regrets the fulfillment of her wish and makes a new one, hoping that he will return. In the end they are reconciled. *Lyle and Humus* is the story of Lyle, a monkey, and Humus, an elephant, who are best friends and in the same act in a traveling circus. One day Humus and Lyle have a misunderstanding and refuse to talk to each other despite the efforts of their friends to effect a reconciliation. Their friendship is finally, and dramatically, restored when Humus rescues Lyle from drowning. An amusing account of misunderstanding between friends is found in *Clancy's Coat*. A farmer and tailor have quarreled because the latter's cow has trampled the former's garden. When the farmer brings his overcoat to the tailor to be mended, the former friends are distant. For a number of reasons, the tailor never gets around to fixing the coat, but the friendship slowly mends as the two men gradually reach out to each other and demonstrate their mutual caring.

A number of other familiar themes have been depicted in children's books. Possessiveness, a common issue among young children is illustrated in *It's Mine* in which two very young friends get along well when they do not have any toys, but instantly fight if they do. Only the impending ruin of a picnic by their refusal to share food finally convinces them to share. In a story about slightly older children, *Katherine's Doll*, the friendship between Molly and Katherine is strained when they argue about who gets to play with Katherine's new doll. After they fight over the doll, they realize that the doll has become more important than their friendship and are able to put the doll into perspective and see that it is less valuable than a friend. Somewhat related to this theme is the problem of competition. In *Battle Day at Camp Delmont* Maude and Sally go to camp together and are inseparable in all of their activities. They also provide physical and emotional support for each other as they face the social and physical challenges at camp. However, on Battle Day, they end up on different teams and have to confront divided loyalties. In a climatic event, they play each other in the decisive tennis match and realize that they can compete, yet still be friends.

Jealousy is another feeling that often undermines both one's self-concept and peer relationships. In *Timothy Goes to School,* the main character feels diminished by the superior talents of Claude, a classmate who taunts him for his inexperience. He discovers that Violet feels the same way about Grace. They play together and unite to ridicule their superior peers. Unfortunately, the book leaves the reader with the conclusion that taunting others is a way of feeling better about oneself. The book would have a more positive message if Violet and Timothy had realized the limitations of uniting against common enemies and had formed an alliance based on mutual respect and interests rather than the common enemy syndrome. If teachers use this book, they should include in a critique of the ending (e.g., "The children are still being mean to each other. What would be a better way to end this story?"). *Happy Birthday, Crystal* shows a different kind of jealousy when Susan, who is friends with Crystal at school goes to her birthday party and becomes aware of Sherri who lives next door and obviously spends a lot more time with Crystal. Her feelings of alienation and jealousy keep her from enjoying the party until Crystal shows her appreciation for Susan. Related to jealousy is children's possessiveness of each other. *The Best Friends Club* illustrates how exclusive relations can be too restrictive and, as one of the protagonists says, "No fun!" This story might be used to help children break out of overly tight friendships and see the advantages of expanding their contacts. Because the original friends are a boy and girl, this book portrays a cross-sex friendship, although the roles are somewhat stereotyped.

Trust in a friendship is another issue that occurs in children's lives and is reflected in children's books. *Tough Eddie* is the story of a boy who likes to play with his doll house, but is afraid that he will be ridiculed by his peers. He makes a point to dress and act in ways that merit him the title of "Tough Eddie." After he proves to himself that he can be truly brave in the face of a bee, he is confident enough to show others his doll house. In *Hound and Bear,* the bear begins to distrust in his friend the hound because the latter is always playing tricks on him. The hound realizes that the friendship is important and makes a genuine gesture that restores the good will between the two friends. In *Octavia Told Me a Secret,* the narrator is tempted to reveal her friend's secret as she is torn between loyalty to her friend and the excitement of knowing a secret. She finally decides not to reveal the secret because the friendship is more important than the agony of not telling a secret.

Teachers can also help children understand that we all approach social interactions in different ways. Several stories illustrate the range of human behavior and the pitfalls that accompany various social approaches. *The Shy Little Girl* is the story of Anne who is very shy and excluded by her peers. When a new girl arrives at school, they discover many things in common and form a close relationship, which, in turn, helps Anne become more assertive in the classroom. In a contrasting story, *Attila the Angry*, an irascible squirrel becomes aware of the social costs of his temper tantrums. He learns how to control his feelings and express them appropriately. This story can be used to illustrate differences in children's affective responses and also as a vehicle for helping children who tend to get angry to learn how to modulate their responses. *Taking Care of Melvin* illustrates the pitfalls of being too altruistic and the need to balance demands of others with one's own needs. Melvin Dog is so generous that he exhausts himself doing favors for other people. When he finally collapses, his friends gather around and take care of him. He then becomes very demanding and exacting, which, in turn, alienates his friends. Through these experiences, he and his friends learn how to balance their own needs and those of their friends.

Activities

Cooperative Games. Children's participation in cooperative activities can provide more concrete experiences to convey the importance of learning particular social skills and social problem solving strategies. As mentioned in Chapters 5 and 6, teachers can prepare children for these activities and projects by discussing these skills and perhaps using enactments and stories to make them more tangible. In their discussions with the children about how the groups are functioning, teachers can also help children see how specific skills and awareness help (or potentially help) groups to function more successfully. *Discovery Sessions* includes many activities to help children learn these skills.

Social Problem-Solving Exercises. The curriculum should also include a program to teach children social problem-solving skills. Several of the methods described in Chapters 5 and 6 can be adapted for this purpose. The DUSO kit also provides many props and stories for engaging children in this kind of learning. Other good programs are *The Lollipop Dragon* film strip series and *Aware: Activities for Social Development*. Teachers can also develop their own programs that reflect the needs and issues of the children in their classroom.

LACK OF FRIENDS

At some point almost all children worry about whether or not they will have friends and how well they are accepted by their peer group. Children may also be concerned about rejected classmates and wonder why that dynamic is happening and perhaps worry about what they can do to help. In other words, concerns about lack of friends are common to all children, not simply those that have been labeled as rejected.

Stories

With books and activities all children can discuss their fears about social isolation and perhaps gain some sensitivity to the plight of children who do not have many or any friends. Unfortunately, few children's books deal directly with the issue of peer rejection. Most often stories about making new friends center on children who are alone because they are new to the community or have had their best friend move away. *Attila the Angry*, mentioned in the previous section is one of the few books that directly addresses the social costs of aggression. Most stories about the lack of friends come to the happy conclusion that many friends are available, and that children can easily initiate new relationships. For some children this salubrious outcome is not a possibility if they are being excluded because of their behavior, abilities, or racial, ethnic, or class background. In short, children's stories often portray easy solutions to more complex problems. Teachers may want to adapt existing stories or have the children write some of their own stories to present a more realistic picture of children's social problems. One book that does not portray a happy ending is *The New Friend* (Zolotow). A close friendship between two girls ends when one finds a new friend. The one left behind dreams of finding a new friend too, but is still mourning the loss of her old companion at the end of the book.

Stories about making new friends, however, do deal with many of the issues and can be used to help children both explore their own social fears and become more sensitive to those of their peers. In *Anna's Secret Friend*, a young Japanese girl is lonely after her family moves to a new community. She begins to receive anonymous gifts and finally discovers her benefactor is a shy little girl in her neighborhood. They happily go off to play. In a somewhat more complex story, *A Tiger Called Thomas*, Thomas has decided that no one in his new neighborhood likes him and refuses to leave his front porch. Finally on Halloween, disguised as a tiger, Thomas ventures forth and discovers that all of his neighbors know his name and are eager to get to know him. This book illustrates the ease with which many people assume no one likes them and the value in learning that this assumption is wrong.

Some stories about making new friends address the issue of initial antag-onisms that occur when children confront unfamiliar people. In *Addie Meets Max*, a young girl is angry when her new next door neighbor's dog barks at her. After a few antagonistic exchanges, Addie and Max discover some common interests and start to become friends. *The New Boy on the Sidewalk* begins with a similar antagonism between a child and a new neigh-bor. After several insulting encounters they realize that they can learn something from each other and then defend each other from the taunts of some older boys. In *Horrible Hannah*, two sisters are mislead by a warning sign to assume that the new girl who has moved in across the street is horri-ble. When they discover their mistake, they learn a lesson about jumping to conclusions about others. Books with these kinds of plots can be used to help children see the importance of not making quick and rigid judgments about peers based on superficial and partial information.

Another theme related to lack of friends is the development of a posi-tive self-image. When children feel unappreciated by their peers, they often feel badly about themselves. At the same time, if they can concentrate on enjoying their own company, they may gain some self-appreciation and, in turn, be more appealing to others. In *The 329th Friend*, Emery Raccoon invites 328 fellow animals to dinner in the hopes of making some friends. He spends days preparing a huge feast only to be ignored by his guests who seem interested only in the food and each other. He retreats to his house and has his dinner by himself and finds that he enjoys his own company. When he returns to his guests, he discovers that they have missed him and are all eager to thank him and to become his friend. After they leave, Emery labors long into the night cleaning up the dishes, but enjoys the time with himself.

Activities

Teachers can adapt techniques described in Chapters 5 and 6 to engage the children in discussions about their fears of not having friends and to recog-nize the pain of peers who are in that position. Children might engage in problem-solving activities that focus on strategies to overcome rejection and on ways in which one might assist a rejected peer. If a new child will be entering the classroom, teachers might want to present a skit about being a new child in order to help children empathize with the newcomer and plan ways to welcome him. For older children who are more consciously worried about what others think of them, a skit about a child who imagines that her classmates are talking about her might help children express these concerns and think of ways to alleviate those anxieties in themselves and others (e.g., "If I think that a group of kids is laughing at me, later I might ask the one I know the best if that was true or not." "If I notice that someone is looking worried and left out, I might go over and talk to him, so he knows that we are not laughing at him."). Children might write stories about the most embarrassing thing that ever happened to them as a way of seeing that everyone sometimes humiliated and "out of it."

APPRECIATION OF DIVERSITY

Respect and appreciation for diversity and the unlearning of stereotypes is a crucial aspect of children's social development. These goals have been woven into all of the applications that have been mentioned in previous chapters. Likewise, activities related to friendship and other social relations can also support these goals.

First, stories, pictures, and examples should all be scrutinized for the people and the life styles they portray. The cumulative message should also convey that people from different groups can form positive relationships. Unfortunately, few books provide examples of positive cross-group relationships. Many of the books cited previously show white same-race, same-age friends. A few books cited below represent more diversity, but they are far less common than the books that depict white middle-class suburban lifestyles.

Stories

Any curriculum on social relations should include efforts to dispel children's stereotypes of other people. *Oliver Button Is a Sissy* illustrates how children who do not conform to traditional gender roles are often scapegoated by their peers. Oliver prefers dancing school to football and is teased by his peers. However, after demonstrating his dancing skills in a local talent show, his peers reevaluate their view of him. In a contrasting story, *Who's Afraid of Ernestine?*, a young boy is terrified of Ernestine with whom he has to do a school project. He is scared by her friendly teasing and imagines her as an evil witch or dragon lady. When he finally gets around to working with her on the project, he discovers that she is pleasant and considerate, and he reverses his opinion. He particularly appreciates the fact that she likes him in spite of his faults. In the classic story *Best Friends for Frances*, Frances is excluded by Albert and his friends because she is a girl. She challenges this rejection by joining with her younger sister, whom she has usually rejected, to engage in an outing that excludes boys. The result of this adventure is that her friend Albert recognizes the foolishness of excluding on the basis of sex, and Frances gains some appreciation for her younger sister. In *Somebody Else's Child*, a much-loved school-bus driver makes a disparaging remark about adopted children only to discover later that one of the children that he has befriended is adopted. The story not only illustrates the pain and misunderstanding that comes from prejudicial beliefs, but also shows a positive relationship between an older person and a child. *Sneetches* is a humorous illustration of the costs and folly of one group setting itself above another one.

A number of stories use animals to illustrate the fact that friends can be very different. The story of *The 329th Friend* mentioned previously is a good example of this theme. The book *May I Bring a Friend?* playfully illustrates what would happen if a child brought his friends from the zoo to various meals with the king and queen. For young children the story of *Play with Me* shows a child's delight when the forest animals come and play with her. *A Boy, a Dog, a Frog and a Friend* is a book without words that shows a humorous series of events in which a fishing trip is disrupted by a snapping turtle. When the turtle appears to be dead as a result of his struggle with the dog and the frog, the boy, dog, and frog mourn its loss. The turtle is then revived and all four cheerfully go off together. In *Friends*, which was originally published in Germany, a rooster, mouse, and pig team up to have a wonderful day bicycling, playing in the village pond, and picking cherries. Their differences in skills and statures complement each other well and they are able to accomplish a number of challenging tasks. However, when they try to spend the night together, they cannot find a place where they can all fit or be comfortable, so they agree that even close friends must sometimes be apart. *Charlotte's Web* is a classic story about friends who are very different, yet use their different abilities to help each other.

Many stories illustrate the value of friendships with people of different ages groups. *Not So Fast Songololo* is the story of a young boy and his grandmother spending a day in the city. As they ride the bus into town and do their errands, the warmth and caring between them is obvious. At the end of the story the grandmother buys her grandchild a pair of new red sneakers. The fact that the sneakers are called tackies (the story was published in England) is intriguing to young children and can be used to show that people use different words for similar items. *Hi, Mrs. Mallory!* portrays a friendship between a young African–American girl and an elderly, poor white woman. Mrs. Mallory teaches Li'l Bits how to say the alphabet backwards, tells wonderful poems and stories, and makes delicious meals. The young girl helps Mrs. Mallory by bringing in wood and writing out her checks and letters. When Mrs. Mallory dies, Li'l Bits is devastated, but comforted by her memories and the presence of Mrs. Mallory's dog. *I Know a Lady* also shows the affection between a young girl and an elderly woman. As the young child recounts all of the kind things that her older neighbor does for her and her friends, she wonders about the childhood of the old lady and if she had a similar friend. A *Special Trade*, described earlier, also illustrates the closeness that can develop between children and older friends. Overcoming an initial reluctance to become friends with an elderly woman is the theme of *Miss Maggie*. This story, which takes place in Appalachia, tells of how young Nat overcame his fears and suspicions of his elderly neighbor Miss Maggie, after he found her mourning the death of her pet bird. The ensuing friendship illustrates the compatibility of interests that often occur between the very young and the very old. *My War with Mrs. Galloway* also shows the evolution from antagonism to affection as it traces the relation between Becca and her babysitter. The initial cycle of rebelliousness and reprimands gives way to a supportive relation when the two look after Becca's cat who is having kittens. Both of these latter books can be used to bring up issues related to stereotyping and prejudice.

Some books illustrate friendships that cross ethnic and racial lines. *Hi, Mrs. Mallory!* is one example in which the relationship seems very warm and spontaneous. *My Little Island* is a story about a child who returns to the Caribbean Island of his birth and brings his white friend with him. The story and pictures mostly portray events and traditions on the island, and though little explicit reference is made to the relationship between the two boys, their shared enjoyment of the island and their experiences is evident in the text and pictures. In *Jamaica's Find*, a young African–American girl finds a stuffed dog. She decides to keep it, but changes her mind when she realizes that it probably belongs to another child who may miss the dog. After she turns the dog into the park guard, she meets the dog's owner, a young white child, and dog and owner are reunited. The story ends with Jamaica and her new friend going off to play together. Some books that depict cross-ethnic relations are written with a focus on describing the life style of a particular ethnic group and are less insightful in terms of portraying a relationship between people. An example of this kind of book is *My Best Friend Martha Rodriguez* which is a detailed account of life in a Mexican–American family and the friendship between Martha and her Anglo–American friend Kathy. Although the book presents a positive and informative picture of Martha's family, the relationship between the two girls seems somewhat contrived. A similar book is *A Day with Ling*, which is informative about a Chinese family living in Great Britain, but the relationship between the two girls (one English and one Chinese) seems stilted and static. These stories are useful in their information about various groups, but do not really portray friendships. In contrast *Blue Willow* is an engaging story about a friendship between a Mexican–American child and the daughter of white migrant farm workers.

Some books, written for slightly older children, describe some of the challenges and misperceptions that are inherent in cross-cultural relations.

Plain Girl is the story of Esther, a young Amish girl, who has her first contact with non-Amish people when she begins school. Because her older brother left the Amish community after he went to school, she is wary of all the temptations of the outside world. As she gets to know other children and learns how other Amish children have negotiated their two worlds, her fears dissipate. A similar theme is found in the story of *Little Navajo Bluebird*, in which a young Navajo girl grieves at the departure of her older sister to boarding school and worries about what will happen to her when her turn comes. Her aunt, who has attended school and has returned to her people, helps her see how she can learn some white ways and yet remain a Navajo. The one problem with this book is that, because it was written in 1940, it accepts of the assumption that Native American children should go to boarding schools, a practice long condemned by many tribal leaders. If teachers use this book, they should balance it with pictures of contemporary tribal schools.

Some books have been written to show children how people are the same yet different. Although they are not really stories, children can enjoy looking at the pictures and making comparisons between the images they see and their own lives. Some examples of these books are *My Friends Live in Many Places*, *A Country Far Away*, and *Why Am I Different?*.

A few stories have tackled more difficult subjects such as friendships that occur between people with different abilities and resources. In *My Friend Jacob* a young African–American boy and an older white boy who is retarded are friends. The story illustrates how each one contributes to the relationship and how they learn from each other. The heroine in *Secrets Aren't Always for Keeps* has to decide if she will tell her Australian penpal about her learning disability when the penpal arrives for a visit. The story describes her fears of being rejected and shows how her secrecy undermines her friendship. In *What's the Hurry, Harry?* a young boy who likes to race around learns from his friend who has to use crutches and cannot move fast that there are some advantages in going more slowly and taking the time to do things well and appreciate the world around him. *About Handicaps* describes in photographs and words a young child's fears about his friend's cerebral palsy. His father helps him express his concerns and finds many ways of reassuring him. The story ends as the two friends, each using their particular skills, jointly make a large structure.

A book that tackles the difficult question of poverty is *Tramp* which portrays a lonely child's friendship with a tramp. The boy's initial reaction to the tramp is one of disgust, and he enlists the other neighborhood children to attack the tramp. Afterwards, however, he feels remorse and begins to bring food to the tramp, despite his anxiety about stealing it from other family members (a good dilemma for discussing moral conflicts). Although the tramp does not talk, he becomes a major figure in the boy's fantasy games. When the tramp leaves, the boy is devastated, but, because of his relation with the tramp, is now able to start making friends with other children in his neighborhood. *The Paper Crane* also shows how people with few material resources can make a great contribution. In this story a restaurant owner and his son's business has been ruined by the rerouting of a highway. One night they give a free dinner to a poor elderly man who cannot pay, but offers instead a paper crane. When the boy claps, the paper crane dances. People come from miles around to see the dancing crane, and the restaurant is prosperous again. *The Gift* is a moving story of a young Vietnamese–American girl who becomes friends with her elderly neighbor Nana Marie. Every day they spend many hours talking, and Anna learns many stories about the elderly woman's life. When Nana Marie becomes ill and loses her sight, Anna is devastated. However, she thinks of a wonderful gift for her friend; she will describe in detail all of the natural changes and phenomena that Nana Marie loves. This book illustrates the warmth and mutual caring that can occur between people of different ages and backgrounds. This story might also be used to begin a language arts activity in which children think of ways to describe what they have seen to a blind person. Not only would this activity help them develop more descriptive skills, but also would heighten their awareness of others' perspectives.

For older children, teachers can include some of the previously mentioned stories and biographies (e.g., *Blue Willow*, biographies of Martin Luther King, Jackie Robinson) that directly describe the effects of discrimination and the isolation that occur when groups are segregated. Children in early elementary grades are very conscious about what is and is not fair and this concern can be fostered by exposing them to some of the injustices of the larger society.

Activities

Efforts to support children's appreciation of diversity need to occur throughout the curriculum and physical setting. All decisions from what photographs to display to the seating arrangement of children should be considered from the perspective of how to foster an appreciation of diversity. For more specific ideas, readers can turn to Louise Derman-Sparks' book *Anti-Bias Curriculum: Tools for Empowering Children*, and my previous book *Teaching and Learning in a Diverse World*.

Thinking Games. Thinking games about friends can include issues of differences. For example, children could consider whether or not two people who are very different might still be friends. For older children this dilemma could also include adult disapproval of the relationship. For example, they could discuss what they would have done if they had been one of Martin

Luther King's white childhood friends who was told that he could no longer play with Martin because of his skin color. They can also address specific stereotypes or misconceptions that the children have. In one preschool classroom (Ramsey, 1986b) some white children assumed that children with darker skin had to "wash their hands a lot to get all that dirt off." The teacher set up a series of water play activities in which children washed baby dolls, some black, some white, and some white ones with water color brown streaks on them. As the children washed the dolls, they noticed that painted streaks came off, but not the color on the darker skinned dolls.

SOCIAL RESPONSIBILITY

In addition to learning how to get along with peers, children also need to see themselves as members of the larger society and assertively express their values and beliefs. As children become aware of situations and actions that are unfair, they need to see themselves as active agents of change. In other words, developing interpersonal skills does not mean simply accommodating to others and conforming to one's cultural social rules. Social competence also means the ability and willingness to recognize and fight for what is fair and collaborate with others to be strong enough to be successful.

Stories

As can be seen by the brevity of this section, few authors have written books on this theme. Some books for children show the value of working together and being assertive to overcome unfair and threatening laws or people. For young children the story of *Swimmy* in which the small fish work together to chase off their predators provides an example of how collaboration can make the weaker and smaller beings strong and powerful.

For older children some biographies illustrate the importance of activism. *Mumbet: The Story of Elizabeth Freeman*, tells of a slave woman who wins her freedom by going to court in 1781 to test the Massachusetts Constitutional guarantee that all men were born "equal and free." Here the power of knowledge of one's rights and the collaboration of like-minded individuals force a change in the existing laws. *The Story of Harriet Tubman: Freedom Train* is another good book to illustrate the power of people taking risks for doing what they believed to be right.

Activities

Community Involvement.   An excellent source of ideas for helping children to develop these skills is *Anti-bias Curriculum: Tools for Empowering*

Children. In the chapter on activism, Derman-Sparks describes numerous ways in which teachers can help their children to become more active to create positive change. Several activities involve teachers helping children recognize discriminatory situations. For example, in one preschool class, the teacher raised the issue about the term "flesh-colored" Band-Aids that are clearly only flesh-colored for some people. She had the children put on Band-Aids and count how many children the Band-Aids actually matched. The children and teachers made a chart and realized that the Band-Aids matched only a few children's skin. The children then dictated a letter about this issue and they sent it to the company that manufactured the Band-Aids. Although the company was only slightly responsive, the children still learned that they were able to take action to address an unfair situation.

Many classroom and community situations lend themselves to this kind of action. Children can write to toy manufacturers and publishers about stereotyped characters and other unfair practices. In one-third grade classroom, some children had sent off for a pair of binoculars that were advertised in a children's magazine. When the binoculars arrived, they were much smaller and less powerful than advertised. Several children wrote a joint letter to the company complaining about their misleading advertising and were able to get their money refunded. Children can become involved in community issues particularly if they directly affect their lives, such as the closing of a school, the curtailment of hours at a branch library, and the demolition of buildings that are providing shelter for people who otherwise are homeless. In one daycare center, the funding agency decided to withdraw its funds because of the political affiliations of the director. The staff and the families, including the children, picketed the agency, gained media coverage, and were successful in getting the decision reversed. In the classroom or while engaged in some social action, children enjoy singing protest songs such as "We Shall Overcome" and "Freedom" and these can often be used as a way of introducing children to stories about movements for social change.

Afterword

Throughout this book, we have focused on individual children, classrooms, and teachers. Ideally, however, attempts to promote children's peer relationships should occur in the context of school-wide programs and family and community support. Thus, a discussion of how to create these optimal environments is a fitting conclusion to this book. To illustrate ways of developing this broad support, I will briefly describe three programs that have multifaceted approaches to promoting positive peer relationships in schools. Because each program has a unique orientation, together they illustrate the diversity of ways in which the principles and research discussed in this book might be applied. Moreover, as each program has a strong evaluation component, these projects have been and will continue to be excellent sources of information about the effectiveness of specific interventions and strategies in particular settings. Finally, the fact that these programs have received funding and are gaining some national attention raises hopes that similar efforts may begin to attract more support both locally and nationally.

The School Development Program headed by James Comer (at the Yale Child Study Center) has been implemented in several elementary schools in New Haven, Connecticut and Benton Harbor, Michigan (Comer, 1985). Started in 1968, this program predated the current research interest in peer relationships, but its goals and methods are compatible with many of the principles generated by this research, and its positive results are encouraging to all researchers and practitioners engaged in promoting peer relationships. The program was initially implemented in two urban elementary schools that served poor African–American children. Prior to the intervention, both schools were plagued with low achievement scores, severe and chronic behavior problems, high truancy rates, and low teacher morale. The overall goal of the School Development Project was to improve children's academic achievement by focusing on their psychological adjustment and the social climate of the school. The primary catalyst for change was a mental health team that worked with the school staff in the areas of school

governance, parent–school relations, and curriculum and staff development. With the guidance and facilitation of the mental health team, the
teachers, administrators, parents, and students made many significant
improvements in the way in which the school and classroom operated. The
specific changes are too numerous to be discussed here, but essentially they
were oriented toward helping all members of the school community work
together more closely and more effectively. For example, parents, teachers,
and administrators formed a school governance committee that established
policies and procedures for the school. The parents' program fostered closer
parent–teacher relations by developing a parent aid program, collaborating
with teachers in planning special events, and increasing the frequency of
parent–teacher conferences and classroom visits. The staff and curriculum
development were oriented around teachers cooperating to create an integrated and innovative curriculum that reflected developmentally appropriate goals and emphasized positive social relationships among teachers and
students. The mental health team also helped staff members and parents
resolve specific classroom problems with interventions similar to some of
those described in Chapter 6. Despite a rocky first year, the schools that
participated in the program have shown "an upward spiral of staff, parent,
and student performance" (Comer, 1985, p. 132). The improvement in the
schools' social climates was dramatically illustrated by a drop in children's
aggressive behavior and truancy, a rise in the morale and attendance record
of the teachers, and an increase in parent involvement in all areas of the
school. The students' academic achievement showed a substantial rise that
was still continuing 15 years after the beginning of the program. This
improvement supported the program's underlying assumption that the quality of social relationships among teachers, students, and parents is critical to
academic success. The role of the mental health team was taken over by
regular school personnel after the program was fully established so the staff
of the Yale Child Study Center is no longer directly involved in these
schools. However, they are disseminating the practices that they developed
during this project by sponsoring a year-long fellowship program for educators who want to develop a similar program in their own schools.

The second program is the Child Development Project in San Ramon,
California. Starting in the early 1980s, a group of educators and researchers
implemented a school-wide program designed to promote children's prosocial behavior and to foster their long-term commitment to social justice
and the rights of others (Battistich, Solomon, Watson, Solomon, & Schaps,
1989; Battistich, Watson, Solomon, Schaps, & Solomon, 1989; Solomon,
Watson, Delucchi, Schaps, Battistich, 1989). Unlike the population in the
School Development Program, the children who participated in this project
were from middle-class families and were not considered a high-risk group

for current or later social problems. This program embodied much of the research done on prosocial development in the 1970s and reflected the belief that all children need support and guidance to develop their prosocial motivation and skills and that schools neglect this area of development. The children in six elementary schools (three control and three program schools) were studied for a period of 5 years. At the three program schools, teachers went through extensive training and changed their classroom practices in several ways. They incorporated more cooperative activities, with a particular emphasis on learning fairness, consideration, and social responsibility. The teachers also gained more skills in developmental discipline, which promotes the internalization of prosocial norms and values by involving children in rule setting and mutual problem solving instead of using external rewards and consequences. In classrooms and throughout the school, teachers emphasized social understanding by using both planned (e.g., class meetings) and unplanned events (e.g., a fight) to enhance children's awareness of other people. Prosocial values were stressed in children's daily interactions; in themes in literature, films, and television; and in expectations that children should assist classmates and teachers and participate in school and community service activities.

Comparisons between the control and program schools throughout the project showed that children in the latter schools were better at resolving social problems, as measured both in problem-solving interviews and in children's responses to issues and concerns that arose in their classrooms, and were more prosocial in their ongoing classroom interactions. At the end of 5 years, the children in the control and intervention groups had similar achievement scores, which is reassuring to teachers and administrators who worry that emphasizing social development might compromise the academic program.

A third program has just started and is geared to the direct application of much of the research discussed in this book, especially in Chapter 4. It is primarily a clinical intervention program for individual children who are considered at-risk for poor social adjustment (Dodge, 1991). This program is a collaborative effort of a number of researchers (Karen Bierman, John Coie, Kenneth Dodge, Mark Greenberg, John Lochman, and Bob McMahon) and institutions in several different areas of the country. It is designed to prevent later problems by intervening with high-risk children at a relatively young age and so is located in urban and rural school districts that have high rates of adolescent behavior problems. Children are screened in kindergarten, and those who are identified as behaving aggressively by teachers and parents are placed in either a control group or an intervention group. One innovative aspect of this program is that both the children and their families in the intervention group receive support services and participate in different kinds of training. First, the parents, who are paid for their participation, are trained in positive discipline strategies. Second, each family is assigned a coordinator who regularly visits them in their home in order to provide support, relief from stress, and help in organizing family life. The coordinators also facilitate closer ties between parents and teachers in a number of ways. Third, to prevent alienation from school due to academic deficiencies, children receive tutoring in reading skills. They also participate in weekly social skills training sessions. In their classrooms, the high-risk children are paired with popular peers for activities and games twice a week in order to facilitate their integration into the peer social life. Furthermore, all class members participate in the PATHS curriculum (Providing Alternative Thinking Strategies), a series of 30-minute activities done four times a week in the classroom and designed to improve self-control, emotional understanding, and social problem-solving skills (Kusche, 1991). Because this project is in its early stages, no research is yet available on its outcomes. However, it promises to be a rich source of information about the causes and remediation of children's social problems.

Although these three programs have different orientations, their approaches are complementary and mutually enhancing. In order to consolidate the gains made in small group and individual sessions, individual children at risk for poor social adjustment (the primary targets of the third program) not only need individual help but also social environments in which classmates and teachers are responsive and caring. Conversely, teachers who are trying to build prosocial classrooms, such as those in the program in San Ramon, will find their efforts thwarted if children with more serious adjustment problems do not receive the necessary help and resources. The effectiveness of both of these approaches, in turn, is highly dependent on the quality of the school social climate and the extent to which children, teachers, and parents feel connected and supported as found in James Comer's project. As illustrated by these programs, we must also be attuned to the larger social context in order to understand how economic inequities and cultural gaps between families and schools may increase some children's vulnerability for social and academic problems. Finally, we need to recognize how the social discord and callousness that characterize our nation's mass culture and economic practices affect all children's orientations and behaviors. As teachers we must work on all of these fronts to change the social conditions that divide and disenchant our youth.

All of us as teachers remember children who did not fit in, groups that just did not get along, and disputes between children that we could never resolve. Likewise, we savor times when children are caring for each other or are cooperating on exciting projects. We recall with joy the momentous day when a very shy child made his first tentative move to join his peers, or the breakthrough when a classmate penetrated the sullenness of an alienated child.

I often think about Lenny, the child described in the Preface of this book, and wonder what happened to him and hope that another more astute and experienced teacher was able to make the critical difference in his life. Recently I had a chance to work with a teacher who had a child who was similar to Lenny. Together we observed Rusty and his peers and identified the situations that seemed to elicit his most negative behaviors. As though we were working on a giant puzzle, we pieced together the information about Rusty, his family, and his friends to create a fairly coherent picture of what Rusty was trying to achieve in his relationships with his peers and the teacher. The teacher made some minor adjustments in the classroom schedule and routines in order to meet Rusty's needs more expeditiously and was able to alleviate some of the most persistent problems. With some skillful seat changes and grouping assignments, she created time and space for Rusty to gain some distance from his usual antagonists and to get to know some of his quieter and more amiable classmates. As these new relationships developed he became more relaxed and less volatile. Meanwhile, the school counselor persuaded Rusty's mother to join a support group for recently divorced parents so that she could get the help and nurturing she needed to provide the reassuring environment that Rusty craved. I cannot say that a miracle happened; Rusty is still difficult and is often antagonistic toward his classmates, but he is happier, more involved in his work, and sees his peers as positive resources, not simply as targets for his anger.

This book was written to help all of us become more effective in helping the Lennies and Rusties participate in peer relationships in a positive way. It was also written with the hope that together we can create more positive social environments in our classrooms, in our schools, and in our communities so that all children can thrive as individuals and enjoy the world of childhood friends.

Appendix 1: Rating Scales

TEACHER–CHILD RATING SCALE ITEMS

Primary Mental Health Project, 575 Mt. Hope Avenue, Rochester, NY 14620

Please rate the child on the following:	Not Problem	Mild	Moderate	Serious	Very Serious Problem
Disruptive in class					
Withdrawn					
Underachieving					
Fidgety, difficulty sitting still					
Shy, timid					
Poor work habits					
Disturbs others while they are working					
Anxious, worried					
Poor concentration, limited attention span					
Constantly seeks attention					
Nervous, frightened, tense					
Difficulty following directions					
Overly aggressive to peers (fights)					
Does not express feelings					
Poorly motivated to achieve					
Defiant, obstinate, stubborn					
Unhappy, sad					
Learning academic subjects					

How well do the following items describe the child?	Not at all	A little	Moderately well	Well	Very well
Accepts things not going his/her way					
Defends own views under group pressure					
Completes work					
Has many friends					
Ignores teasing					
Comfortable as a leader					
Well organized					
Is friendly toward peers					
Accepts imposed limits					
Participates in class discussions					
Functions well even with distractions					
Makes friends easily					
Copes well with failure					
Expresses ideas willingly					
Works well without adult support					
Classmates wish to sit near this child					
Tolerates frustration					

Child Rating Scale Items

	Usually No	Sometimes	Usually Yes

1. I behave in school
2. I get scared in school
3. I have many friends
4. I like to do school work

5. I bother classmates who are working
6. I'm afraid of making mistakes
7. My classmates tease me
8. I get bored in class

9. I do what I'm supposed to in school
10. I worry about things at school
11. Other kids are mean to me
12. School is fun

13. I get in trouble in class
14. My feelings get hurt easily
15. My classmates like me
16. I like to answer questions in class

17. I follow the class rules
18. I'm nervous at school
19. Other kids choose me last for games
20. I hate school

21. I call other students names
22. I feel like crying at school
23. I make friends easily
24. I get tired of going to school

Appendix 2: Forms for Recording Observations

Times and Locations of Aggressive Acts							
Date: _____							
Time	Books	Science	Math	Games	Tables	Water	Hall
8:00–8:15							
8:15–8:30							
8:30–8:45							
8:45–9:00 ⋮ 11:15–11:30							

Individual Record of Aggressive Behavior						
Name of child: _____				Date: _____		
Time	Area	Type of Aggression		Target	Focus of Aggression		
		Physical	Verbal		Object	Territ	Soc. Control

Anecdotal Record

Name of Child: _____

Other children present: _____

Date: _____

Description of what occurred:

Interpretation/Comments/Pattern:

Observer:

Duration of Aggressive Episodes

Name of Child: _____   Date: _____

Location	Time	Type of Aggression	Duration

Appendix 3: Children's Books and Resources Discussed in Chapter 7

THE NATURE OF DIFFERENT SOCIAL RELATIONSHIPS

Douglass, Barbara. *Good as New*. Illus. Patience Brewster. New York: Lothrop, Lee, and Shepard Books, 1982.

Dragonwagon, Crescent. *I Hate My Brother Harry*. Illus. Dick Gackenbach. New York: Harper and Row, Publishers, 1983.

Goldman, Susan. *Grandma Is Somebody Special*. Chicago: Albert Whitman, 1976.

Greenfield, Eloise. *Me and Neesie*. Illus. Moneta Barnett. New York: Thomas Y. Crowell Co., 1975.

Greenfield, Eloise. *She Come Bringing Me That Little Baby Girl*. Illus. John Steptoe. New York: Lippincott, 1974.

Hurd, E.T. *I Dance in My Red Pajamas*. Illus. E. A, McCully. New York: Harper and Row, Publishers, 1982.

Keats, Ezra Jack. *Peter's Chair*. New York: Harper and Row, 1967.

Jenness, Aylette. (1990). *Families: A Celebration of Diversity, Commitment, and Love*. Boston: Houghton Mifflin, 1990.

Johnson, Angela. *Do Like Kyla*. Illus. James E. Ransome. New York: Orchard Books, 1990.

Thomas, I. *Hi, Mrs. Mallory!* Illus. A. Toulmin-Rothe. New York: Harper and Row, 1979.

Wittman, Sally. *A Special Trade*. Illus. Karen Gundersheimer. New York: Harper and Row, 1978.

Zolotow, Charlotte. *Timothy Too!* Illus. Ruth Robbins. Oakland: Parnassus Press, 1986.

THE POWER AND IMPORTANCE OF RELATIONSHIPS

Appiah, Sonia. *Amoko and Efua Bear*. Illus. Carol Easman. New York: Macmillan, 1988.

Davidson, Margaret. *Jackie Robinson, Bravest Man in Baseball*. Illus. Floyd Cooper. New York: Parachute Press, 1988.

deKay, James. *Meet Martin Luther King, Jr*. Illus. Ted Burwell. New York: Random House, 1969.

Graf, Stewart and Polly Anne. *Helen Keller*. New York: Dell, 1965.

Iwamura, Kazuo. *Ton and Pon: Two Good Friends*. Scarsdale: Bradbury Press, 1980.

Schlank, Carol Hilgartner and Barbara Metzger. Martin Luther King, Jr.: *A Biography for Young Children*. Illus. John Kastner. Maryland: Gryphon House, 1990.

Steig, William. *Amos and Boris*. New York: Farrar, Straus, and Giroux, 1971.

Williams, Vera B. *A Chair for My Mother*. New York: Greenwillow Books, 1982.

THE EFFECTS OF EXTERNAL EVENTS AND PRESSURES ON RELATIONSHIPS

Aliki. *We Are Best Friends*. New York: Greenwillow Books, 1982.

Cohn, Janice. *I Had a Friend Named Peter*. Illus. Gail Owens. New York: William Morrow, 1987.

Ganley, Helen. *Jyoti's Journey*. London: Andre Deutsch, 1986.

Gates, Doris. *Blue Willow*. Illus. Paul Lantz. New York: Viking Press, 1940.

Hickman, Martha Whitmore. *My Friend William Moved Away*. Illus. Bill Myers. Nashville: Abingdon, 1979.

Slate, Joseph. *Lonely Lulu Cat*. Illus. Bruce Degan. New York: Harper and Row, 1985.

Stanley, Diane. *A Country Tale*. New York: Macmillan, 1985.

Varley, Susan. *Badger's Parting Gifts*. Great Britain: Andersen Press, 1984.

Weissman, Bari. *Sam Comes to Dinner*. Boston: Little, Brown, 1977.

Zelonky, Joy. *My Best Friend Moved Away*. Illus. Angela Adams. Milwaukee: Raintree Publishers, 1980.

LEARNING TO BE A GOOD FRIEND

Bonsall, Cosby. *It's Mine...A Greedy Book*. New York: Harper and Row, Publishers, 1964.

Bunting, E. *Clancy's Coat*. Illus. L. B. Cauley. New York: Rederick Warne, 1984.

Clifton, Lucille. *Three Wishes*. Illus. Stephanie Douglas. New York: The Viking Press, 1974.

Cohen, Miriam. *Best Friends*. Illus. Lillian Hoban. New York: Macmillan, 1971.

Eriksson, Eva. *Jealousy*. Minneapolis: Carolrhoda Books, 1985.

Gackenbach, Dick. *Hound and Bear*. New York: Seabury Press, 1976.

Giff, Patricia Reilly. *Happy Birthday, Ronald Morgan!* Illus. Susanna Natti. New York: Viking Penguin, 1986.

Gordon, Shirley. *Happy Birthday, Crystal*. Illus. Edward Frascino. New York: Harper and Row, 1981.

Hayes, Geoffrey. *Patrick and Ted*. New York: Four Winds Press, 1984.

Kellogg, Steven. *Best Friends*. New York: Dial Books for Young Readers, 1986.

Krasilovsky, Phyllis. *The Shy Little Girl*. Illus. Trina Schart Hyman. Boston: Houghton Mifflin, 1970.

Lobel, Arnold. *Frog and Toad Are Friends*. New York: Harper and Row, 1970.

Myers, Bernice. *Not at Home*. New York: Lothrop, Lee, and Shepard, 1981.

Sharmat, Marjorie Weinman. *Attila the Angry*. Illus. Lillian Hoban. New York: Holiday House, 1985.

Sharmat, Marjorie Weinman. *I'm Not Oscar's Friend Anymore*. Illus. Tony de Luna. New York: E.P. Dutton ,1975.

Sharmat, Marjorie Weinman. *Octavia Told Me a Secret*. Illus. Roseanne Litzinger. New York: Four Winds Press, 1979.

Sharmat, Marjorie Weinman. *Rollo and Juliet Forever!* Illus. Marilyn Hafner. New York: Doubleday, 1981.

Sharmat, Marjorie Weinman. *Taking Care of Melvin*. Illus. Victoria Chess. New York: Holiday House, 1980.

Viorst, Judith. *Rosie and Michael*. Illus. Lorna Tomei. New York: Atheneum, 1981.

Weiss, N. *Battle Day at Camp Delmont*. New York: Greenwillow Books, 1985.

Weiss, N. *Maude and Sally*. New York: Greenwillow Books, 1983.

Wells, Rosemary. *Timothy Goes to School*. New York: Dial Press, 1981.

Winthrop, Elizabeth. *The Best Friends Club*. Illus. Martha Weston. New York: Lothrop, Lee, and Shepard, 1989.

Wild, Margaret. *The Very Best of Friends*. Illus. Julie Vivas. San Diego: Harcourt Brace Janovich, 1989.

Winthrop, Elizabeth. *Katharine's Doll*. Illus. Marilyn Hafner. New York: E. P. Dutton, 1983.

Winthrop, Elizabeth. *Tough Eddie*. Illus. Lillian Hoban. New York: E. P. Dutton, 1985.

Zalben, J.B. *Lyle and Humus*. New York: Macmillan, 1974.

Zalben, J.B. *Oliver and Allison's Week*. Illus. E. A. McCully. New York: Farrar, Strauss, Giroux, 1980.

Zolotow, Charlotte. *The Hating Book*. Illus. Ben Shecter. New York: Harper and Row, 1969.

LACK OF FRIENDS

Bottner, B. *Horrible Hannah*. Illus. J. Drescher. New York: Crown, 1980.

Craig, M. Jean. *The New Boy on the Sidewalk*. Illus. Sheila Greenwald. New York: W.W. Norton, 1967.

Robins, Joan. *Addie Meets Max*. Illus. Sue Truesdell. New York: Harper and Row, 1985.

Sharmat, Marjorie Weinman. *Attila the Angry*. Illus. Lillian Hoban. New York: Holiday House, 1985.

Sharmat, Marjorie Weinman. *The 329th Friend*. Illus. Cyndy Szekeres. New York: Four Winds Press, 1979.

Tsutsui, Yoriko. *Anna's Secret Friend*. Illus. Ahiko Hayashi. New York: Viking Penguin, 1987.

Zolotow, Charlotte. *The New Friend*. Illus. Emily Arnold McCully. New York: Thomas Y. Crowell, 1968.

Zolotow, Charlotte. *A Tiger Called Thomas*. Illus. Kurt Werth. New York: Lothrop, Lee, and Shepard, 1966.

APPRECIATION OF DIVERSITY

Aiello, Barbara. *Secrets Aren't Always For Keeps*. Illus. Loel Barr. Frederick, MD: Twenty-First Century Books, 1988.

Bang, Molly. *The Paper Crane*. New York: Greenwillow Books, 1985.

Carrick, Malcolm. *Tramp*. New York: Harper and Row, 1977.

Clark, Ann Nolan. *Little Navajo Bluebird*. Illus. Paul Lantz. New York: Viking Press, 1943.

Clifton, Lucille. *My Friend Jacob*. Illus. Thomas D. Grazia. New York: E. P. Dutton, 1980.

Coutant, Helen. *The Gift*. Illus. Vo-Dinh Mai. New York: Alfred A. Knopf, 1983.

Daly, Niki. *Not So Fast Songololo*. New York: Macmillan, 1985.

de Paola, Tomie. *Oliver Button Is a Sissy*. New York: Harcourt Brace Janovich, 1979.

de Regniers, Beatrice Schenk. *May I Bring a Friend?* Illus. Beni Montresor. New York: Macmillan, 1964.

Ets, Marie Hall. *Play with Me*. New York: Viking Press, 1955.

Gates, Doris. *Blue Willow*. Illus. Paul Lantz. New York: The Viking Press, 1940.

Gray, Nigel. *A Country Far Away*. Illus. Philippe Dupasquier. New York: Orchard Books, 1988.

Havill, Juanita. *Jamaica's Find*. Illus. Anne Sibley O`Brien. Boston: Houghton Mifflin, 1986.

Heine, Helme. *Friends*. New York: Macmillan, 1982.

Hoban, R. *Best Friends for Frances*. Illus. L. Hoban. New York: Harper and Row, 1969.

Lessac, Frane. *My Little Island*. London: Macmillan, 1984.

Macmillan, Diane and Dorothy Freeman. *My Best Friend Martha Rodriguez*. Illus. Warren Fricke. New York: Julia Messner, 1986.

Mayer, Mercer and Marianna Mayer. *A Boy, a Dog, a Frog, and a Friend*. New York: Pied Piper Printing, 1971.

Mitchell, Barbara. *A Pocketful of Goobers: A Story About George Washington Carver*. Illus. Peter Hanson. Minneapolis: Carolrhoda Books, Inc., 1986.

Orgel, Doris. *My War with Mrs. Galloway*. Illus. Carol Newsom. New York: Viking Kestral, 1985.

Raynor, Dorka. *My Friends Live in Many Places*. Chicago: Albert Whitman , 1980.

Rylant, Cynthia. *Miss Maggie*. Illus. Thomas DiGrazia. New York: E. P. Dutton, 1983.

Seuss, Dr. *The Sneetches*. New York: Random House.

Sharmat, Marjorie Weinman. *The 329th Friend*. Illus. Cyndy Szekeres. New York: Four Winds Press, 1979.

Sharmat, Marjorie Weinman. *Who's Afraid of Ernestine?* Illus. Maxie Chambliss. New York: Coward-McCann, 1986.

Silman, Roberta. *Somebody Else's Child*. Illus. Chris Conover. New York: Frederick Warne, 1976.

Simon, Norma. *Why Am I Different?* Illus. Dora Leder. Illinois: Albert Whitman and Co., 1976.

Sorensen, Virginia. *Plain Girl*. Illus. Charles Geer. New York: Harcourt, Brace, 1955.

Stein, Sara Bonnett. *About Handicaps*. Illus. Dick Frank. New York: Walker and Co., 1974.

Steiner, Charlotte. *What's the Hurry, Harry?* New York: Lothrop, Lee, and Shepard, 1968.

Thomas, I. *Hi, Mrs. Mallory!* Illus. A. Toulmin-Rothe. New York: Harper and Row, 1979.

Tsow, Ming. *A Day with Ling*. Illus. Christopher Cormack. Great Britain: Harnish Hamilton, 1982.

White, E. B. *Charlotte's Web*. Illus. Garth Williams. New York: Harper and Row, 1952.

Wittman, Sally. *A Special Trade*. Illus. Karen Gundersheimer. New York: Harper and Row, 1978.

Zolotow, Charlotte. *I Know a Lady*. Illus. James Stevenson. New York: Greenwillow Books, 1984.

SOCIAL RESPONSIBILITY

Felton, Harold W. *Mumbet: The Story of Elizabeth Freeman*. Illus. Donn Albright. New York: Dodd, Mead, 1970.

Lionni, Leo. *Swimmy*. New York: Pantheon, 1968.

Sterling, Dorothy. *The Story of Harriet Tubman: Freedom Train*. New York: Scholastic, 1954.

ACTIVITY BOOKS AND KITS

Crary, E. *Kids Can Cooperate*. Seattle: Parenting Press, 1984.

DUSO Discover Understanding of Self and Others, Don and Don Dinkmeyer, American Guidance Service, Circle Pines, MN 55014.

Elardo, P., Cooper, M. *Aware: Activities for Social Development*. Reading, MA: Addison-Wesley, 1977.

Luvmour, S., & Luvmour, J. *Everyone Wins*. Philadelphia: New Society Publishers, 1990.

Orlick, T. *The Cooperative Sports and Games Book*. New York: Pantheon, 1978.

Orlick, T. *The Second Cooperative Sports and Games Book*. New York: Pantheon, 1982.

Pirtle, S. *Discovery Sessions: K–8 Lesson Plans for Building Cooperation and Conflict Resolution Skills*. Available from the author, 54 Thayer Road, Greenfield, MA 01301 (undated).

Society for Visual Education. *Lollipop Dragon*. Film strip series, Society for Visual Education, Inc., Chicago, IL 60614.

Wichert, S. *Keeping the Peace: Practicing Cooperation and Conflict Resolution with Preschoolers*. Philadelphia: New Society Publishers, 1989.

Zeitlin, P. *A Song Is a Rainbow: Music, Movement, and Rhythm Instruments in the Nursery School and Kindergarten*. Glenview, IL: Scott, Foresman, 1982.

References

Aboud, F. (1987). The development of ethnic self-identification and attitudes. In J. S. Phinney & M. J. Rotheram (Eds.), *Children's ethnic socialization: Pluralism and development* (pp. 32–55). Beverly Hills, CA: Sage.

Allport, G. W. (1945). Catharsis and the reduction of prejudice. *Journal of Social Issues, 1*, 3–10.

Asarnow, J. R. (1983). Children with peer adjustment problems: Sequential and nonsequential analyses of school behaviors. *Journal of Consulting and Clinical Psychology, 51*, 709–717.

Asher, S. R. (1985, November). *Children without friends: Teaching children social skills.* 1985 Pickering Lecture, Carleton University. Unpublished manuscript.

Asher, S. R. (1990). Recent advances in the study of peer rejection. In S. R. Asher & J. D. Coie (Eds.), *Peer rejection in childhood* (pp. 3–14). New York: Cambridge University Press.

Asher, S. R., & Coie, J. D. (Eds.). (1990). *Peer rejection in childhood.* New York: Cambridge University Press.

Asher, S. R., & Gabriel, S. W. (1989, March). *The social world of peer rejected children as revealed by a wireless audio-visual transmission system.* Paper presented at the annual meeting of the American Educational Research Association, San Francisco.

Asher, S. R., & Hymel, S. (1981). Children's social competence in peer relations: Sociometric and behavioral assessment. In J. D. Wine & M. D. Smye (Eds.), *Social competence* (pp. 125–157). New York: Guilford.

Asher, S. R., Oden, S. L., Gottman, J. M. (1977). Children's friendships in school settings. In L. G. Katz (Ed.), *Current topics in early childhood education* (Vol. 1, pp. 33–61). Norwood, NJ: Ablex.

Asher, S. R., Parkhurst, J. T., Hymel, S., & Williams, G. A. (1990). Peer rejection and loneliness in childhood. In S. R. Asher & J. D. Coie (Eds.), *Peer rejection in childhood* (pp. 253–273). New York: Cambridge University Press.

Asher, S. R., Singleton, L. C., Tinsley, B., & Hymel, S. (1979). A reliable sociometric measure for preschool children. *Developmental Psychology, 15*, 443–444.

Asher, S. R., & Wheeler, V.A. (1985). Children's loneliness: A comparison of rejected and neglected peer status. *Journal of Consulting and Clinical Psychology, 53*, 500–505.

Asher, S. R., & Williams, G. A. (1987, April). New approaches to identifying rejected children at school. Paper presented in G. W. Ladd (Chair), *Identification and treatment of socially rejected children in school settings.* Annual meeting of the American Educational Research Association, Washington, D.C.

Bakeman, R., &. Brownlee, J. (1980). The strategic use of parallel play: A sequential analysis. *Child Development, 51,* 873–878.

Ballard, M., Corman, L., Gottlieb, J., & Kaufman, M. J. (1977). Improving the social status of mainstreamed retarded children. *Journal of Educational Psychology, 69,* 605–611.

Barden, R. C., Zelko, F. A., Duncan, S. W., & Masters, J. C. (1980). Children's consensual knowledge about the experimental determinants of emotion. *Journal of Personality and Social Psycholgy, 39(5),* 968–976.

Bar-Tal, D., Raviv, A., & Goldberg, M. (1982). Helping behavior among preschool children: An observational study. *Child Development, 53,* 396–402.

Battistich, V., Solomon, D., Watson, M., Solomon, J., & Schaps, E. (1989). Effects of an elementary school program to enhance prosocial behavior on children's cognitive–social problem-solving skills and strategies. *Journal of Applied Developmental Psychology, 10,* 147–169.

Battistich, V., Watson, M., Solomon, D., Schaps, E., & Solomon, J. (1989). The child development project: A comprehensive program for the development of prosocial character. In W.M. Kurtines & J.L. Gerwitz (Eds.), *Moral development and behavior: Advances in theory, research, and application* (Vol 1, pp. 289–322). Hillsdale, NJ: Erlbaum.

Baumrind, D. (1967). Child care practices anteceding three patterns of preschool behavior. *Genetic Psychology Monographs, 75,* 43–88.

Becker, W. C. (1964). Consequences of different kinds of parental discipline. In M. L. Hoffman and L. W. Hoffman (Eds.), *Review of child development research* (Vol. 1). New York: Russell Sage Foundation.

Bergen, D. (1988). Designing play environments for elementary-age children. In D. Bergen (Ed.), *Play as a medium for learning and development.* Portsmouth, NH: Heinemann Educational Books.

Bergen D., & Oden, S. (1988). Designing play environments for elementary-age children. In D. Bergen (Ed.), *Play as a medium for learning and development* (pp. 241–269). Portsmouth, NH: Heinemann Educational Books.

Berndt, T. J. (1986). Children's comments about their friendships. In M. Perlmutter (Ed.), *Minnesota Symposia on Child Psychology,* (Vol. 18, pp. 189–212). Hillsdale, NJ: Erlbaum.

Bierman, K. L., & Furman, W. (1984). The effects of social skills training and peer involvement on the social adjustment of preadolescents. *Child Development, 55,* 151–162.

Birch, L. L., & Billman, J. (1986). Preschool children's food sharing with friends and acquaintances. *Child Development, 57,* 387–395.

Boivin, M., & Begin, G. (1989). Peer status and self-perception among early elementary school children: The case of the rejected children. *Child Development, 60,* 591–596.

Borke, H. (1971). Interpersonal perception of young children: Egocentrism or empathy? *Developmental Psychology, 9,* 263–269.

Bossert, S. T. (1979). *Tasks and social relationships in classrooms: A study of instructional organization and its consequences.* New York: Cambridge University Press.

Bronfenbrenner, U. (1979). *The ecology of human development.* Cambridge: Harvard University Press.

Bronfenbrenner, U. (1986). Ecology of the family as context for human development. *Developmental Psychology, 22,* 723–742.

Bryant, B. (1989, April). Conflict resolution strategies in relation to children's peer relations. Paper presented at the biennial meeting of the Society for Research in Child Development, Kansas City, MO.

Budd, K. S. (1985). Parents as mediators in the social skills training of children. In L. L'Abate & M. A. Milan (Eds.), *Handbook of social skills training and research* (pp. 219–244). New York: Wiley.

Buzzelli, C. A., & Fine N. (1989). Building trust in friends. *Young children, 44(30),* 70–75.

Cartledge, G. (1986a). Assessment and evaluation of social skills. In G. Cartledge (Ed.), *Teaching social skills to children* (pp. 29–71). New York: Pergamon Press.

Cartledge, G. (1986b). *Teaching social skills to children.* New York: Pergamon Press.

Cochran, M., & Riley, D. (1988). Mother reports of children's personal networks: antecedents, concomitants, and consequences. In S. Salzinger, J. Antrobus, & M. Hammer (Eds.), *Social networks of children, adolescents, and college students* (pp. 113–145). Hillsdale, NJ: Erlbaum.

Coie, J. D. (1985). Fitting social skills intervention to the target group. In B. H. Schneider, K. H. Rubin, & J. E. Ledingham (Eds.), *Children's peer relations: Issues in assessment and interaction* (pp. 141–156). New York: Springer–Verlag.

Coie, J. D. (1990). Toward a theory of peer rejection. In S. R. Asher & J. D. Coie (Eds.), *Peer rejection in childhood* (pp. 365–401). New York: Cambridge University Press.

Coie, J. D., & Dodge, K. A. (1983). Continuities and changes in children's social status: A five-year longitudinal study. *Merrill–Palmer Quarterly, 29,* 261–282.

Coie, J. D., & Dodge, K. A. (1988). Multiple sources of data on social behavior and social status in the school: A cross-age comparison. *Child Development, 59,* 815–829.

Coie, J. D., Dodge, K. A., & Kupersmidt, J. B. (1990). Peer group behavior and social status. In S. R. Asher & J. D. Coie (Eds.), *Peer rejection in childhood,* (pp. 17–59). New York: Cambridge University Press.

Coie, J. D., & Koeppl, G.K.K. (1990). Adapting intervention to the problems of aggressive and disruptive children. In S. R. Asher & J. D. Coie (Eds.), *Peer rejection in childhood* (pp. 309–337). New York: Cambridge University Press.

Coie, J. D., & Kupersmidt, J. B. (1983). A behavioral analysis of emerging social status in boys' groups. *Child Development, 54,* 1400–1416.

Comer, J. (1985). Empowering black children's educational environments. In H. P. McAdoo & J. L. McAdoo (Eds.), *Black children: Social, educational, and parental environments* (pp. 123–138). Newbury Park, CA: Sage.

Cook, S. W. (1985). Experimenting on social issues: The case of school desegregation. *American Psychologist, 50,* 452–460.

Corsaro, W. A. (1981). Friendship in the nursery school: Social organization in a peer environment. In S. R. Asher & J. M. Gottman (Eds.), *The development of children's friendships* (pp. 207–241). New York: Cambridge University Press.

Corsaro, W. A. (1985). *Friendship and peer culture in the early years.* Norwood, NJ: Ablex.

Costin, S. E., & Jones, D.C. (1989, April). *Friendship and emotion-control interventions among young children.* Paper presented at the biennial meeting of the Society for Research in Child Development, Kansas City, MO.

Crary, E. (1984). *Kids can cooperate.* Seattle: Parenting Press.

Crick, N. R., & Dodge, K. (1989, March). *Rejected children's expectations and perceptions of peer interaction.* Paper presented at the annual meeting of the American
Educational Research Association, San Francisco.

Damon, W. (1977). *The social world of the child.* San Francisco: Jossey–Bass.

Damon, W. (1980). Patterns of change in children's social reasoning: A two-year
longitudinal study. *Child Development, 51,* 1010–1017.

Damon, W. (1983). *Social and personality development: Infancy through adolescence.*
New York: Norton.

Dawe, H. (1934). An analysis of two hundred quarrels of preschool children. *Child
Development, 5,* 139–157.

Day, D. E. (1983). *Early childhood education: A human ecological approach.* Glenview,
IL: Scott, Foresman.

Derman-Sparks, L., & A.B.C. Task Force (1989). Anti-bias curriculum: Tools for
empowering young chldren. Washington, D.C.: NAEYC.

Dodge, K. A. (1991, April). *On the empirical basis for preventive intervention.* Paper
presented at the biennial meeting of the Society for Research in Child Development, Seattle, WA.

Dodge, K. A., & Coie, J. D. (1989, April). *Bully–victim relationships in boys' play
groups.* Paper presented at the biennial conference of the Society for Research
in Child Development, Kansas City, MO.

Dodge, K. A., Murphy, R. R., & Buschbaum, K. (1984). The assessment of inten-
tion-cue detection skills in children: Implications for developmental psy-
chopathology. *Child Development, 55,* 163–173.

Dodge, K. A., Pettit, G. S., McClaskey, C. L., & Brown, M. M. (1986). Social competence in children. *Monographs of the Society for Research in Child Development,
51* (2, Serial No. 213).

Dodge, K. A., Schlundt, D. C., Schocken, I., & Delugach, J. D. (1983). Social competence and children's sociometric status: The role of peer group entry strategies. *Merrill–Palmer Quarterly, 29,* 309–336.

Doyle, A. (1982). Friends, acquaintances, and strangers: The influence of familiarity
and ethnolinguistic background on social interaction. In K. H. Rubin & H. S.
Ross (Eds.), *Peer relationships and social skills in childhood* (pp. 229–252). New
York: Springer–Verlag.

Dunlop, K. H., Stoneman, Z., & Cantrell, M. L. (1980). Social interaction of exceptional and other children in a mainstreamed preschool classroom. *Exceptional
Children, 47(2),* 132–141.

Edelman, M. S., & Omark, D.R. (1973). Dominance hierarchies in young children.
Social Science Information, 12, 103–110.

Eder, R. A., & Jones, M. (1989, April). *The early emergence of self-monitoring: Individual differences in the recognition and production of emotional expressions.* Paper
presented at the biennial meeting of the Society for Research in Child Development, Kansas City, MO.

Edwards, C. P. (1986). *Promoting social and moral development in young children: Creative approaches for the classroom.* New York: Teachers College Press.

Eisenberg, A. R., & Garvey, C. (1981). Children's use of verbal strategies in resolving conflicts. *Discourse Processes*, *4*, 149–170.

Eisenberg, N., & Mussen, P. H. (1989). *The roots of prosocial behavior in children*. New York: Cambridge University Press.

Elgas, P. M., Klein, E., Kantor, R., & Fernie, D. E. (1988). Play and the peer culture: Play styles and object use. *Journal of Research in Childhood Education*, *3 (2)*, 142–153.

Epstein, J. L. (1986). Friendship selection: Developmental and environmental influences. In E. C. Mueller & C. R. Cooper (Eds.), *Process and outcome in peer relationships* (pp. 129–160). New York: Academic Press.

Epstein, J. L. (1989). The selection of friends: Changes across the grades and in different school environments. In T. J. Berndt & G. W. Ladd (Eds.), *Peer relationships in child development* (pp. 158–187). New York: Wiley.

Erikson, E. H. (1963). *Childhood and society* (2nd ed.), New York: Norton.

Evans, I. M., Engler, L. B., & Okifuji, A. (1991, April). *Experimental evaluation of a preventative home–school partnership program for at-risk elementary-aged children*. Paper presented at the biennial meeting of the Society for Research in child Development, Seattle.

Fein, G. (1985). Learning in play: Surfaces of thinking and feeling. In J. L. Frost & S. Sunderlin (Eds.), *When children play* (pp. 45–53). Wheaton, MD: Association for Early Childhood International.

Fein, G. G., & Stork, L. (1981). Sociodramatic play: Social class effects in integrated preschool classrooms. *Journal of Applied Developmental Psychology*, *2*, 267–279.

Fernie, D. E., Kantor, R., Klein, E. L., Meyer, C., & Elgas, P. M. (1988). Becoming students and becoming ethnographers in a preschool. *Journal of Research in Childhood Education*, 3(2), 132–141.

Field, T. M. (1980). Preschool play: Effects of teacher/child ratios and organization of classroom space. *Child Study Journal*, *10*, 191–205.

Finkelstein, N. W., & Haskins, R. (1983). Kindergarten children prefer same-color peers. *Child Development*, *54*, 502–508.

Fischer, K. W., Shaver, P. R., & Carnochan, P. (1989). A skill approach to emotional development: From basic- to subordinate-category emotions. In W. Damon (Ed.), *Child development today and tomorrow*, pp. 107–136. San Francisco: Jossey–Bass.

Foot, H. C., Chapman, A. J., & Smith, J. R. (1977). Friendship and social responsiveness in boys and girls. *Journal of Personality and Social Psychology*, *35*, 401–411.

Fox, D. J., & Jordan, V. B. (1973). Racial preference and identification of black, American Chinese, and white children. *Genetic Psychology Monographs*, *88*, 229–286.

French, D. C. (1988). Heterogeneity of peer-rejected boys: Aggressive and nonaggressive subtypes. *Child Development*, *59*, 976–985.

Furman, W., & Gavin, L.A. (1989). Peers' influence on adjustment and development. In T. J. Berndt & C. W. Ladd (Eds.), *Peer relationships in child development* (pp. 319–340). New York: Wiley.

Furman, W., Rahe, D. F., & Hartup, W.W. (1979). Rehabilitation of socially withdrawn preschool children through mixed-age and same-age socialization. *Child*

Development, 50, 915–922.

Gelman, R. (1978). Cognitive development. In R. Rosenzweig & L. W. Porter (Eds.), *Annual Review of Psychology, 29,* 297–332.

Gelman, R. (1979). Preschool thought. *American Psychologist, 34(10),* 900–905.

Gelman, R., & Gallistel, C. R. (1978). *The child's understanding of numbers.* Cambridge, MA: Harvard University Press.

Gerber, P. J. (1977). Awareness of handicapping conditions and sociometric status in an integrated preschool setting. *Mental Retardation, 15,* 24–25.

Getz, J. A., Goldman, J. A., & Corsini, D. A. (1983, April). *Interpersonal problem solving in preschool children: A comparison of assessment procedures using two-dimensional vs. three-dimensional stimuli.* Paper presented at the biennial meeting of the Society for Research in Child Development, Detroit.

Gibbs, J. T., & Huang, L. N. (1989). *Children of color: Psychological interventions with minority youth.* San Francisco: Jossey-Bass.

Goodenough, F. L. (1931). *Anger in young children.* Minneapolis: University of Minnesota Press.

Goodman, H., Gottlieb, J., & Harrison, R. H. (1972). Social acceptance of EMR's integrated into a non-graded elementary school. *American Journal of Mental Deficiency, 76,* 412–417.

Gottman, J. D., Gonso, J., & Rasmussen, B. (1975). Social interaction, social competence, and friendship in children. *Child Development, 46,* 708–718.

Gottman, J. D., & Parkhurst, J. T. (1980). A developmental theory of friendship and acquaintanceship processes. In W. A. Collins (Ed.), *Minnesota symposia on child development: Volume 13: Development of cognition, affect, and social relations* (pp. 197–253). Hillsdale, NJ: Erlbaum.

Gresham, F. M., & Nagel, R. J. (1980). Social skills training with children: Responsiveness to modeling and coaching as a function of peer orientation. *Journal of Consulting and Clinical Psychology, 48,* 718–729.

Guralnick, M. J. (1980). Social interactions among preschool children. *Exceptional Children, 46,* 248–253.

Guralnick, M. J. (1981). The social behavior of preschool children at different developmental levels: effects of group composition. *Journal of Experimental Child Psychology, 31,* 115–130.

Guralnick, M. J., & Groom, J. M. (1987). The peer relations of mildly delayed and nonhandicapped preschool children in mainstreamed playgroups. *Child Development, 58,* 1556–1572.

Hallinan, M. T., & Teixeira, R. A. (1987). Opportunities and constraints: Black-white differences in the formation of interracial friendships. *Child Development, 58,* 1358–1371.

Harrison, A. O. (1985). The black family's socializing environment: Self-esteem and ethnic attitude among black children. In H. P. McAdoo & J. L. McAdoo (Eds.), *Black children: Social, education, and parental environments* (pp. 174–193). Newbury Park, CA: Sage.

Hart, C. H., Ladd, G. W., & Burleson, B. R. (1990). Children's expectations of the outcomes of social strategies: Relations with sociometric status and maternal disciplinary styles. *Child Development, 61,* 127–137.

Hartup, W. W. (1974). Aggression in childhood: Developmental perspectives. *American Psychologist, 29*, 336–341.

Hartup, W. W., Laursen, B., Stewart, M. I., & Eastenson, A. (1988). Conflict and the friendship relations of young children. *Child Development, 59*, 1590–1600.

Hatch, J. A. (1986, April). *Alone in a crowd: analysis of covert interactions in a kindergarten*. Paper presented at the annual meeting of the American Educational Research Association, San Francisco.

Hatch, J. A. (1988). Learning to be an outsider: Peer stigmatization in kindergarten. *Urban Review, 20*, 59–72.

Hay, D. F. (1984). Social conflict in early childhood. In G. J. Whitehurst (Ed.) *Annals of child development* (Vol.1, pp. 1–44). Greenwich, CT: JAI.

Hazen, N., Black, B., & Fleming–Johnson, F. (1984). Social acceptance: Strategies children use and how teachers can help children learn them. *Young Children. 39*, 26–36.

Hoffman, M. L. (1981). Is altruism part of human nature? *Journal of Personality and Social Psychology, 40*, 121–137.

Hold, B. (1976). Attention-structure and rank specific behaviour in preschool children. In M. R. C. Chance & R. R. Larsen (Eds.), *The social structure of attention* (pp. 177–201). London: Books Demand UMI.

Holliday, B. G. (1985). Developmental imperatives of social ecologies: Lessons learned from black children. In H. P. McAdoo & J. L. McAdoo (Eds.), *Black children: Social, education, and parental environments* (pp. 53–69). Newbury Park, CA: Sage.

Holloway, S. (1991, April). *Social resistance in cooperative group learning: An interpretive study*. Paper presented at the annual meeting of the American Educational Research Association, Chicago.

Honig, A. S. (1987). The shy child. *Young Children, 42 (4)*, 54–64.

Hops, H., & Finch, M. (1985). Social competence and skill: A reassessment. In B. H. Schneider, K. H. Rubin, & J. E. Ledingham (Eds.), *Children's peer relations: Issues in assessment and interaction* (pp. 23–39). New York: Springer–Verlag.

Howes, C. (1983). Patterns of friendship. *Child Development, 54*, 1041–1053.

Howes, C. (1987a). Peer interaction of young children. *Monographs of the Society for Research in Child Development, 53*, (1, Serial No. 217).

Howes, C. (1987b). Social competence with peers in young children. *Developmental Review, 7*, 252–272.

Howes, C., Unger, O., & Seidner, L. B. (1989). Social pretend play in toddlers: Parallels with social play and with solitary pretend. *Child Development, 60*, 77–84.

Humphreys, A. P., & Smith, P. K. (1987). Rough and tumble, friendship, and dominance in schoolchildren: Evidence for continuity and change with age. *Child Development, 58*, 201–212.

Hymel, S., Wagner, E., & Butler, L. J. (1990). Reputational bias: View from the peer group. In S. R. Asher & J. D. Coie (Eds.), *Peer rejection in childhood* (pp. 156–186). New York: Cambridge University Press.

Iano, R. P., Ayers, D., Heller, H. B., McGettigan, J. F., & Walker, V. S. (1974). Sociometric status of retarded children in an integrative program. *Exceptional Children, 40(4)*, 267–271.

Izard, C. (1977). *Human emotions*. New York: Plenum.

Jenness, Aylette. (1990). *Families: A Celebration of Diversity, Commitment, and Love*. Boston: Houghton Mifflin.

Johnson, D. W. (1981). Student–student interaction: The neglected variable in education. *Educational Researcher, 10*, 5–10.

Kantor, R., Elgas, P. M., & Fernie, D. E. (1989). First the look and then the sound: Creating conversations at circle time. *Early Childhood Research Quarterly, 4*, 433–448.

Katz, P. A. (1976). The acquisition of racial attitudes in children. In P. A. Katz (Ed.), *Towards the elimination of racism* (pp. 125–154).

Katz, P. A. (1983). Developmental foundations of gender and racial attitudes. In R. L. Leahy (Ed.), *The child's construction of social inequality* (pp. 41–78). New York: Academic Press.

Kendall, F. (1983). *Diversity in the classroom: A multicultural approach to the education of young children*. New York: Teachers College Press.

Kennedy, P., & Bruininks, R. H. (1974). Social status of hearing impaired children in regular classrooms. *Exceptional Children, 40*, 336–342.

Kinsman, C. A., & Berk, L. E. (1979). Joining the block and housekeeping areas. *Young Children, 35 (1)*, 66–75.

Kritchevsky, S., Prescott, D., & Walling, L. (1977). *Planning environments for young children: Physcial space*. Washington, D.C.: National Association for the Education of Young Children.

Kupersmidt, J. B., Coie, J. D., & Dodge, K. A. (1990). The role of poor peer relationships in the development of disorder. In S. R. Asher & J. D. Coie (Eds.), *Peer rejection in childhood* (pp. 273–305). New York: Cambridge University Press.

Kusche, C. A. (1991, April). Improving classroom behavior and emotional understanding in special needs children: The effects of the PATHS Curriculum. Paper presented at the biennial meeting of the Society for Research in Child Development, Seattle, WA.

La Greca, A. M., & Santogrossi, D. A. (1980). Social skills training with elementary school students: A behavioral group approach. *Journal of Consulting and Clinical Psychology, 48*, 220–227.

Ladd, G. W. (1981). Effectiveness of a social learning method for enhancing children's social interaction and peer acceptance. *Child Development, 55*, 71–82.

Ladd, G. W. (1983). Social networks of popular, average, and rejected children in school settings. *Merrill–Palmer Quarterly, 29*, 283–307.

Ladd, G. W. (1990). Having friends, keeping friends, making friends, and being liked by peers in the classroom: Predictors of children's early school adjustment? *Child Development, 61*, 1081–1100.

Ladd G. W., & Asher, S. R. (1985). Social skill training and children's peer relations. In L. L'Abate & M. A. Milan (Eds.) *Handbook of social skills training and research* (pp. 219–244). New York: Wiley.

Ladd, G. W., & Mize, J. (1983). A cognitive–social learning model of social skill training. *Psychological Review, 90*, 127–157.

Ladd, G. W., & Oden, S. L. (1979). The relationship between peer acceptance and children's ideas about helpfulness. *Child Development, 50*, 402–408.

Ladd, G. W., & Price, J. M. (1987). Predicting children's social and school adjustment following the transition from preschool to kindergarten. *Child Development*, *58*, 1168–1189.

LaFreniere, P., & Charlesworth, W. R. (1983). Dominance, attention, and affiliation in a preschool group: A nine-month longitudinal study. *Ethology and Sociobiology*, *4*, 55–67.

LaFreniere, P. J., & Sroufe, L. A. (1985). Profiles of peer competence in the preschool: Interrelations between measures, influence of social ecology, and relation to attachment history. *Developmental Psychology*, *21*, 56–69.

Lamb, M. E., & Campos, J. L. (1982). *Development in infancy: An introduction.* New York: Random House.

Lambert, W. E., & Klineberg, O. (1967). *Children's views of foreign people.* New York: Appleton–Century–Crofts.

Langlois, J. H., & Stephan, C. W. (1981). Beauty and the beast: The role of physical attractiveness in the development of peer relations and social behavior. In S. S. Brehm, S. M. Kassin, & F. X. Gibbons (Eds.), *Developmental social psychology* (pp. 152–168). New York: Oxford University Press.

Lasquade, C. A. (1988). *Power and popularity: The development of the relationship between dominance and sociometric status.* Unpublished master's thesis, Mount Holyoke College, South Hadley, MA.

Lee, P. (1989). Is the young child egocentric or sociocentric? *Teachers College Record*, *90*, 375–391.

Lewin, K., Lippitt, R., & White, R. (1939). Patterns of aggressive behavior in experimentally created social climates. *Journal of Social Psychology*, *10*, 271–299.

Lochman, J. E. (1985). Effects of different treatment lengths in cognitive behavioral interventions with aggressive boys. *Child Psychiatry and Human Development*, *16*, 45–56.

Lochman, J. E., Burch, P. R., Curry, J. F., & Lampron, L. B. (1984). Treatment and generalization effects of cognitive–behavioral and goal-setting interventions with aggressive boys. *Journal of Counseling and Clinical Psychology*, *52*, 915–916.

Longstreet, W. S. (1978). *Aspects of ethnicity.* New York: Teachers College Press.

Maccoby, E. E. (1980). *Social development: Psychological development and the parent–child relationship.* New York: Harcourt Brace Jovanovich.

Maccoby, E. E. (1986). Social groupings in childhood: Their relationship to prosocial and antisocial behavior in boys and girls. In D. Olewus, J. Block, & M. Radke–Yarrow (Eds.), *Development of antisocial and prosocial behavior* (pp. 263–284). New York: Academic.

Masters, J. C., & Furman, W. (1981). Popularity, individual friendship selection, and specific peer interaction among children. *Developmental Psychology*, *17*, 344–350.

McGee, P. E. (1979). *Humor: Its origin and development.* San Francisco: W. H. Freeman.

McHale, S. M. (1981). Social interactions of autistic and nonhandicapped children during free play. *American Journal of Orthopsychiatry*, *53 (1)*, 81–91.

McLoyd, V. C. (1982). Social class differences in sociodramatic play: A critical review. *Developmental Review*, *2*, 1–30.

McLoyd, V. C. (1990). The impact of economic hardship on black families and children: Psychological distress, parenting, and socioemotional development. *Child Development*, *61*, 311–346.

Middleton, H., Zollinger, J., & Keene, R. (1986). Popular peers as change agents for the socially neglected child in the classroom. *Journal of School Psychology, 24,* 343–350.

Midlarsky, E., & Hannah, M.E. (1985). Competence, reticence, and helping by children and adolescents. *Developmental Psychology, 21,* 534–541.

Mize, J., & Ladd, G. W. (1990). Toward the development of successful social skills training for preschool children. In S. R. Asher & J. D. Coie (Eds.), *Peer rejection in childhood* (pp. 338–361). New York: Cambridge University Press.

Mize, J., Ladd, G. W., & Price, J. M. (1985). Promoting positive peer relations with young children: Rationales and strategies. *Child Care Quarterly, 14,* 221–237.

Moss, J. F., & Oden, S. (April, 1983). Children's story comprehension and social learning. *The Reading Teacher,* 784–789.

Naimark, H. (1983). *Children's understanding of social class differences.* Paper presented at the biennial meeting of the Society for Research in Child Development, Detroit.

Newman, M. A., Liss, M. B., & Sherman, F. (1983). Ethnic awareness in children: Not a unitary concept. *The Journal of Genetic Psychology, 143,* 103–112.

O'Connor, R. D. (1969). Modification of social withdrawal through symbolic modeling. *Journal of Applied Behavior Analysis, 2,* 15–22.

O'Connor, R. D. (1972). Relative efficacy of modeling, shaping, and the combined procedures for modification of social withdrawal. *Journal of Abnormal Psychology, 79,* 327–334.

Oden, S. (1986). Developing social skills instruction for peer interaction and relationships. In G. Cartledge & J. F. Milburn (Eds.), *Teaching social skills to children: Innovative approaches* (2nd ed., pp. 246–269). New York: Pergamon Press.

Oden, S. (1988). Alternative perspectives on children's peer relationships. In T. D. Yawkey & J. E. Johnson (Eds.), *Integrative processes and socialization: Early to middle childhood.* Hillsdale, NJ: Earlbaum.

Oden, S., & Asher, S. R. (1977). Coaching children in social skills for friendship making. *Child Development, 48,* 495–506.

Odom, S. L., Jenkins, J. R., Speltz, M. L., & DeKlyen, M. (1982). Promoting social interaction of young children at risk for learning disabilities. *Learning Disability Quarterly, 5,* 379–387.

Ogbu, J. U. (1978). *Minority education and caste.* New York: Academic Press.

Ogbu, J. U. (1983). Socialization: A cultural ecological approach. In K. M. Borman (Ed.), *The social life of children in a changing society* (pp. 253–267). Norwood, NJ: Ablex.

Olewus, D. (1990). Bully/victim problems among schoolchildren: Basic facts and effects of a school based intervention program. In K. Rubin & D. Pepler (Eds.), *The development and treatment of childhood aggression.* Hillsdale, NJ: Erlbaum.

Olson, S. L. (1989, April). *Behavioral antecedent of peer status, impulsivity, and aggression in preschool boys.* Paper presented at the biennial meeting of the Society of Research in Child Development, Kansas City, MO.

Omark, D. R., Omark, M., & Edelman, M. (1975). Formation of dominance hierarchies in young children. In T. R. Williams (Ed.), *Psychological anthropology* (pp. 289–315). The Hague: Moulton Press.

Osman, B. B. (1982). *No one to play with.* New York: Random House.

Paley, V. G. (1984). *Boys and girls: Superheroes in the doll corner*. Chicago: University of Chicago Press.

Parke, R. D., & Bhavnagri, N. P. (1989). Parents as managers of children's peer relationships. In D. Belle (Ed.), *Children's social networks and social supports*. New York: Wiley.

Parker, J. G., & Asher, S. R. (1987). Peer relations and later personal adjustment: Are low-accepted children at risk? *Psychological Bulletin, 102*, 357–389.

Parker, J. G., & Gottman, J. M. (1989). Social and emotional development in a relational context: Friendship interaction from early childhood to adolescence. In T. J. Berndt & G. W. Ladd (Eds.), *Peer relationships in child development* (pp. 95–131). New York: Wiley.

Parkhurst, J., & Gottman, J. (1986). How young children get what they want. In J. M. Gottman & J. G. Parker (Eds.), *Conversations of friends: Speculations on affective development* (pp. 315–345). New York: Cambridge.

Parten, M. (1933). Social play among preschool children. *Journal of Abnormal and Social Psychology, 28*, 136–147.

Patterson, G. R., & Stouthamer–Loeber, M. (1984). The correlation of family management practices and delinquency. *Child Development, 55*, 1299–1307.

Pellegrini, A. D. (1984). The social cognitive ecology of preschool classrooms: Contextual relations revisited. *International Journal of Behavioral Development, 7*, 321–332.

Perry, D. G., Perry, L. C., & Rasmussen, P. (1986). Cognitive and social learning mediators of aggression. *Child Development, 57*, 700–711.

Perry, D. G., & Williard, J. C. (1989). *Victims of peer abuse*. Paper presented at the biennial meeting of the Society of Research in Child Development, Kansas City, MO.

Peters, M. F. (1985). Racial socialization of young black children. In H. P. McAdoo & J. L. McAdoo (Eds.), *Black children: Social, educational, and parental environments* (pp. 159–173). Newbury Park, CA: Sage.

Pettit, G. S., Bakshi, A., Dodge, K. A., & Coie, J. D. (1990). The emergence of social dominance in young boys' play groups: Developmental differences and behavioral correlates. *Developmental Psychology, 26*, 1017–1025

Pettit, G. S., Dodge, K. A., & Brown, M. M. (1988). Early family experience, social problem solving patterns, and children's social competence. *Child Development, 59*, 107–120.

Pettit, G. S., Harris, A. W., & Childers, L. K. (1989, April). *Social networks and social–cognitive problem solving in early childhood*. Paper presented at the biennial meeting of the Society for Research in Child Development.

Phinney, J. S., & Rotheram, M. J. (1982). Sex differences in social overtures between same-sex and cross-sex preschool pairs. *Child Study Journal, 12*, 259–269.

Piaget, J. (1951). *The child's conception of the world*. New York: Humanities.

Price, J. M. (1989). *A behavioral analysis of socially controversial boys in small peer groups*. Paper presented at the biennial meeting of the Society for Research in Child Development, Kansas City, MO.

Price, J. M., & Dodge, K. A. (1989). Peers' contributions to children's social maladjustment: Description and intervention. In T. J. Berndt & G. W. Ladd (Eds.),

Peer relationships in child development (pp. 341–370). New York: Wiley.

Putallaz, M. (1983). Predicting children's sociometric status from their behavior. *Child Development, 54,* 1417–1326.

Putallaz, M. (1987). Maternal behavior and sociometric status. *Child Development, 58,* 324–340.

Putallaz, M., & Heflin, A. (1990). Parent–child interaction. In S. R. Asher & J. D. Coie (Eds.), *Peer rejection in childhood* (pp. 189–216). New York: Cambridge University.

Putallaz, M., & Wasserman, A. (1989). Children's naturalistic entry behavior and sociometric status: A developmental perspective. *Developmental Psychology, 25,* 1–9.

Putallaz, M., & Wasserman, A. (1990). Children's entry behavior. In S. R. Asher & J. D. Coie (Eds.), *Peer rejection in childhood* (pp. 60–89). New York: Cambridge University Press.

Radke–Yarrow, M., & Zahn–Waxler, C. (1983). Roots, motives, and patterns in children's prosocial behavior. In J. Reykowski, T. Karylowski, D. Bar-Tal, & E. Staub (Eds.), *Origins and maintenance of prosocial behaviors.* New York: Plenum.

Ramsey, P. G. (1980). Beyond winning and losing: Confidence without competition. *Day Care and Early Education, 8,* 50–54.

Ramsey, P. G. (1986a). Possession disputes in preschool classrooms. *Child Study Journal, 16,* 173–181.

Ramsey, P. G. (1986b). Racial and cultural categories. In C. P. Edwards, *Promoting Social and Moral Development in Young Children: Creative Approaches for the Classroom.* New York: Teachers College Press.

Ramsey, P. G. (1987). *Teaching and Learning in a Diverse World: Multicultural Education for Young Children.* New York: Teachers College Press.

Ramsey, P. G. (1988). Social skills and peer status: A comparison of two socioeconomic groups. *Merrill–Palmer Quarterly, 34,* 185–202.

Ramsey, P. G. (1989a, April). *Friendships, groups, and entries: Changing social dynamics in early childhood classrooms.* Paper presented at the biennial meeting of the Society for Research in Child Development, Kansas City, MO.

Ramsey, P. G. (1989b, March). *Making friends in preschools: Outcomes of entry attempts.* Paper presented at the annual meeting of the American Educational Research Association, San Francisco.

Ramsey, P. G. (1989c, April). *Successful and unsuccessful entry attempts: An analysis of behavioral and contextual factors.* Paper presented at the biennial meeting of the Society for Research in Child Development, Kansas City, MO.

Ramsey, P. G. (1990, April). *Changing levels of social participation in early childhood classrooms.* Paper presented as part of Invited Symposium "Social Competence in the Context of Schooling," Angela Taylor, Chair, at the annual meeting of the American Educational Research Association, Boston.

Ramsey, P. G. (1991a). Salience of race in young children growing up in an all-white community. *Journal of Educational Psychology, 83,* 28–34.

Ramsey, P. G. (1991b, April). *What they do and what they say: A comparison of children's classroom behaviors and interview responses.* Paper presented at the biennial meeting of the Society for Research in Child Development, Seattle.

Ramsey, P. G. (1991c). Young children's awareness and understanding of social class differences. *Journal of Genetic Psychology, 152,* 71–82.

Ramsey, P. G., & Myers, L. C. (1990). Salience of race in young children's cognitive, affective and behavioral responses to social environments. *Journal of Applied Developmental Psychology, 11,* 49–67.

Ramsey, P. G., & Reid, R. (1987). Designing play environments for preschool and kindergarten children. In D. Bergen (Ed.) *Play as a Medium for Learning and Development* (pp. 213–239). Portsmouth, NH: Heinemann Educational Books.

Rheingold, H. L. (1982). Little children's participation in the work of adults, a nascent prosocial behavior. *Child Development, 53,* 114–125.

Rheingold, H. L., Hay, D. F., & West, M. J. (1976). Sharing in the second year of life. *Child Development, 47,* 1148–1158.

Rist, R. C. (1973). *The urban school: A factor for failure,* Cambridge, MA: MIT Press.

Rizzo, T. A. (1989). *Friendship development among children in school.* Norwood, NJ: Ablex.

Rizzo, W., & Corsaro, W. A. (1991, April). *Social support processes in early childhood friendships.* Paper presented at the biennial meeting of the Society for Research in Child Development, Seattle.

Rogers, P. J. ,& Miller, J. V. (1984). Playway mathematics: Theory, practice and some results. *Educational Research, 26,* 200–207.

Rogosch, F. A., & Newcomb, A. F. (1989). Children's perceptions of peer reputations and their social reputations among peers. *Child Development, 60,* 597–610.

Roopnarine, J. L. (1984). Becoming acquainted with peers in the nursery classroom. In T. Field, J. L. Roopnarine, & M. Segal (Eds.), *Friendships in normal and handicapped children* (pp. 81–87). Norwood, NJ: Ablex.

Roopnarine, J. L., & Field, T. M. (1984). Play interactions of friends and acquaintances in nursery school. In T. Field, J. L. Roopnarine, & M. Segal (Eds.), *Friendships in normal and handicapped children* (pp. 89–98). Norwood, NJ: Ablex.

Rosenfield, D., & Stephan, W. G. (1981). Intergroup relations among children. In S. S. Brehm, S. M. Kassin, & F. X. Gibbons (Eds.), *Developmental social psychology* (pp. 271–297). New York, Oxford University.

Rotheram-Borus, M. J., & Phinney, J. S. (1990). Patterns of social expectations among blacks and Mexican–American children. *Child Development, 61,* 542–556.

Rubin, K. H. (1977). Play behaviors of young children. *Young Children, 32,* 16–24.

Rubin, K. H. (1983). Recent perspectives on social competence and peer status: Some introductory remarks. *Child Development, 54,* 1383–1385.

Rubin, K. H. (1985). Socially withdrawn children: An "at risk" population? In B. H. Schneider, K. H. Rubin, & J. E. Ledingham (Eds), *Children's peer relations: Issues in assessment and intervention.* New York: Springer–Verlag.

Rubin, K. H., Hymel, S., & Mills, R. S. L. (1989). Sociability and social withdrawal in childhood: Stability and outcomes. *Journal of Personality, 57:2,* 237–255.

Rubin, K. H., LeMare, L. J., & Lollis, S. (1990). Social withdrawal in childhood: Developmental pathways to peer rejection. In S. R. Asher & J. D. Coie (Eds.), *Peer rejection in childhood,* (pp. 217–249). New York: Cambridge University Press.

Rubin, K. H., Maioni, T. L., & Hornung, M. (1976). Free play behaviors in middle– and lower–class preschoolers: Parten and Piaget revisited. *Child Development, 47,* 414–419.

Sackin, S., & Thelen, E. (1984). An ethological study of peaceful associative outcomes to conflict in preschool children. *Child Development, 55,* 1098–1102.

Sagi, A., & Hoffman, M. L. (1976). Empathic distress in newborns. *Developmental Psychology, 12,* 175–176.

Sapon–Shevin, M. (1986). Teaching cooperation. In G. Cartledge (Ed.), *Teaching social skills to children* (pp. 270–302). New York: Pergamon Press.

Schaffer, M., & Sinicrope, P. (June, 1983). *Promoting the growth of moral judgment: An inservice teacher training model.* Paper presented at the annual meeting of the Jean Piaget Society, Philadelphia.

Schofield, J. (1981). Complementary and conflicting identities: Images and interactions in an interracial school. In S. R. Asher & J. M. Gottman (Eds.), *The development of children's friendships* (pp. 53–90). New York: Cambridge University Press.

Selman, R. L. (1980). *The growth of interpersonal understanding.* New York: Academic Press.

Selman, R. L. (1981). The child as a friendship philosopher. In S. R. Asher & J. M. Gottman (Eds.), *The development of children's friendships* (pp. 242–272). New York: Cambridge University Press.

Selman, R. L., & Demorest, A. P. (1984). Observing troubled children's interpersonal negotiation strategies: Implications of and for a developmental model. *Child Development, 55,* 288–304.

Serbin, L. A., Tonick, I. J., & Sternglanz, S.H. (1977). Shaping cooperative cross-sex play. *Child Development, 48,* 924–929.

Shaffer, D. R. (1988). *Social and personality development* (2nd ed.). Pacific Grove, CA: Books/Cole.

Shannon, K., & Kafer, N. F. (1984). Reciprocity, trust, and vulnerability in neglected and rejected children. *Journal of Psychology, 117,* 65–70.

Shantz, C. U. (1987). Conflicts between children. *Child Development, 58,* 283–305.

Shantz, C. U., & Shantz, D. W. (1985). Conflict between children: Social–cognitive and sociometric correlates. In M. W. Berkowitz (Ed.), *Peer conflict and psychological growth: New directions for child development* (pp. 3–21). San Francisco: Jossey–Bass.

Shure, M., & Spivak, G. (1974). *Preschool interpersonal problem-solving test manual.* Philadelphia: Department of Mental Health Sciences, Hahnemann Community Mental Health/Mental Retardation Center.

Singer, J. L. (1984). *The human personality.* New York: Harcourt, Brace, Jovanovich.

Singleton, L. C., & Asher, S. R. (1977). Peer preferences and social interaction among third-grade children in an integrated school district. *Journal of Educational Psychology, 69,* 330–336.

Singleton, L. C., & Asher, S. R. (1979). Racial integration and children's peer preferences: An investigation of developmental and cohort differences. *Child Development, 50,*936–941.

Siperstein, G. N., Brownley, M. V., & Scott, C.K. (1989, April). *Social interchanges between mentally retarded and nonretarded friends.* Paper presented at the biennial meeting of the Society for Research in Child Development, Kansas City, MO.

Slaughter-Defoe, D. T., Nakagawa, K., Takanishi, R., & Johnson, D. J. (1990). Toward cultural/ecological perspectives on schooling and achievement in

African– and Asian–American children. *Child Development, 61,* 363–383.

Slavin, R. E. (1983). *Cooperative learning.* New York: Longman.

Slavin, R.E. (1988). Student team learning: An overview and practical guide. Washington, D.C.: National Education Association.

Smilansky, S. (1968). *The effects of sociodramatic play on disadvantaged preschool children.* New York: Wiley.

Smith, P. K., & Lewis, K. (1985). Rough-and-tumble play, fighting, and chasing in nursery school children. *Ethology and Sociobiology, 6,* 175–181.

Solomon, D., Watson, M., Delucchi, K., Schaps, E., Battistich, V. (1988). Enhancing children's prosocial behavior in the classroom. *American Educational Research Journal, 25,* 527–554.

Sorensen, Virginia. *Plain Girl.* Illus. Charles Geer. New York: Harcourt, Brace, 1955.

Spencer, M. B. (1990). Development of minority children: An introduction. *Child Development, 61,* 267– 269.

Spivak, G., & Shure, M. B. (1974). *Social adjustment of young children.* San Francisco: Jossey–Bass.

Sroufe, L. A., & Fleeson, J. (1986). Attachment and the construction of relationships. In W. W. Hartup & Z. Rubin (Eds.), *Relationships and development* (pp. 51–71). Hillsdale, NJ: Erlbaum.

Sroufe, L. A., Schork, E., Motti, F., Lawroski, N., & LaFreniere, P. (1984). The role of affect in social competence. In C. E. Izard & J. Kagan (Eds.), *Emotions, cognition, and behavior.* New York: Cambridge.

Stabler, J. R., Zeig, J. A., & Johnson, E. E. (1982). Perceptions of racially related stimuli by young children. *Perceptual and Motor Skills, 54,* 71–77.

Strain, P. S. (1985). Programmatic research on peers as intervention agents for socially isolate classmates. In Schneider, N. H., Rubin, K. H., Ledingham, J. E. (Eds.), *Children's peer relations: Issues in assessment and intervention* (pp. 193–205). New York: Springer–Verlag.

Strayer, F. F., & Strayer, J. (1976). An ethological analysis of social agonism and dominance relations among preschool children. *Child Development, 47,* 980–989.

Swadener, E. B., & Johnson, J. E. (1989). Play in diverse social contexts: Parent and teacher roles. In M. N. Bloch & A. D. Pellegrini (Eds.), *The ecological context of children's play,* pp. 214–244. Norwood, NJ: Ablex.

Taylor, A., & Gabriel, S. (1989, April). *Cooperative versus competitive game-playing strategies of peer accepted and peer rejected children in a goal conflict situation.* Paper presented at the biennial meeting of the Society for Research in Child Development, Kansas City, MO.

Taylor, A. R., Asher, S. R., & Williams G. A. (1987). The social adaptation of mainstreamed mildly retarded children. *Child Development, 58,* 1321–1334.

Taylor, A. R., & Trickett, P. K. (1989). Teacher preference and children's sociometric status in the classroom. *Merrill–Palmer Quarterly, 35,* 343–361.

Tegano, D., & Parsons, M. (April, 1989). *The effects of structure and play period duration on preschoolers' play.* Paper presented at the biennial meeting of the Society for Research in Child Development, Kansas City, MO.

Theokas, C. (1991). *Modifying sex-typed behavior and contact patterns in a kindergarten classroom with an outer space intervention curriculum.* Unpublished Masters Thesis, Mount Holyoke College.

Thorne, B. (1986). Girls and boys together... but mostly apart: Gender arrangements in elementary schools. In W. W. Hartup & Z. Rubin (Eds.), *Relationships and development* (pp. 167–184). Hillsdale, NJ: Erlbaum.

Tietjen, A. M. (1989). The ecology of children's social support networks. In D. Belle (Ed.), *Children's social networks and social supports* (pp. 37–69). New York: Wiley.

Tschantz, L. L. (1985, April). Preschool play behaviors and sociometric status. Paper presented at the annual meeting of the American Educational Research Association, Chicago.

Urbain, E. S., & Kendall, P.C. (1980). Review of social–cognitive problem-solving interventions with children. *Psychological Bulletin, 88,* 109–143.

Vandenberg, B. (1981). Environmental and cognitive factors in social play. *Journal of Experimental Child Psychology, 31,* 169–175.

Vygotsky, L. S. (1978). *Mind in society: The development of higher psychological processes.* Cambridge, MA: Harvard University.

Waters, E., Wippman, J., & Sroufe, L. A. (1979). Attachment, positive affect, and competence in the peer group: Two studies in construct validation. *Child Development, 50,* 821–829.

Wexler–Sherman, C., Gardner, H., & Feldman, D. (1988). A pluralistic view of early assessment: The project spectrum approach. *Theory into Practice, 27 (1),* 77–83.

Whiting, B. B., & Whiting, J. W. M. (1975). *Children of six cultures.* Cambridge: Harvard University.

Wichert, S. (1989). *Keeping the peace: Practicing cooperation and conflict resolution with preschoolers.* Philadelphia: New Society Publishers.

Wilkinson, L. C., Lindow, J., & Chiang, C. (1985). Sex differences and sex segregation in students' small-group communication. In L. C. Wilkinson & C. B. Marrett (Eds.), *Gender influences in classroom interaction* (pp. 185–207). New York: Academic.

Willems, E. (1967). Sense of obligation to high school activities as related to school size and marginality of student. *Child Development, 38,* 1247–1260.

Wright, J. C., Giammarino, M., & Parad, H. W. (1986). Social status in small groups: Individual–group similarity and the social "misfit." *Journal of Personality and Social Psychology, 50,* 523–536.

Yarrow, M. R., & Waxler, C. Z. (1976). Dimensions and correlates of prosocial behavior in young children. *Child Development, 47,* 118–125.

Zahn, G. L., Kagan, S., & Widaman, K. F. (1986). Cooperative learning and classroom climate. *Journal of School Psychology, 24,* 351–362.

Zahn–Waxler, C., Cummings, E. M., & Cooperman, G. (1984). Emotional development in childhood. In G. J. Whitehurst (Ed.) *Annals of child development* (Vol.1, pp. 45–106). Greenwich, CT: JAI.

Zahn–Waxler, C. Iannotti, R., & Chapman, M. (1982). Peers and prosocial development. In K. Rubin & H. Ross (Eds.), *Peer relationships and social skills in childhood* (pp. 133–162). New York: Springer–Verlag.

Zimbardo, P., & Radl, S. L. (1981). *The shy child.* New York: McGraw Hill.

Index

About the Author

PATRICIA G. RAMSEY is Associate Professor of Psychology and Education and Director of Gorse Child Study Center at Mount Holyoke College in South Hadley, Massachusetts. Formerly, she taught in the Early Childhood Education Departments at Wheelock College, Indiana University, and the University of Massachusetts. She hold a Masters Degree from California State University in San Francisco and a doctorate in early childhood education from the University of Massachusetts in Amherst. She is a former preschool and kindergarten teacher.